The
Mother

Based on a true story

By: Amanda Hutcheson

To my two miracles, Kristi and JJ,

for renewing my hope and faith in humanity.

I also would like to thank my two best friends,

Peggy Richardson and Carla Middleton,

for believing in me when I didn't believe in myself.

Prologue

The earliest memory I have is also one of the happiest memories I have. I was very young and don't remember a lot of the details. I remember a man and feelings of safety and love. I am sitting on the floor, a man with a big and bushy reddish brown mustache is sitting on a chair in front of me. He has a guitar. He says he loves me and wants to give me a present. His present is a short song that runs through my mind almost every day.

Samantha,

Light up my life.

If God made an angel,

You would be one.

Hello, my name is Samantha Amelia Anderson. I survived but I didn't survive. It is a long story.

Chapter 1

It all began when I was around 4 years old. I spent the day playing with my sisters. My Mom was gone again. I had three sisters who I loved. Stacy Anderson was my oldest sister. Although we had the same last name, we had different fathers. Her father was the brother of my father. She was a teenager and in high school. Then there was my brother Benjamin Brentner, who we called Benny, he was in his early teens and was different. He was violent and he didn't act normal. He kept to himself in the shed taking apart old electronics. Sometimes I caught Benny looking at my sisters and me

funny. I had even caught him watching us change. Then there was Krista Brentner. She was four years older. She could be mean but she was also so cool. She had the most Barbie doll clothes. Then my favorite sister, Shayla Brentner. She was my best friend and we always played together. She was two years older than me.

We played all day. Then Mom came home. She was acting funny. She was mad and smelled funny, bad funny. It was late and we were in bed. Suddenly, the door to the room that we four girls shared banged open. Mother stormed in super mad. She threw me and Shayla out of the bed we shared. Krista and Stacy jumped out of bed quickly. The four of us huddled together in the middle of the room waiting to hear what we had done wrong.

"You ungrateful, selfish, stupid bitches! You stupid slobs! You come home expecting me to clean up your shit that you throw all over this house. I slave away all day and come home to this fucking shit house." Mom ranted as she ran around the room throwing toys out of the toy box, throwing clothes out of the drawers and closet, and stripping the bed clothes.

As Mom ranted and tore up the room I whispered to my sister Stacy, "What's wrong? Why is Mommy angry? Stacy, I am scared."

"Shh, be quiet. Mom is drunk. Just be quiet and stay together." Stacy whispered back as she held me close, "I will protect you."

Mom had stopped throwing things. She turned to us and screamed "Look at this mess, you ungrateful bitches! I want this shit cleaned up immediately!" Mom stormed out of the room.

I started to cry. Stacy dried my tears.

"Stop being a baby, Brat!" Krista said angrily.

"I am not a baby." I whimpered back.

"Both of you stop. Let's just get this mess cleaned up before she returns. Krista will help me remake the beds. Shayla and Samantha, you guys put the toys back in the toy box."

We started cleaning the room. Mom had also thrown everything off the top of the dressers. The room looked like a tornado had blown through it. After the beds were made, Krista

picked up everything that went on the dressers. Stacy went and got a broom to sweep everything up in a big pile. After about an hour all that was left was folding and hanging up the clothes that were thrown around. The clothes were in a big pile in the middle of the room. We were folding them and I must have dozed off onto the pile. I woke to a nightmare.

"AAAAHHHHHHHHH!"

I awoke to a blood chilling scream of horror. Then I felt it too. The belt hit me in the shoulder and upper back. I screamed.

"I told you to clean up your mother fucking mess. You stupid, ungrateful bitches." Mom was running around swinging the belt like a whip. The four of us girls were running around in circles trying to escape. She kept swinging that belt and we were all screaming. The belt caught Stacy across the face. Stacy fell and Mom started kicking her and swinging the belt over and over. The rest of us huddled in the corner but I was scared because Stacy stopped screaming. I ran forward and grabbed at the belt.

I caught the belt and pulled. Mom turned from Stacy, picked me up and threw me into the wall. I remember everything just going black.

"Samantha, Samantha, are you ok?" "Can you move?" "What if she is dead?"

I heard the voices from a distance. I slowly rose to the surface. It was like I was swimming into consciousness. The pain in my head was bad. "Owwww" I mumbled.

"She is alive." My sister Shayla exclaimed, sounding relieved.

"Can she move?" My sister Krista said from across the room.

I opened my eyes. Stacy was sitting beside me holding a washcloth to the back of my head and a wet washcloth to her own face which now was swollen and red. It was beginning to bruise. Shayla was in front of me crying. Krista was across the room hanging up the rest of the clothes.

"We were worried when you would not wake up. Are you ok, sweetheart?" Stacy said worriedly. She was always more like a

mother to me then a sister. She took care of us all. I felt better in her arms.

"My head hurts." I cried as tears slid down my cheeks.

"I know, sweetheart, but the bleeding has stopped so you should feel better soon. Can you stand up?" Stacy asked.

Shayla and Stacy helped me stand up. The four of us tiptoed quietly to the bathroom. Mom was passed out on the couch. We cleaned up the best we could. Then we tiptoed back to the room. I asked what happened. Krista said that after Mom threw me into the wall she stomped out of the room and passed out on the couch. Stacy tucked Shayla and me into bed and we all went to sleep.

The next morning, Stacy woke us all up and helped me get ready for the day. They all had school except me. My head still hurt. Mom was still asleep on the couch. Stacy fed us all cereal in the kitchen.

"Samantha, I want you to spend the day outside today. Don't come inside until I come home. Try to stay out of sight of Mom." Stacy said after breakfast. She handed me a sack with some food in it and took me out to the backyard, "Remember to be very quiet and try to keep your head clean so your head can heal." Then the three of them went to school.

My head hurt and I still felt sleepy so I curled up on a chair on the back porch. I soon fell asleep. I woke up with the hot sun high in the sky. I felt sick and threw up off the edge of the porch on the grass. Mom came out of the house.

"What is wrong with you?" She said.

"My head hurts, Mommy." I replied.

"My head hurts, too, Sissy. Here come inside and you can watch TV with Mommy." Mom then turned and walked into the house. I knew the offer was not optional so I followed her inside.

Mom was on the couch. She was in different clothes then the night before and her hair was wet. She was watching a game show on TV. I sat next to her and she gave me her glass of water. She got up and made herself a cup of coffee before sitting herself back down

beside me. We spent the rest of the day curled up on the couch. I fell asleep a few times and threw up once more, slowly my pain faded to a dull ache. Then it was time to go pick up my siblings from school.

We picked up Shayla and Krista first. Benny went to a different school, so we picked him up next. When we got to the high school to pick up Stacy, Mom parked like usual then she started to cuss. I held Shayla's hand and looked out the window. I saw Stacy walking out of the school with a woman in a suit. There was a police car and a black car in front of the school. Stacy got in the black car with the woman. Suddenly Mom turned the car around and went quickly back home. She told us we had ten minutes to pack because we were moving. That was the last time I saw Stacy and it was the beginning of the end for the rest of us. I lost my protector that day.

Chapter 2

We were given one trash bag each and told to pack as much as we could. Shayla and I worked together and managed to pack most of our clothes and a few toys. Krista helped by telling us what to pack. When everyone was loaded in the car we drove away from the house. Shayla and I had grabbed the blanket from the bed and we huddled under the blanket every time Mom yelled at Krista. Since Stacy was not there, Krista was in the front seat reading the map as Mom drove. Krista had never been in charge of navigation so she kept getting us lost. Every time she misread the map Mom would yell and sometimes slap her across the face. I was seated by the window in the back, Shayla was in the middle and Benny was at the other window.

We drove all night. I remember Mom ranting in the front seat on and off. She kept cursing out Stacy and repeatedly said that the government needed to keep the hell out of her business. The more we drove the more agitated she became. I dozed off to the sound of her cursing and yelling. I woke up in the middle of the night. Everyone else was asleep. Mom was driving.

"Where is Stacy, Mommy?" I asked.

"When did you wake up? You should go back to sleep." My mom said. Sometimes Mom was mean but sometimes she could almost be nice in an annoyed, frustrated sort of way.

"I miss Stacy. Are we going to go back to get her?" I was scared without Stacy.

For the longest time I thought Mom was just going to ignore my questions. The silence seemed to go on and on. Finally, Mom spoke. "Do you remember when we went to pick her up at school?" Mom asked.

"Yes, Mommy," I replied.

"Well, she was being taken by the police. They are going to lock her away and we will never see her again. That is what the police do. That is why you should never trust the police. Stacy will probably be dead in a week. The police are going to torture her relentlessly. She should have kept her stupid, ugly, ignorant goddamned mouth shut. Because of that bitch, we are going to have to start all over. I hate her......." Mom started to rant and seemed not to remember me. What she said terrified me. I was still young enough to believe everything she said. I fell asleep imagining my beloved sister screaming in pain while police officers hit her over and over.

The next morning we arrived at a tiny two bedroom white farmhouse in the middle of nowhere. It was barely furnished. There was a small TV, a VHS player, and a sofa in the front room. The kitchen had a small, round, wobbly table. The two rooms had only one bed in each with no sheets. Mom dropped us off and told us that Benny and her would take the first bedroom, Shayla and I would take the second room, and Krista could take the couch. She told us that we should unpack and prepare to stay for a while. She then left to go to town for some food.

We unpacked in silence and then went outside to explore. I was thinking about everything Mom had said about what was happening to Stacy. Benny found an old shed out back that had some old stuff inside. He spent the day inside the shed. Krista was tired

and took a nap on the couch. Shayla and I decided to pick flowers. We stayed outside for hours just running through the field and playing games. When we were hungry we went back. Krista was watching TV. Mom had not returned.

Krista, Shayla and I looked in the kitchen for some food. We found an old can of peaches and a can of peas but nothing else. We couldn't even find a can opener. The three of us tried everything we could to open the cans but couldn't. Finally, we gave up. We left the cans on the counter and watched TV with Krista. Benny came in two cartoons later. He took the cans out to the shed. We followed him to the shed hoping he could open the cans. He used a knife to open them but then would not share the food. We begged him but he just shut the door to the shed and ignored us. Mom still was not back by dark. We all went to our respective sleeping spots. Shayla and I huddled under our blanket.

Right before we fell asleep Shayla whispered in my ear "What if Mommy never returns?"

The next morning Mom was there. She had returned in the night. "Good morning. Time for breakfast." We ran to the kitchen and saw her pouring milk into cereal bowls.

"Mommy, where were you?" Shayla asked.

"I had to work so I could afford some food. Now eat while I take a nap. Krista do the dishes after breakfast. All of you, I want complete silence. I am very tired. If you wake me up, I swear I will beat you within an inch of your life." She then went into the bathroom and turned on the water. After breakfast Shayla and I were putting on our shoes to go outside, when Mom walked naked out of the bathroom and went into the first bedroom and shut the door. Shayla and I giggled as we went outside.

Shayla and I were making flower dolls when Krista came outside. We usually avoided Krista because she was often cruel and violent without warning or provocation. Usually Stacy protected us from Krista. Now that Stacy was gone I worried about Krista's anger, she often seemed worse than Mom. However, Shayla and I

were both saddened by the loss of Stacy. I told Shayla what Mom had said in the car and we were both having nightmares of the torture of our sister who was more of a Mom in our eyes. Stacy had been our protector, caregiver, and friend. Now, she was surely dead. We missed her. So, we hoped Krista would take care of us.

"What are you guys doing?" Krista asked when she was close enough.

"We are making dolls out of flowers and then we are going to play princess with them. Do you want to play?" I replied while smiling. Shayla looked up to Krista hopefully.

"That's dumb. You are so childish. I am going to look for some neighbors. There's got to be someone around here. I hate the country." Krista said, then she walked away towards a small hill in the distance.

Shayla and I went back to playing. After a few minutes Shayla looked up at me and said, "Why did we move here?"

"I don't know, but we will be ok." I soothed. The truth was I was scared. Without Stacy to watch and protect us, Mom could lose control and no one would be there to help. I felt alone. While Shayla was my best friend, I knew that there was something different about her. She was simpler. It was almost like she couldn't grasp concepts that I could. Although she was older, it was like she was the younger sister and I was the older one. I worried about us. I kept these worries to myself. What is the point in worrying her unnecessarily?

"Who is going to take care of us?" Shayla asked. She seemed to be more worried than I thought.

"We will take care of each other. Let's make a promise to always be there for each other." I said.

"Okay." She replied. We shook pinkies on our promise.

We played in the field for the rest of the morning. We were avoiding the house for fear of angering Mom. We even went potty outside. We were playing tag when we saw Krista returning from her search.

"Hey, Krista, do you want to play tag with us?" I yelled.

She did not reply so we ran over to her, "Hey, Krista, do you want to play tag with us?" I asked again. I was slightly out of breath.

"No, I am too tired and hungry. Have you been back to the house?" She answered.

"No, we were too scared." Shayla said.

"Is Mom still here?" Krista understood our fear.

"Yeah. Did you find any neighbors?" I clung to the hope that there may be someone nearby. Someone with kids to play with and maybe food to share.

"Not that I could see. Come to the house with me and we can get something to eat. If we go together it might be ok. Maybe she is still asleep." Krista said.

"Ok, but if she is awake and mad, promise you won't leave us." I pleaded.

"Just come on and stop acting like a baby." Krista agreed.

Shayla and I walked hand in hand as Krista walked immediately behind us. The house was quiet and yet ominous. I opened the screen door and released Shayla's hand. We quietly entered and paused in the living room as our eyes adjusted. Mom was at the kitchen table drinking coffee. Mom saw me so I walked slowly towards the table. Shayla and Krista followed me inside but stood by the door. I was on my own.

"Good morning, Mommy," I spoke when we were close.

"Actually, it is the afternoon, princess. It is already one. What have you kids been up to?" Mom seemed like she was in a good mood. The key was to not anger her. Even as young as I was I knew to always try not to anger her.

"We were playing in the field. We made flower dolls and played tag." I purposely did not tell Mom about Krista looking for neighbors. I knew it would make Mom mad and I also realized that we were here because Mom was hiding from something. I just did not know what we were hiding from.

"That's nice. Maybe you could pick some flowers to brighten this dump. Have you had lunch?" Mom was sad. I did not know why. The way she said it and the look on her face made it obvious.

"No, Mommy," I replied.

"Ok, wash your hands and sit down. I will make you some sandwiches before I go to work. Krista, go outside and get your brother." Mom said as she got up.

Shayla and I ran into the bathroom and I helped Shayla clean her hands. Krista came in just as we were drying our hands. Shayla and I went and sat at the table and watched Mom finish making us peanut butter and jelly sandwiches. Krista and Benny joined us just as Mom was serving the plates.

"I am going to work. Be on your best behavior. Krista, you are the oldest girl so make sure the house is clean for when I return." Mom then turned and grabbed her purse. She came back to the table and gave me a kiss on the forehead. She then walked out the front door. We heard her car start and drive down the gravel driveway.

"Why do I have to do the chores? That isn't fair!" Krista exclaimed.

"I will help if you need it," I offered.

"What can you do? You're just a baby. Besides if Mom found out you helped she would be mad. You're her 'baby'," Krista snickered. I quietly finished my sandwich.

Chapter 3

After lunch, Shayla and I went to our room. We opened the window and colored in our coloring books. We could hear Krista in the kitchen running water. After a while the water turned off. A few minutes later we heard the front door open and shut. Shayla and I went to the living room and turned on the TV. We found a cartoon and sat on the couch to watch it. Krista returned after we had been watching for a while. She sat down on the couch silently and watched TV with us.

Mom had bought peanut butter, jelly, a loaf of bread, a gallon of milk, and three boxes of cereal. She had not returned so Krista and I worked together to pour cereal for everyone for dinner while Shayla went to get Benny. We ate and the evening progressed as usual. However, when we awoke the next day Mom was not home. She was gone day after day. We ran out of food on day five. Shayla and I discover that some of the flowers in the field were actually edible, in other words they did not make us sick. The little yellow flowers actually did not taste too bad. Searching for flowers to eat actually distracted us a little from how hungry we were. On the eighth morning, Krista woke me up early.

"Hey, wake up. Wake up," Krista was sitting on our bed and shaking me. It was still dark outside.

"What are you doing?" I groggily asked.

"We need to talk," Krista replied.

I sat up in bed and looked at Krista, "What is wrong? Is Mom back? Is she mad?" I feared that Mom would not return and I feared how she would be if she did return.

"Shhhhhh," Shayla said as she rolled over and pulled the blanket over her head.

"Come on, let's talk out here," Krista said as she rose and walked to our bedroom door.

I rose and put on my shirt and skirt. Shayla and I would get hot at night so we were sleeping in just our underwear. Once my clothes were on, I went looking for Krista in the dim house. The sun was not up yet and the lights were out. I found Krista in the kitchen at the table. I sat down beside her.

"We have to find food today, and I don't mean the flowers you and Shayla have been eating." Krista began.

"There is no food. What are we supposed to do?" I answered.

"I think we should fill the old milk gallon with water and follow the road. It has to lead somewhere. If we stay here we could starve." Krista was obviously panicked.

"Mom could return," I argued.

"She might not, we can't wait." Krista was right.

"But if Mom does return and she learns we left she will be mad." I was afraid.

"We won't get caught. We will go together and leave Benny and Shayla here. That way if Mom does return we can just tell her we went for a walk." Krista seemed to have it all planned out.

"Ok, but let's go now before the others get up." I agreed.

I went to tell Shayla that I was going for a walk and would return later. Shayla went back to sleep. Our constant hunger actually made us sleep longer. I was worried. When I left our room Krista was already in the living room with half a gallon of water. We started down the driveway. We walked in silence, both lost in the same nagging worries. We reached the end of the drive just as the sun brightened the sky behind us.

"Which way do we go?" I asked.

"We came from the left but we never passed the town so the town must be right. That way. Besides left was the way I went last week and I didn't see anyone," Krista pointed to the left.

"What if there is nothing to the right?" I asked.

"We will walk this way, if we don't find anything then tomorrow we will try the other way." Krista started walking and I followed.

We walked beside each other. We would climb each hill in the hopes of seeing a town on the other side. At the top of each hill we only saw more fields and hills. After a while we grew tired and decided to take a break. I saw some trees in the distance and we walked over to that shade to rest.

"Krista, should we turn around?" I was worried Mom would return and know we were gone.

"There is no point. If we don't find food we will die." She said in despair.

I looked into the woods around us and noticed a small red ball.

"Krista, look," I exclaimed.

"What? Oh, a ball. So what?" Krista sounded annoyed.

"So, how did it get here? We are too far from the road. Someone must have left it here. Maybe there is a house nearby. Come on let's go look." I welcomed exploring in the woods more than the road because the shade was much cooler.

"You go ahead and let me know what you find. I need to rest." With that Krista leaned against a tree and relaxed.

I went over to the ball and looked around. I decided to go towards the sun. The sun had only risen a little so I thought if I went straight towards it I would not get lost. I did not walk far before the trees began to thin. At the edge of the trees I paused and looked around. In the distance I could see a two story yellow house. It was beautiful. The house had a porch that seemed to wrap all around. The Porch had white railings and there were blue shutters on all the windows of the house. It looked like a fairy tale house. I almost thought it was not real. The house lay in a large valley surrounded by hills. It was beautiful. I ran back to tell Krista what I found. Krista followed me back through the woods. We arrived at the edge of the woods and paused.

"Should we knock on the door and ask for help?" I asked.

"We can't, what if they call the cops. You know what happened to Stacy." Krista whispered back to me.

Just then the front door opened and a boy and a girl ran outside. Krista and I ducked behind the trees. We watched as a man and a woman carrying a baby came outside as well. The boy and father were wearing ties and jackets with matching pants. The baby, woman and little girl were wearing beautiful dresses. We watched as they all got in the car and drove down the driveway. The car had a weird fish sticker on the back window. We watched as the car faded from view.

"Quick, now's our chance," Krista grabbed my hand and the water gallon and pulled me to the house.

"What are we going to do?" I asked as I ran to keep up.

"Just be quiet and follow my lead," Krista replied. When we got to the house Krista put the water down and rang the doorbell.

"What are you doing?" I whispered.

"Shush," Krista hissed before ringing the doorbell again.

When no one answered the door, Krista started to walk around the porch towards the back door while looking through the windows. The back door was unlocked. We went inside. The house was incredible. There was food everywhere in the kitchen. There were toys strewn everywhere. It looked like paradise to me. I had never seen so much of everything.

"No one is home. Go grab those two wagons on the porch. We will take some food and they will never know we were here." Krista was older and I wanted to make her happy so I did not argue. Besides, they had so much, surely they would not miss a little. We packed as much food as we could in the wagons. I remembered to grab the water gallon from the front porch. When the wagons were full, Krista and I explored the rest of the house.

"Look at how much they have. Can we take a few things?" I asked as we were exploring the girls room.

"Ok, but only a few things." Krista anxiously said as she looked out the windows.

She found us each a backpack. I found some red shampoo with a princess on the bottle that smelled like strawberries and some beautiful clothes that would fit Shayla and me. Then I packed four Barbie dolls and as many clothes and shoes for them that I could. I also grabbed two pairs of tennis shoes and two pairs of sandals for Shayla and I. Krista found some clothes, a hair brush, some lip gloss, toothpaste, new toothbrushes for each of us, and a baby doll with clothes. There were no shoes there that fit her so she grabbed some flip flops from the big bedroom. Then we left quickly. Krista was worried that the family might return at any moment. We decided to go over the hill in the hopes of getting home quicker.

"Are we thieves?" I asked, feeling guilty for everything we took. I pulled one wagon loaded with food while Krista pulled the other. We each were wearing the backpacks we packed.

"We don't have a choice. Besides, they have everything. They probably won't even notice this stuff missing," Krista puffed. The wagons and backpacks were heavy.

Krista had a point. Those people seemed to have everything. I could not help but wonder about them. What was it like to live there? Was it nice? Were they happy? They seemed to have everything.

We eventually made it back to the house. Mom was not back. Benny and Shayla marveled at our tale of the magical house filled with food and toys and clothes. The magical house that was chilly inside despite the heat outside. The house that was beautiful and magical. Benny and Shayla helped us unpack the food. When we finished unpacking the food, we ate apples and oranges for lunch. It was wonderful.

Benny grabbed some chips and apples and said he was going to camp in the shed. He said there was a cot out there and left. Shayla, Krista and I unpacked the book bags we brought. Shayla loved the new clothes and shoes even though they were a little tight on her. We changed into the new clean clothes. I wore a blue cotton dress with little red flowers all over it. Shayla wore purple shorts with a yellow and white lace top. Krista was wearing a jean skirt and a rainbow tank top. We felt so beautiful in the new clothes. We then went to the porch to play with our new toys.

The sky was starting to grow darker. After a little while it started to storm so we went inside. We played in the living room while watching cartoons for the rest of the day. We ate bologna sandwiches and chips for dinner. Then for dessert we each had a chocolate bar. Benny stayed in the shed. We went to bed happy and full of hope that night.

Mom was still gone in the morning. Krista, Shayla, and I ate pop tarts for breakfast. Then Shayla and I took a bath together. I wanted to try the princess shampoo. I thought it might turn us into princesses. We took the Barbie dolls into the tub with us. We washed each other's hair and then played until the water turned too cold.

Then we got out and dressed in our new clothes. I loved my new blue dress and declared blue was my new favorite color. The new shoes were a little big but very comfortable. I regretted not getting new underwear and socks. Krista and Shayla went to try and wash our dirty clothes in the kitchen sink. I grabbed my now empty backpack and snuck out when they were distracted. I wanted to see the magic house and the mysterious family again.

Chapter 4

I avoided the road and went through the fields and over the hills. When I reached the top of the last hill and could see the house I ducked down and ran to the trees. I sat hidden in the trees and watched the house. The sun was high in the sky but it felt cool in the shade of the trees. I regretted not grabbing something to eat and drink before I left but I did not want to let Krista know where I was going and why. I just wanted to see the family again.

When I saw the family yesterday, I had a feeling that I could not understand. They all looked so happy as they were leaving. Almost like they did not have a worry in the world. They were laughing and joking as they went to their car. I had had a dream last night that I was part of their family. I did not worry about food. I dreamed that the mother had held me and read me a book then she tucked me into bed and kissed my forehead like Stacy used to. I woke up saddened and just wanted to return. So, here I was watching the house.

At first I did not see much. Then I heard a door open and shut. I could not see anyone so I decided to get closer. I crept closer and peeked around the side of the house. I heard a woman singing a song I had never heard before. I still didn't see anyone. I ran up the porch steps and tiptoed around the house towards the backyard where the singing was coming from. When I got to the corner, I peeked. The mother was hanging clothes on a clothes line and singing. Her back was to me. I looked in the window of the house

and did not see anyone. I made a split decision and quietly went to the back door and entered the house.

I grabbed some juice boxes and some apples, oranges, and peaches. I then ran towards the stairs. The baby was in a playpen sleeping. I must have made noise because when I started up the stairs the baby awoke and started to cry. I ran to the girls room and hid in the closet. I thought for sure I'd been discovered. After a while of not being found I tiptoed to the door of the room and looked toward the stairs. I did not see anyone so I went quietly to the top of the stairs and peeked down. The mother was holding the baby and talking silly to the baby. I went back to the girls room and quietly shut the door. I went around the room slowly looking and touching everything. I imagined growing up in such a wonderful room. When I got to the dresser I made sure to grab some socks and underwear. I also grabbed some nightgowns. I went back to the closet and grabbed a few more dresses. I put everything into my backpack. I wanted her life, her room, her mother. This girl was a princess. She was cared for. She was loved.

I spent the day in that room. I pretended it was my room. I found some books with colorful pictures and put 9 of them in my backpack. I could not read but I hoped Krista would read to me. Then I heard the front door open. I looked out the window and saw the boy and girl walking down the driveway in the distance. They were wearing backpacks. I grabbed my backpack full of treasure, and dashed to the stairs. The mother had stepped off the porch to greet the kids so I quietly went downstairs and darted out the back door. I ran as fast as I could up the hill and ducked behind it. I did not know if I was seen. I quickly made my way home.

Shayla saw me coming and ran towards me. Krista was on the porch and looked mad. The shed door was open but I did not see Benny. Mom's car was still gone.

"Where were you? Did you go to the magic house?" Shayla said excitedly.

Before I could answer Krista shouted from the porch, "Samantha get your ass over here now, you selfish stupid ass!"

I walked quickly to the porch. I knew I should not have gone. I knew Krista would be mad. I just did not know how mad.

When I reached the porch Krista turned and said, "Follow me." Shayla stayed on the porch as I followed Krista into the room I shared with Shayla. Krista shut the door. I turned to face her and suddenly felt a sharp pain across my cheek. Krista had slapped me. I fell on the floor and she was immediately on top of me. She hit me twice more than she wrapped both of her hands around my throat until I could not breathe.

"You had no right to go back to that house! You could have been caught! You are so selfish! You are not to leave this house without my permission again! You are the stupidest most selfish......" She said while choking me. I clawed at her face and hands but she wouldn't loosen her grip. She was still yelling at me when I blacked out.

I regained consciousness slowly. My eyes were closed but I heard the sound of voices, crying and a weird thudding noise. Also, I was curled up on my side on a cold metal surface. My head and neck hurt and there was a roaring in my ears. I was thirsty and dizzy. I did a quick inventory of my body with my eyes closed. I tried not to move. I seemed fine, just sore and in pain.

"I don't want to," I recognized Shayla's terrified voice.

"Just shut up and dig. She deserved it. She shouldn't have run away." Krista sounded annoyed.

"What do we tell Mommy?" Shayla sounded so upset and scared. My throat hurt so much. I tried to swallow.

"We will just tell her she ran away. That is true." I heard Krista say.

I started to cough and opened my eyes. Krista and Shayla were a few feet away digging with little shovels. I was on the wagon. I touched my throat and my face where the pain was. There must have been blood on my face because my hand came back with blood

on it. I looked at my sisters. Shayla looked shocked and amazed. Krista looked shocked and annoyed.

"You're alive!" Shayla exclaimed and ran over and hugged me. Krista stood up and threw down the shovel, "Well, you just wasted my whole day. You better have learned your lesson. You are not allowed to return to that house without me again." Krista angrily stormed off towards the house.

"Are you ok?" Shayla asked as she helped me off the wagon.

"What happened? How did I get here?" I felt headachy and confused.

"Krista killed you. She made me get the wagon. We put you on it. We got shovels from Benny in the shed then Krista made me pull the wagon out here. She said we had to bury you so Mom wouldn't find out." Shayla explained.

I looked at the hole that would have been my grave. I felt scared.

"I am thirsty, let's go inside," I croaked.

Shayla pulled the wagon while we walked slowly to the house. Inside Krista was watching TV and eating a sandwich on the couch. She barely looked at me before turning back to the TV. Shayla and I went into the bathroom. I looked in the mirror. There was a small cut on the left side of my face just a small distance from my eye. My neck was bruised and looked like it may have a few cuts from Krista's nails. I took a washcloth and cleaned up the best I could. Then Shayla and I went to the kitchen. Shayla poured some juice while I peeled the last of the oranges. We ate in silence. It hurt to swallow but the juice tasted good and I began to feel better.

After we ate, Shayla and I went to our room. I showed her the stuff I got from the magic house. She loved the nightgown and dress. I then took the nightgown and dress I got for Krista out to the living room. Krista was still on the couch.

"I am sorry I went back without telling you," I said, fearing she may still be mad but hoping that I could calm her down. I wanted her to

love me. "I got you something. Do you like them?" I said as I handed her the dress and nightgown.

"If we take too much they will find out and we won't be able to get what we need. You need to stay away. You are so dumb sometimes." She said this and then looked down at the items I had given her. "This is a nightgown."

"We didn't have anything to sleep in so I went back to get us something," I replied.

"Thanks. I like the dress too. Red is my favorite color. Did you know that?" She asked.

"Yes, most of your clothes are red," I said.

"Well, thanks. Go to your room and play. I will call you for dinner." She returned her attention to the TV.

I walked back to the bedroom and spent the rest of the afternoon playing dolls and looking at the pictures in the books I got. I was going to ask Krista to read us one but worried that she was still mad. I decided to ask tomorrow. I hid the books under the bed. They were a secret treasure. When Krista called us to dinner a short time later, we went and ate in silence. When I finished, I asked if I could go for a walk but Krista said I was grounded and had to stay in the house. Benny had taken his food to the shed. I wondered what he did out there all the time.

I went to bed early. The sun was still setting in the sky. Shayla was watching TV with Krista. I curled up on the bed and fell asleep picturing the beautiful girls room where I had spent hours today. I remembered the feel of the soft comforter on the bed. I recalled how thin the pink curtains were, they were so soft and billowy. I loved the feel of the silky nightgown on my skin. It made the memories more vivid. I dreamed of living there where the nice mother would care for me and no one would hurt me. I was tired of having to be strong. Stacy always used to say that dwelling on the life we wanted only made the reality worse.

I awoke suddenly to a loud bang. It was dark outside. Shayla was asleep beside me. I slipped out of bed without waking her. I

crept to the door slowly and peeked out. Krista was asleep on the couch in the new nightgown I gave her. Then I heard the sound of footsteps coming toward the front door. A minute later I saw Mom approach the door carrying her purse and one bag of groceries. I quickly went to the door and opened the door for her.

"Hello, Mommy. Can I help?" I was excited. Throughout my life my mom had been routinely abusive, but she was the only Mom I had and I loved her. I needed a Mom.

"Thank you, Sissy. What are you doing up? It is 5:30 in the morning." She said as she handed me her purse.

"I heard your car door shut," I answered as I put her purse on the floor beside the couch. It was very heavy.

"Well, take the groceries out of the bag while I go to the restroom," She then turned and went into the bathroom.

The bag of groceries was on the table. I climbed on a chair and began taking everything out of the bag slowly so I would not break anything and make her mad. I missed her. I took out two boxes of cereal, one loaf of bread, one package of bacon, a carton of eggs, a half gallon of milk, some oil, coffee and a small bag of potatoes. Mom returned from the bathroom and grabbed the eggs and milk to put them in the refrigerator.

"What the hell?!?" She said when she saw the food we had taken from the magic house. "Samantha, where did all this shit come from?" Mom exclaimed.

I turned terrified. I wished I had stayed in bed, "You were gone and there was no food. We were hungry so Krista and I found a magic house and got the food from there. The magic house had so much that Krista said they would not even miss what we took. I am sorry Mommy. We were hungry. Please don't be mad," I stood on the chair facing my mom terrified that she would be mad as I desperately tried to explain.

Mom turned and put the eggs and milk in the refrigerator without a word. She then took the empty bag off the table. She went outside and retrieved two more paper bags full of groceries. I held

the door open and then emptied the bags as she put the food and supplies away quietly. I was so scared that she was getting angrier. However, when I got up the courage to look her in the face she looked sad and I saw tears running down her cheeks.

Chapter 5

When she finished putting up the groceries she made a pot of coffee in the coffee maker. As the coffee brewed she folded the empty bags and put them in an empty drawer. She poured herself a cup of coffee and sat at the table. She looked so sad. I know many people will not understand this, but even though my mother hurt us a lot I loved her. She was my mom and I wanted everyone I loved to be happy. Seeing her sad made me want to comfort her.

I got down from my chair where I was sitting and walked the few feet to my mom's chair. I put my hand on her hand and she looked up at me. She had been staring into her coffee cup lost in her own mind.

"Mommy, why are you sad?" I asked in a small sweet voice.

She reached down and pulled me onto her lap and gave me a hug. I felt the tears on my shoulder and back. Mom quietly cried for a few minutes while I held her confused to why she was sad. Then she took a few deep breaths and stopped hugging me. I was still on her lap but now we were sitting face to face.

"Mommy, what's wrong?" I asked again. This whole scene was confusing to me.

"I am just sad that I am failing as a mother. I can't afford to feed my own children. I used to make hundreds of dollars a night. Now, I barely make anything. I am too old and no one wants me anymore. It took me this long just to be able to afford to pay the rent, buy gas and buy the few groceries I did. I have been sleeping in my car since I left because I did not have the gas to return. I thought about you kids everyday but there was nothing I could do. I had to make money. I know you don't understand all this but I don't know what

to do. I need to make some more money or they will turn off the water and electricity." Mom paused to take a drink of her coffee. "Mommy, why don't you get a different job?" I did not know what my mom's job was but I thought that there had to be different jobs. "Oh, Sissy, it is not that simple. I don't have any experience. I have technically never had a job. Nowadays you have to have experience. Besides, no one wants to hire me." Mom seemed to be getting agitated. "I made so much money when I was younger. I wish I could go back and be smarter. I would have done everything different."

"Mommy, is there another way to make money? Can I help? I can get a job?" I saw Mom getting upset and wanted to calm her down before it got bad.

"You're too young, Sissy. I will figure it out." She pushed me off her lap and I sat down on the chair beside her. I watched in silence as my mom slowly finished her coffee. She was no longer staring at her coffee. Instead she was staring at the couch where Krista was still sleeping. I wondered what she was thinking. She seemed deep in thought and had a funny look I could not identify on her face. The sun began to rise. "Tell the rest that I went for a drive. I will be back in a few hours. Tell Krista to get the clothes off the clothes line. Then you girls get this house cleaned up before I return." With that Mom got up and grabbed her purse on her way outside.

I went to my room and woke up Shayla. We got ready for the day in our new dresses. We also wore our new underwear and socks. We put on our shoes and went to the living room. Krista was already up and wearing her new dress. I told them that Mom was here that morning and about the instructions she gave before she left. Krista asked where Mom had gone but I told her I did not know.

Krista gave Shayla and I the empty laundry basket and sent us outside to get the laundry off the line. Shayla and I went outside but could not quite reach the line so I went inside and got a chair. We then took the clothes off the line. Shayla would stand on the chair and hand me the clean clothes that I would then put in the

basket. When the clothes were off the line I carried the chair back inside while Shayla carried the clothes basket. Krista was almost done sweeping the floors. Krista gave me a cloth and told me to wipe everything off. She said it was called dusting. When she finished the floors, Shayla and Krista began to put up the clothes. Afterwards, Krista took my cloth and the rest of the dirty clothes and put them in the hamper which she then put in the closet. Then we washed our hands and went to get breakfast.

"Samantha, put Mom's coffee cup in the sink then put cups for us on the table. Shayla, I want you to take some pop tarts and juice to Benny. Tell him Mom will be back soon." Krista said as she poured the juice and got everyone a package of pop tarts. I took the cups of juice to the table one at a time. Then we sat down and began to eat.

After breakfast Krista did the dishes while Shayla and I took our dolls to the porch to play in the cool breeze. When the dishes were done, Krista brought her doll outside to play on the porch as well. Eventually we heard the sound of an engine approaching. Soon we saw Mom's car coming down the driveway. We all rushed to organize all our toys into a single pile so Mom would not think we were making a mess. Then we stood up and went to greet her at her car door.

"Mommy!"Shayla and I exclaimed when we approached. We each smiled big, eager to engender goodwill.

"Hi, Mommy. We miss you. I cleaned everything like you said." Krista did not mention that Shayla and I helped because she knew she would be punished if she did. I was not supposed to do chores unless Mommy told me to. I was the baby. Shayla was not suppose to do chores because Mom said she was too stupid to do anything right. Mom did not like Shayla much for some reason. She called Shayla retarded all the time. I did not know what that meant but it seemed to be an insult. I thought Shayla was fun to play with.

"Hey, kids. It is nice to see you," Mom got out of the car and gave us one big group hug. Then she reached into the car and got out a bag and her purse.

"Can I carry the bag?" I asked, curious to peek inside.

"No. I want you and Shayla to gather your dolls and go play in the field. I don't want you to come back to the house until I call you. Krista, I want you to go sit on the couch. I will be right behind you." Mom said.

Krista looked at me fearfully. There was nothing to do. Mom's orders had to be followed but I feared for Krista. I quickly grabbed our dolls. Shayla and I carried all the toys to the field. Krista and Mom went inside the house. I did not hear screaming but I was still worried yet I had to protect Shayla.

"Shayla, I need to see what is happening?" I whispered to Shayla.

"No, Mom will get mad." Shayla said fearfully.

"I have to. You stay here. I will sneak and peek in the window. I have to make sure Mom is not hurting Krista. Stacy is gone so it is my job to protect us. I will yell if it is bad. If you hear me yell, then you run to the trees in the distance and hide until I come and get you. You will be safe." I then got up and wiped the dirt and grass from my knees.

Shayla was silent as she watched me walk to the house. When I reached the side of the house I looked back to see Shayla standing and holding a doll close to her chest. I knew she was scared. I was scared as well, but had to help Krista if I could. I ducked down and quietly made my way to the living room window on the side of the house. The window was open to let in the breeze. I heard weird noises and occasional giggling but it did not sound like Mom or Krista.

"Stop closing your eyes and watch. You have to learn how to do it," Mom's voice was close.

"Mom, it looks so gross. Doesn't it hurt? I don't want to watch it," Krista sounded scared and confused.

"Stop complaining or I will give you something to complain about!" Mom sounded upset.

I heard footsteps retreating so I took that moment to peek through the window. Krista was on the couch watching Mom's retreat. Mom went to the kitchen and disappeared for a minute.

"Krista, are you ok?" I whispered.

Krista turned towards my voice, "What are you doing? You are going to get us both in trouble."

"I was worried," I whispered back.

"Mom is making me watch this awful movie with naked people hurting each other with their private parts. Oh, no, she's coming back, duck." Krista whispered back seconds before Mom returned with her coffee cup in her hand. She must have reheated the coffee because there was steam rising from the cup.

I ducked back down but now I was curious. What did Krista mean? What movie? After a few minutes I slowly peeked through the window again. Mom was on the couch sipping her coffee. Krista was wincing but watching TV anyway. I turned my attention to the TV. There was a man and a woman. The man was on top of the woman and the woman was groaning. They were sweating and the man kept calling the woman mean names. It looked gross. I quickly ducked down. I made my way back to the field where Shayla was. I told Shayla what I saw. Shayla asked me to show her with the dolls what the people on TV were doing. I took the clothes off two dolls. We only had girl Barbie dolls so I told her to pretend one was a boy. Then I demonstrated what the people on TV were doing. Shayla said that maybe they were glued together and stuck. It did not make sense to us. We decided to wait and ask Krista about it later. We played with our dolls until Mom called us in for lunch.

Chapter 6

Mom had made spaghetti for lunch. There were only four chairs at the table. Benny was already in one chair. Krista was helping Mom put the food on the table. Shayla and I went to wash our hands. When we returned to the table, Mom and Krista had

finished setting the table. Mom was sitting in the chair next to Benny. Krista was sitting across from Mom looking down at her plate. That left one chair. I knew what was about to happen and hated it.

"Come sit by me, Samantha. Shayla, you can sit on the floor over there," Mom pointed to the corner on the other side of the table.

Shayla rarely got to sit at the table with the rest of us when Mom was home. I did not like it because it made me feel sad for Shayla. Shayla was my friend.

"Mommy, could I please share a seat with Shayla. I don't mind really," I just wanted a new arrangement.

"That is ridiculous. Just come sit down and eat. Shayla get in the corner." Mom then began to eat.

"Mommy, could Shayla at least sit by my chair. I like having her close. Please, Mommy," I said giving Mom my most angelic baby face.

"I can't say no to my little perfect princess. It is fine if you want that mongrel to sit beside you." Mom said as she continued to eat.

Benny ate and told Mom all the stuff he had found in the old shed. Shayla sat on the floor and ate her food quickly. She always got far less food than the rest of us so when she finished I secretly passed her food from my plate. Krista occasionally glanced my way but spent most of the time just staring at her food. She did not eat much and I began to worry. What had happened? Did the movies make her sick? Did Mom hurt her? I ate my food silently just watching everyone around me. When we were done, Krista got up to clear the table.

"Mom, I am going back outside," Benny said as he got up.

"Hold up, I am going into town to make some phone calls. I want you to go with me. Go take a shower and put on some clean clothes," Mom said. Benny turned and went into his room for some clean clothes before he went to the bathroom and closed the door. Mom turned to Krista, "I will be back late. Have the leftover spaghetti for dinner. Also wash some more clothes and sweep the porches." Then

she poured herself a cup of coffee. She paused on her way to the living room to kiss my forehead.

Krista cleaned up the kitchen while Shayla and I went outside to gather all of our dolls. We took them to the porch. We played quietly as we waited for Mom and Benny to leave. We were playing dress up with our dolls when Mom and Benny came out of the house. Benny had on clean jeans and a t-shirt. Mom gave me a hug and then walked to the car. She turned the car around then drove out of sight.

"Shayla, take the dolls into our room. I need to talk to Krista," I was in a hurry to talk to her.

"Ok" Shayla replied as she gathered the toys.

I ran to the kitchen and found Krista almost finished cleaning the kitchen. The dishes were clean, the kitchen was wiped down and now she was just drying and putting away the dishes.

"Krista, Mom is gone. What was that movie about and why did she make you watch it?" my curiosity was overpowering.

Krista put up the cup she was drying and turned towards me, "Are you sure she is gone?"

"We watched her drive out of sight before we came in. Shayla is bringing the toys in from outside," I reassured her.

Krista put down the dish towel. She then walked to the table and sat down. I sat beside her anxious for answers. She had her hands on the table and was looking at them. She had a look of sadness and embarrassment on her face. What had happened? Krista finally looked up at me. The look on her face made me feel pity for her.

"Mom said that she could not afford to take care of us anymore. She said she needed my help. She said that since I was older it was my job. She then made me watch that movie. She said the people were having sex. She said that I had to watch it. Every time I looked away or closed my eyes she would hit me. I am scared. It looks so painful. It is gross. The men kept peeing white pee on the women. The women were making weird faces. One women put a man's private in

her mouth and he peed white pee in her mouth. It must have tasted bad because she spit it out. I don't want to do that? Mom says I have to. What do I do?" Krista buried her face in her hands during the last few sentences.

I got down from my chair and hugged her. I did not know how to help her. I didn't really understand everything she said. I thought pee was yellow. Did boys pee a different color? Why would they pee a different color? Is it because they liked taking things apart and being dirty. Krista sobbed into her hands. Shayla came into the room and saw us like this.

"Don't tell Shayla. It will scare her," I whispered into Krista's ear.
"Hey, Shayla, did you bring in all the toys?" I asked loudly while returning to my chair.
"I think so. Can you check for me?" Shayla asked.
"Sure, why don't you come with me," I walked over to Shayla and took her hand. I wanted to give Krista some time to calm down.
"What's wrong with Krista?" Shayla worried.
"Krista is just tired. Mom made her do a lot of chores by herself today," I took Shayla's hand and led her to the door.

Shayla had missed a few toys so I helped her take them in. Shayla had just thrown the toys into the room so I also had to help clean the room. Shayla and I took about ten minutes to finish cleaning everything up. We then went back to the kitchen. Krista was folding the dish towel. The rest of the dishes were put up.
"Why don't we watch some cartoons?" I suggested.
"I have to start the laundry. I will join you soon," Krista said walking away.

Shayla and I grabbed our crayons and coloring books and went to the living room. We turned on the TV and Krista eventually returned from washing the clothes in the sink and hanging them up outside to dry. A new cartoon had just started when I noticed Krista staring off into space. She looked so sad. When the cartoon was almost over, Krista suddenly stood up.
"I think I am going to go for a walk." Krista announced.

"Do you want me to go with you?" I asked.

"No, I want to be by myself," She was clearly agitated.

"Ok," I was unsure what to do. I did not think she should be alone but she seemed hurried.

Krista went outside. Shayla and I continued watching TV. I kept looking out the window in the direction I saw Krista go. She was not home when we got hungry. We ate cold leftover spaghetti and drank a juice box for dinner.

"I am going to get Krista. If Mom returns just tell her we went for a walk together. I will be back as soon as possible," I decided.

"You can't leave me here all alone. I am scared," Shayla said quickly.

"I need to go. I will be back soon. You are ok," I could not be two places at once.

"I can go with you?" Shayla said hopefully.

"No, if we are all gone when Mom gets back then she might get mad. I will be back before you even miss me," I turned and left before she could argue.

Chapter 7

I did not want Shayla to know where I was going. I was thinking about it and knew there was only one place where Krista would go. Only one place she could go. I had watched the direction she had gone. I knew my sister. I ran through the fields and up and down the hills. When I got to the last hill I went around to the side before going over the hill. I was about 15 feet from the trees so I ran low and fast.

When I got to the trees, I looked around. I did not see anyone so I went deeper into the trees. I found the red ball. I picked it up and carried it. I found Krista sitting beside a tree a few feet into the trees. She was staring at the magic house. I sat down beside her. The dad was home and playing with the kids. We could hear the kids

laughing. The Mom was pushing the baby in a red baby swing. It looked like a perfect movie.

"Are you ok?" I did not look at her but just continued to watch the perfect family. The dad was holding the girls hands and swinging her around and around.

"I don't know. I can't do what Mom is making me do," She sounded so lost.

"I don't think there is anything we can do. Maybe Mom will change her mind," I said.

"I could tell them. Maybe they will help us," she said desperately. "Maybe they will adopt us and then we could live here. We would be safe here."

"I don't want to lose you. You know what happened to Stacy. You have to come back with me," I feared for my sister.

"You don't understand. This might be my only chance." She said as a tear rolled down her cheek.

"I will talk to Mom. I will convince her to change her mind. Trust me, I will protect you," I urged.

"Promise?" Krista was really crying now.

"I promise," I honestly thought I could convince my mother not to do what she was about to do.

I did not know it at the time but that one promise would forever separate my sister and I. I learned to forgive and forget early but Krista had a temper and never truly forgot. That promise made from a naive belief of goodness in everyone would become my curse. It was a promise said to comfort my beloved sister. I thought I could convince my mom. I would be wrong.

Krista and I got up. We walked hand in hand. We took our time returning. We did not talk. When we got home Krista went inside to eat. Shayla was on the porch watching us approach. I stayed outside and threw the ball back and forth with Shayla until we heard an engine approaching. I quickly went inside to put the ball in our closet. I returned outside just as Mom was parking the car. Krista

was on the porch with Shayla. She looked at me intensely and then turned to greet Mom.

Benny jumped out of the car and ran towards the back of the house. I knew he was headed to his shed. Benny was weird. Mom got out of the car and opened the back door. She grabbed a bag. Then she headed towards us.

"Welcome home, Mommy. Did you have fun?" I greeted.

"Actually, I am tired. But thanks for asking, Sissy," Mom looked tired but she still paused to caress my face.

"Can I help?" Krista said quietly.

"Yes. Take this bag into my room and try on these clothes. They are for you to wear when we go to town tomorrow," Mom handed the bag to Krista then she walked into the house.

Krista looked sadly at me and then went inside.

I turned to Shayla, "When we go inside I want you to go play in our room. I need to talk to Mom. Stay there until I come and get you," I was worried I would upset Mom and did not want Shayla to get hurt.

"Why?" Shayla was confused.

"Just trust me," I whispered.

"Ok, but will you tell me later?" Shayla was obviously curious.

"I will try," I did not know how much I could tell her.

Shayla and I went into the house. Mom was in the kitchen. Shayla went to our bedroom. I went into the kitchen. Mom was warming the cold coffee on the stove. I sat down at the table and watched her.

"Mommy, can we talk?" I hesitantly said.

"Sure, Sissy, what do you want to talk about?" Mom sounded tired but seemed to be in a good mood. So now was my chance.

"Mommy, I talked to Krista. She said you were going to make her do stuff tomorrow," I felt awkward talking about it and did not know what words to use but I had to try for Krista's sake.

"What did she tell you?" Mom was eyeing me.

"She said you wanted her to have..........uh.......um......sex," I looked down at my feet when I said sex. I felt so embarrassed even saying the word.

Mom turned back to her coffee and turned off the stove. She poured it into her cup and came and sat at the table. She looked at me with a smile, "Oh, Sissy, she must have misunderstood. Your sister is getting older and I just have to teach her to be a woman. You are too young to understand. Your sister clearly lied to you," Mom took a sip of her coffee.

"Then where are you taking her tomorrow?" Could Mom be telling the truth. Was Krista mistaken? Krista has always been a good liar. But, I saw the movie through the window. Was it really just a lesson?

"I just want to show her where I work," Mom answered then she turned when she heard her bedroom door open.

Krista came into the kitchen wearing a beautiful white dress. The dress went down to just above her knees. It had spaghetti straps and was lacey. She looked so young and innocent.

"Krista, you're beautiful!" I exclaimed.

"It will do. Now go take it off. I don't want you to make it dirty." Mom then turned back to her coffee.

I did not want to believe what Krista had said. Mom could be mean but I did not believe she could be that mean. I decided Krista was wrong. I choose to believe Mom. I actually started to be a little jealous. Mom never talked about her job and I did not know what her job was. I wondered why Krista got to go and not me. My sister gets a new beautiful dress and gets to go to work with Mom.

I went into the room to talk to Krista. Her new dress was on the bed and she was putting back on her clothes.

"Did you talk to Mom?" She asked when she saw me.

"Yes," I replied.

"Did she change her mind?" She asked anxiously.

"She said you misunderstood. She said she isn't going to do what you said. She said you were lying. She just wants to show you where she works," I said as I ran my hand over the new dress.

"I did not misunderstand. You said you would help. You promised!" Krista was angry.

"I did. You are wrong. Stop being silly. You are just selfish," I argued and then I turned and went quickly to my room and shut the door.

It was getting late so Shayla and I decided to take a bath. Shayla and I grabbed some toys and went to the bathroom. I put a little shampoo in the water while the water was running to make it a bubble bath. We played in the tub until Mom told us to get out because Krista needed a bath too. We got out and quickly got dressed. Shayla and I wrapped the toys in a towel to dry and carried them into our room. I wanted to avoid Krista. I was upset and jealous.

When we got to the room I grabbed a book that I had taken from the magic house. I took it to the living room and asked Mom if she would read Shayla and I a bedtime story. She agreed. So, Shayla sat on one side of Mom and I sat on the other side and we listened as Mom read about little red riding hood and the evil wolf. When she finished we hugged her good night and went to bed. I put the book back under the bed.

Chapter 8

Shayla and I always slept side by side sharing our one blanket. We did not have sheets. The mattress was lumpy and smelled funny. We cuddled together for warmth at night.

"You have not told me yet," Shayla whispered to me.

"Told you what?" I had been lost in thought and was not expecting her to talk.

"What happened to Krista?" She insisted.

"Oh, that, Krista was just making up stories. Mom said she was lying," I said angrily.

"What did she lie about?" Shayla sounded confused.

"It does not matter. Let's not play with her tomorrow. That will teach her not to be a liar," I said angrily.

Shayla was silent. I knew she was confused but I also knew she would listen to me. Shayla and I were closer to one another than Shayla and Krista. I was jealous of Krista and wanted to punish her. It was petty and childish but I did not care at the time.

Shayla fell asleep a little while later. I lay in bed listening to the noises in the house. I heard the TV turn off and knew Mom would go to bed soon. I fell asleep a few minutes later. I was dreaming about the magic house and I dreamed that the dad was spinning me around and around. I wanted a daddy. I had never had one.

"Samantha, Samantha, wake up, Samantha," someone was shaking my shoulder and whispering in my ear.

"Shhhh, I am asleep," I pushed someone away.

"Please wake up, please." I recognized Krista's voice.

I was too tired to remember I was upset. I rubbed my eyes and sat up. I looked over. Shayla was snoring softly beside me. I looked around the room while my eyes adjusted. The night was dark outside the window. I could see lightning bugs outside the window. I looked over at Krista. She was kneeling by the bed.

"What do you want? I was sleeping," I said groggily.

"I am sorry about our argument. I am scared about tomorrow. Please help me," Krista whispered.

"I did help. I talked to Mom. She said you were wrong," I wanted to go back to sleep.

"Tell me exactly what she said," Krista urged.

"Ok, fine. Sit down," I scooted over so Krista could sit down on the side of the bed. "I asked Mom if we could talk. She said yes. Then I told her what you said she wanted you to do tomorrow. I asked her if it was true. She said you were wrong. She said you lied. She said

since you were getting older you needed to know how to be a woman. She said you get to see her work tomorrow. It is not fair. I want to go. I don't want to talk to you." I said petulantly.

"Do you believe her?" Krista wondered.

"Yes, now leave me alone," I laid back down and turned away from her.

Recounting the conversation for her left the feelings of jealousy ripe. I was upset all over again. I could feel Krista sitting on the bed. I pretended to go to sleep. After a while I started to actually fall asleep. Then I felt movement. Krista laid down beside me. She got under the cover and put her arm around me.

"I hope you're right," I heard her whisper as she drifted off to sleep.

Her words echoed in my mind. I began to replay the conversation with Mom in my mind. I knew Mom lied but had a hard time believing Krista. Looking back, I think a part of me just did not want to believe that my mom was capable of that. I awoke early from a nightmare I could not remember. Shayla and Krista were still asleep. I climbed out of bed and went down the hall to the bathroom. When I returned I shook Krista awake.

"What?" She said sleepily.

"You have to go back to the couch before Mom wakes up," I whispered.

"Ugh, ok," Krista stood up and slowly left the room.

I heard her go to the bathroom. I quietly got dressed for the day. I did not want to go back to bed. I left the room. I saw Krista had returned to the couch and was lying on her side with her back to the rest of the room. I peeked in Mom's room. She was still asleep. Benny was not there so I figured he had slept in the shed. I walked to the door. I went outside and waited for the day to begin.

Soon the sun had risen behind the house. I heard noises so I went inside. Mom was in the kitchen. Krista was putting on some clothes but not the pretty white dress. Shayla was coming out of the bathroom. I went to our room and helped her find clothes. I helped her with her shoes. We walked to the kitchen and sat at the table to

watch Mom make breakfast. She was scrambling the eggs when we got there. The coffee was finished brewing and Mom was already drinking a cup. There was a plate of bacon on the counter. Krista came in and Mom told her to make the toast. Mom saw Shayla at the table and sent her out to get Benny. Mom gave me some cups and told me to pour some juice for everyone. Krista came over and helped me as the bread toasted.

When the eggs were done Mom made a plate for each of us. We all sat where we had the day before. Mom had given me an extra piece of bacon so I was really excited. When we were done eating Shayla and I took the red ball outside. We played catch. After her chores were done, Krista came outside.

"Hey, throw the ball to me," Krista wanted to play.

"No," Shayla and I said giggling.

"I want to play," Krista said.

"Fine, let's play hide and seek," I suggested. "I'm it. Go hide." I walked over to Shayla and whispered, "Run around the house but don't hide. We are going to trick her."

I walked to the porch and covered my eyes. I counted to ten twice.

"Ready or not, here I come," I shouted.

I opened my eyes. Shayla was approaching from the side of the house but Krista was nowhere to be seen.

"Did you see where she went?" I giggled at Shayla.

"She went behind the shed," Shayla giggled back.

"Come on," I said.

I grabbed her hand and took Shayla inside. We went into our room and took out our coloring books. We colored on the floor. We were spread out and having fun when we heard Krista calling our names outside. We both giggled. Eventually, we heard the front door open and shut.

"Mom, have you seen Shayla and Samantha?" We heard Krista ask Mom in the living room.

"They're in their room," Mom answered.

Krista came into our room a moment later, "I thought we were playing?" She sounded sad. Shayla and I just giggled.

"Can I color with you?" she asked softly.

"We don't want to play with you," I said snottily.

Krista knelt down beside me, "I'm sorry. Please forgive me." She looked so sad.

"Ok, fine. We are tired of coloring anyway. Do you want to play house?" I relented.

"Ok." She answered.

We cleaned up the colors and coloring books and took out our Barbie dolls and Barbie clothes. We played together until Mom called Krista. Shayla and I put up the dolls and went out of the room to find out what was happening. Krista was in the kitchen making everyone sandwiches while Mom was at the table drinking coffee. Shayla carried a plate outside to the shed for Benny. We ate our lunch in silence. After Krista cleaned up from lunch Mom told her to put on her new dress. Krista and Mom gave me a hug and they both got in the car to leave. I looked in Krista's face through the windshield. She looked so scared. I hoped I was right about Mom. I watched them drive out of sight.

Chapter 9

Benny stayed in the shed all evening. Shayla and I played hide and seek and tag outside until we got too hungry. We went into the house. We ate pop tarts and juice for dinner. Then we decided to make popcorn and watch TV. When it started to get dark outside Shayla and I got ready for bed. I put Shayla to bed and told her I was not tired and wanted to watch more TV. The truth is that I was worried about Krista. The look Krista had given me through the windshield haunted me. I kept seeing it over and over. I turned on the TV to a kids movie. I turned the volume low. Then I quietly walk out to the front porch. I sat on the chair that was there. I watched the night come alive. It was a beautiful night.

The moon was a large crescent. The sky was almost cloudless and the stars were bright. The crickets were chirping. There was a breeze that tickled the tall grass causing it to sway in the wind. The air smelled crisp and cool. In the distance an owl hooted. The scene was captivating. Yet, my mind was lost to the beauty.

I replayed the conversations with Mom. Usually Stacy talked to Mom. Stacy said Mom lied all the time but she also said Krista lied sometimes. Who was telling the truth? Who was lying? Did my jealousy get the best of me? Is my sister safe? These questions and more echoed in my mind. I did not have an answer for even one question. I missed Stacy. She would have known the answers. I could feel the tears run down my cheeks.

Bang. Bang. I awoke with a start. I rubbed my eyes. Mom's car was back and Mom and Krista were walking towards the house. They did not see me yet. Krista was holding her stomach and had what looked like tears running down her cheeks. Mom was walking fast and had a smile on her face.

"Hi," I greeted them quietly as they reached the porch. Krista was a few steps behind Mom. She barely looked at me.

"What are you doing up?" Mom asked in reply.

"I couldn't sleep so I was sitting on the porch and must have fallen asleep," I answered quickly.

"Well, go into bed. It is after 2," Mom went inside.

I followed Krista inside. When I saw Mom go to the bathroom, I stepped beside Krista and whispered, "Are you ok? Did Mom make you......" I could not finish the sentence.

"I don't want to talk to you. I hate you. You made me go with her. I could have gotten help. You suck. I will never forgive you for this. It is all your fault." Krista hissed.

She then turned and headed for the bathroom. Mom was exiting the bathroom just as Krista reached the door. Krista went in and closed the door. I stood there in shock just staring at the door. Did this mean Krista did not lie? Did I do this to my sister? Was it my fault? Mom saw me standing there and told me to go to bed. I

walked stiffly to my room. I felt like I was in shock. I felt so sad. What had I done?

After a long while I heard Krista exit the bathroom. I wanted to go to her. I wanted to hold her. I could not move. I lay there staring at the ceiling. I just could not bring myself to move. I felt like I was drowning. I felt like I was lost. I felt more alone than I had ever felt. I did this. It was my fault. I hurt my sister.

I laid in bed until the sun started to brighten the sky. I could not sleep. I lay there riddled with guilt. Krista would never forgive me for this. Shayla was waking up so I went with her to the bathroom. I helped Shayla find some clothes. I put on my new blue dress, the one I took from the magic house. I chose to wear it because I wished I could go back and let Krista go to that family for help. Even if that meant losing her forever like we lost Stacy. Maybe it would have been better. Shayla and I went to the kitchen for breakfast.

Krista was lying on the couch in a fetal position. She was still asleep. There were water tracks on her face. She must have cried herself to sleep. I opened Mom's door a crack. I looked in Mom's room and saw she was asleep. I took Shayla's hand and went to the kitchen. I grabbed two bowls and the cereal. Shayla got two spoons and the milk. We ate quietly. No one was awake when we finished so we cleaned up. Shayla wanted to play with the dolls so I helped her take them to the porch so she would not wake anyone up.
"Shayla, I want to go for a walk. Are you ok staying here?" I whispered.
"Where are you going?" Shayla asked.
"I just need to think," I did not want her to tell anyone where I was going.
"Think about what," Shayla was distracted putting a dress on her doll.
"Just some stuff. Are you ok out here?" I said.
"Ok, can we play tag later?" Shayla asked, distracted.
"Yes, later," I hopped off the porch and headed across the yard.

Chapter 10

I knew where I was going. I just did not know what I would do when I got there. I just knew I had to go. I got to the stand of trees quicker than I expected. I was so lost in my head I forgot to duck down and run. Instead I did not realize I was there until I was among the trees. I went to the spot I found Krista sitting the other day. I sat down and watched the house. Could these people help us? Would they want to? I expected the kids to go to school soon but they did not leave. I saw movement in the house but no one was coming outside.

The dad came out first. He got in his car and drove away. What would I even tell them if I did go there? We took their stuff without asking? Maybe they thought we were ghosts? What if they were mad? What do you say in this situation? I don't even know what happened.

"That is my sister's dress," the little boy was standing off to my right just out of the trees.

I was so lost in my thoughts I had not even seen him come outside. I jumped up ready to run.

"Don't be scared. Lacy did not like it anyway. She prefers pink," the boy smiled at me and I paused unsure what to do. "My name is Brian. What is your name?"

"Um....Uh....Samantha," I felt scared.

"Hi, Samantha. I saw you here talking to someone the other day. Was that your sister?" Brian sounded nice.

"Yes," I answered. "Why didn't you go to school today?"

"Schools out for the summer," Brian came closer. He was only a few feet in front of me now.

"Where is your sister?" I asked, looking towards the house.

"She is helping Mom with the baby," Brian said. "Where do you live? Are you close? There is no one to play with here. Do you have a brother?"

Brian was curious but I didn't know what to tell him. He seemed so nice and seemed friendly. He smiled at me and seemed to like me.

"I live over that way," I said pointing. "I have a brother but he does not like people."

"That sucks. Do you want to play?" Brian smiled.

"Ok," I answered, "But what if your sister sees my dress. Will she be mad?"

"No, just say you got it at the mall. They have hundreds of them there." Brian seemed so cool.

I played tag and kick ball with Brian. I had so much fun that for a little while I forgot why I had come. It was so much fun just having fun. I met his sister Lacy. She said she used to have a dress like mine but that she could not find it. Brian's Mom was named Sally. The baby was called Sandra. I lost track of the time. It wasn't until Sally asked if I wanted to stay for lunch that I realized how late it was. I said I had to go and ran over the hill towards the house.

I was half way home when something hit me from behind. I fell to the ground hard. My breath rushed out of me. There was a heavy weight on my back.

"You bitch! You backstabbing whore! You traitor!" I heard Krista yell.

"Please let me up," I begged.

"Have you been talking to them this whole time?" Krista said as she held me down.

"No, I swear, please, I can't breathe," my voice was barely more than a whisper.

"I saw you, don't lie to me you selfish whore!" Krista was yelling right in my ear as she pulled my hair.

"Please, let me explain, please, Krista, please," I begged.

"Explain fast or I swear I will kill you and drop your body on the doorstep of your new family," Krista hissed in my ear before rolling off of me and sitting just a foot away.

I sat up. I was sore in a few spots and my ankle hurt really bad. My ankle twisted when I fell. I dusted the dirt and grass off my face and dress. Then I looked up into the angry face of my sister. She was glaring at me with hate in her eyes.

"I went there for you. I remembered what you said about asking for help. I did not know what to say so I sat down to think. The boy found me and he was nice. I just did not know what to say so I just did not say anything. I got distracted. He was nice." I tried to explain.

"That is a lie. I hate you. You just wanted to keep them for yourself. I wish you were dead." Krista punched me in the face then she stood up and ran towards our house.

I stood up. It hurt too much to put pressure on my ankle so I limped home. Shayla was no longer on the porch but our dolls were. I went inside. Everyone was sitting down for lunch.

"What happened to you?" Mom asked when she saw me.

I looked at Krista. She was not looking my way. "I fell down and hurt my ankle" I said looking at Mom.

"Let me see," Mom came close and knelt down. "It looks sprained. Krista get your sister a bag of ice."

Mom picked me up and put me on the couch. Mom then went to get my lunch off the table so I could eat on the couch. She went to the bathroom to grab a wet washcloth to clean me off. Krista returned with my bag of ice when Mom was out of the room. Krista threw the bag of ice and hit me hard in the chest. I quickly put it on my ankle. When Mom returned with the washcloth I used the wet washcloth to clean my face, hands, arms, legs, and dress. I then took my plate and began to eat my sandwich and chips. Shayla was sitting on the floor in the corner of the kitchen. My seat was empty and Mom still would not let Shayla sit at the table. Krista was at the table. Every once in a while she would glare at me. I could not finish my lunch. I felt sick to my stomach.

Chapter 11

After Mom finished lunch she got another cup of coffee and came to sit with me on the couch. She turned on a game show channel and watched TV. She began chain smoking one cigarette after another. Shayla brought our dolls in from the porch. Then Shayla came and sat on the floor in front of me. Krista was doing the kitchen chores. For the first time in my life I did not feel guilty for not helping. I felt relieved. Krista was so angry that I was afraid of her. I felt guilty for becoming distracted at the house. If I had told them maybe Krista would not hate me. However, I still did not know what to tell them. How do you tell perfect strangers about a living nightmare?

When Krista was done with the kitchen, she came into the living room. She did not sit down. She just stood there looking at everyone sitting around me.

"Can I go outside?" Krista asked Mom.

"Yes, just stay where I can see you. I don't want you going far," Mom sounded annoyed with Krista.

"Come with me, Shayla," Krista urged.

"No, I want to stay with Samantha. I don't want to go outside," Shayla reached up and held my hand.

"Fine," Krista replied angrily before going outside.

Did Shayla see what Krista had done? Did she suspect? I did not know and could not ask in front of Mom. Mom ignored Shayla. When she got up to get more coffee she grabbed me some juice. She did not even acknowledge Shayla's presence. I shared my juice with Shayla.

"You should not share your drink with animals," Mom said when she saw Shayla take a drink.

"Mommy, Shayla is my friend. She isn't an animal," I defended my sister. Shayla put the drink down on the coffee table and looked down at her hands. I knew it hurt her how Mom saw her.

"You're wrong about that, Sissy," Mom said. "You will see it my way when you are older."

I just put my hand on Shayla's shoulder. I knew if I fought Mom Shayla would suffer. Besides arguing with Mom was pointless, she never listened and usually resorted to violence. Mom got up and grabbed her purse from the floor. She put the purse on the coffee table and started digging inside. She started pulling out a lot of money.

"Here, Sissy, help Mommy count this," Mom was putting bills in my lap.

"Wow," Shayla stared wide eyed at the money.

"Get away from that, you stupid retard. You're worse than a dog. I never should have had you." Mom snapped at Shayla. Mom was still digging the money out of the bag.

I started to organize the bills. I separated the bills in ones, fives and twenties.

"Is this real?" I was holding up a bill with 100 on it. I had never seen one.

"Yep. I had more business than I knew what to do with last night," Mom sounded so proud.

I began to count the bills. There were fifty-seven ones. There were fifteen fives. There were three tens. There were seventeen twenties. And there were four hundreds. Mom was so excited.

"I made more last night than I made all month. A few more nights like last night and I won't have to work all month. We might even be able to move into town. This is great," Mom was smiling.

Mom looked so happy but what she said made me feel sick. I looked towards the door where Krista disappeared. What do I do? How can I protect her? She was too angry to let me help her. I still wasn't sure what had happened. How much of what Krista thought would happen actually happened? Mom was determined to do whatever she did last night again. Then I did the only thing I could.

"Mommy, what happened last night hurt Krista," I said. I looked at Mom, she barely glanced at me as she put the money in her wallet.

"Don't be silly," Mom replied.

"Mommy, take me next time. Not Krista. It is not fair. I love my sister," I pleaded.

Mom finally looked at me. She stared at me like she was finally seeing me. She looked at me and I saw an expression I had never seen before.

"Why would you say that?" She said slowly.

"I just know that it hurt her, whatever it was. Please don't hurt her. Hurt me," I was holding Shayla's hand.

I was terrified by what I was saying but I loved Krista even if she no longer loved me. There was only one way I could think of saving her. I had seen the delight and excitement in Mom's face when we counted the money. Mom was going to do it again. There was no way to prevent that, but maybe I could save Krista. Mom was still looking at me but her look was changing.

"I did not hurt Krista. She is just a stupid whiner. Damn, you are all ungrateful bitches. I go out every night and do the same thing your sister did last night. You don't see me complaining. I don't recall you asking to take my place. No, you and your ungrateful sisters just take, take, take," Mom stood up and started to pace.

I leaned down and whispered in Shayla's ear, "Quickly and quietly, go outside now. Hide in the trees. Don't let Mom see you. If you see Krista tell her to hide as well." I released her hand and she left as soon as Mom turned her back.

Mom came over and sat back down. She looked at me intently, "What did Krista tell you?"

"Nothing, Mommy, honest. She just looked like she was in pain. I swear Mommy. Please don't be mad. I'm sorry. You're right. I misunderstood. I made a mistake. Please forgive me," I pleaded. My fear was making tears spring to my eyes.

"That little bitch. Just can't keep from whining. I will give that bitch something to complain about," Mom yelled before storming out of the house.

I could not see anything. I hoped that Shayla had managed to hide well. I also hoped that Krista had managed to hide. She may

hate me but I still loved her. Mom stormed back into the house. She grabbed her purse. Oh no, what if she was taking Krista again. She stormed back out the door before I could rise. I jumped up and hobbled to the door, ignoring the searing pain in my ankle as much as possible. The ice had helped but the way I was moving was making it worse. I rushed to the door and burst through it just as Mom was starting the car. I frantically looked in the passenger seat. It was empty. I tried to see into the back seat but could not see before she was driving down the driveway. She disappeared as I stared. Were my sisters safe?

Chapter 12

It took me a minute to calm my frantic heart. The pain in my ankle actually helped. I concentrated on the pain until my breathing slowed. I took a deep breath. Then I ignored the pain and stepped down off the porch. I had to find my sisters. I had to believe they were safe. They had to be safe. I loved them more than they knew. "Krista, Shayla, Are you alright? Please answer. Please," I shouted as loud as I could. "Krista, Shayla." I limped to the nearest stand of trees.

"Samantha!" I heard Shayla yell behind me.

She ran to me as I limped to her. I was so relieved. We hugged each other tightly. I had tears running down my cheeks. I was so scared.

"Krista! Where is Krista?" I pulled back to look at Shayla's face. She was crying too.

"I couldn't find her before I heard Mom come outside so I hid behind the house," Shayla said quickly.

"I'm here," Krista said angrily as she stomped past us to the house.

"Are you ok?" I asked anxiously. "Did Mom hurt you?"

"Like it matters to you. I saw her come out and ducked into the tall grass. Just shut up. I knew you would make her mad eventually. You're such a bitch!" Krista stomped towards the house.

"Krista, wait," I called.

"WHAT!" Krista turned to glare at me.

"Mom is really mad. It might not be safe to sleep at the house tonight," I was worried about what would happen if Mom returned in the middle of the night. "Maybe we should sleep somewhere else. Just for tonight."

"Oh, yah, like where?" Krista said sarcastically. "Like I would even listen to you let alone trust you. You're probably just trying to get us in trouble. If I were you, Shayla, I would not trust that bitch." Krista pointed at me.

Krista went quickly back to the house. I watched her walk away. I did not know what to say. I had lost my sister. I felt that loss deep in my heart. Stacy was gone so it was my job to protect my sisters but I had failed. I hurt Krista. I broke our family. I did this.

"Come on. We need to go before Mom gets back," I said as I turned my attention back to my other sister.

"What about Krista?" Shayla was confused and hurt by Krista's reaction.

"I don't know." I admitted, "We have to go. Maybe she will be ok."

Shayla helped me back to the house. I was getting used to the pain in my ankle which made the pain easier to ignore. It was a trick I learned early in life. If you embrace the pain you can eventually learn to ignore the pain. You can even use the pain to distract yourself from other pain. Pain can give you strength.

I emptied Shayla's old school backpack and handed it to her. I grabbed my new backpack. We packed our three favorite outfits. Then we grabbed our toothbrushes and toothpaste. After that we went into the kitchen. Krista was in the living room packing her own backpack. Shayla and I packed as much food and drink that we could fit in our book bags. We walked into the living room.

"Shayla, go grab the blanket off our bed. We will use it as a sleeping bag," Shayla went into our room.

"Are you coming with us?" I asked Krista. She had her back to me.

"No," She said angrily.

"We can protect each other," I suggested.

"Like you protected me last night. You could have stopped it. You let it happen. You caused it. Mom said it was all your idea so don't act all innocent. She told me how you gave her the idea. She said you talked to her. I trusted you," Krista started out sounding angry but in the end she was crying.

I stood there shocked. Before I could reply, Krista grabbed her backpack and ran out of the house. I stared after her. Was it my idea? I thought back to the conversations I had with Mom but could not even think of one thing I said that would suggest this nightmare. Was it true?

Shayla returned from the bedroom. We folded the blanket. I carried the blanket and we went outside. We headed across the fields. I knew where we would be safe from Mom. The safest place I knew. I was relieved when we made it over the first hill. If Mom did return she would not see us. I slowed down a little. The walking made my ankle throb and I felt the pressure against my shoe as my ankle swelled up. I felt the pain but knew I could not concentrate on it until Shayla and I were safe.

"Where are we going, Samantha?" Shayla asked.

"Would you like to see the magic house?" I asked with a smile on my face. I knew it would excite her and I liked making her happy.

"Really!" She exclaimed excitedly.

"Really, Really. Are you excited?" I smiled bigger. Shayla's happiness was contagious.

"Yes, can we go inside?" She asked.

"I don't think so, but we can watch the house and if the kids are there we will play with them. But you can't tell them we are camping out or anything that is happening at home. I don't want to lose you like we lost Stacy." I warned her.

"Ok," Shayla said as she literally bounced around with excitement.

We were halfway there and walked the rest of the way without talking. I could not run so we walked around the last hill before walking to the grove of trees. I did not see anyone and hoped

no one saw me. We walked to the spot where I sat last time. I walked a little ways into the trees and sat down the blanket and my heavy book bag. Shayla followed me and did the same. I took out two juice boxes and two small bags of chips. I took two slices of cheese from Shayla's bag. I sat down where I sat earlier that day and Shayla sat beside me. We divided the food. I stretched out my ankle and loosened the velcro strap on my shoe. My ankle was red and swollen.

"Does it hurt?" Shayla asked.

"Yes," I said simply.

"Did you really fall by yourself?" Shayla was staring at her slice of cheese as she asked. I wished I had remembered to grab bread.

"No," I admitted quietly.

"Was it Krista?" Shayla asked. She was still looking at her cheese. She was not eating. She just stared at the cheese looking sad.

"Yes, but she did not mean it. I hurt her worse and she just reacted. She still loves you," I tried to reassure her.

"No one loves me except you. You love me," a tear rolled down her cheek.

"I do love you. Krista loves you, too, you know," I hated to see Shayla cry.

"She finds me annoying and she ignores me," Shayla said barely above a whisper.

"She does not mean it. She just does not see others well. She forgets to think of others," I could not think of anything else to say.

"She's mean to both of us. She says bad words. She acts like Mommy," Shayla said a little louder.

"Don't say that. Listen, let's just change the subject. Look there is the magic house. Would you like me to describe it to you?" I suggested.

"I guess," Shayla said sadly.

"Hey, would you like my food? I am not hungry so I just want my juice." I was eager to make her happy again.

"Thanks" She said as she gave me a small smile.

Shayla was different from Krista and I in the way her mind worked. However, sometimes, like now, she amazed me about how much she perceived. She might be smarter than us all. She saw the world the way it was. She did not make excuses. She quietly watched the world and judged it for what it was. I loved her.

I distracted her by describing everything I knew about the inside of the magic house. Their car was gone so I knew they were not home. I told her about everyone in the family. I described the girls room for her. I told her the names of everyone. We talked until the sun was about to sit. We then cleared out a small section under the trees. We laid down the blanket. We laid on half the blanket and covered ourselves with the other half. It was cold so we huddled together. I put my ankle outside of the blanket. The cool night air felt great on my ankle. I was exhausted and fell asleep quickly.

Chapter 13

When the sky began to lighten I awoke. I had propped my ankle on my backpack before I fell asleep. It was still sore and I drew back the covers to look at it. It was no bigger than it was the night before and the color had changed to a light bluish. I eased my ankle off the backpack and looked around. Shayla was still asleep so I gently covered her head with the blanket so the sun would not wake her up. I stood up slowly and moved my backpack off the blanket. I walked deeper into the trees and went potty behind a tree. Then I limped back and found my shoes. I put them on. I made sure that the shoe was loose on the foot with the hurt ankle. Then I walked to the edge of the trees and looked toward the magic house. Their car had returned during the night.

I liked waking before the rest of the world. You saw the world come alive. I stood there watching the sun rise behind the house. The sky came alive with breathtaking colors of light pink, blue, purple and yellow. It was like a promise every morning that today would be better than the day before. When the day did turn out

bad, the sunset would hold an apology in its hands. The sun rose and fell with a message to bear. You just needed to listen.

The lights in the house began to turn on. I watched the windows hoping to see who was awake. As I watched I heard movement behind me. I quietly made my way back to the makeshift campsite. Shayla was turning over trying to stay asleep. I leaned against a tree to take my weight off my ankle. I watched my sister begin to wake. I wondered if she would be ok. Could I really protect her when I had failed so miserably before? We would eventually have to return to the house. We could not camp here forever.

"Are you awake?" I asked when I saw Shayla open her eyes.

"No," she answered and rolled over. She pulled the blanket over her head.

"It's morning sleepy head," I smiled at my beloved sister.

"No, it's not," I heard her mumble through the blanket.

I giggled at her. She was never much of a morning person. I woke up early and could never go back to sleep after I was awake. Shayla was different. She could shut her mind off and actually go back to sleep. She didn't worry. To be perfectly honest, sometimes I wished I was more like that. I also wished Stacy was here. I felt a tear roll down my cheek. I quickly dried my face and put on a smile.

"Wake up, sleepyhead," I said as cheerfully as I could. I did not have time to be sad. I would be sad tomorrow.

"What are you guys doing here?" A loud voice boomed behind us.

I jumped a foot in the air and actually fell.

"Ahhhh," I screamed on my way down. I was smart enough not to land on my ankle. I landed on my butt hard. "Ow!"

"Are you ok?" it was the dad. He came over to me and helped me up. "What are you doing out here?" He said again.

"Um....Uh.....We....um.......Mom said....our Mom......she...uh said we could camp outside ......uh......so we were camping," I lied horribly.

The dad looked around at our makeshift campsite. Shayla was sitting up holding the blanket like a shield. Shayla was staring wide eyed at the man. The man saw our backpacks.

"Are you runaways?" He asked gently, still holding me up.

"Not exactly," I said. I was a horrible liar. I took a step back and leaned one hand against a tree so I could take my weight off my ankle. "Please don't be mad. We just needed a safe place to stay for the night." Sometimes the truth is all you have.

He watched me closely for a minute then he looked around again. "You're Samantha, right?"

"Yes," I said. Shayla stood up and moved right behind me.

"My son told me about you. Why don't you come up to the house so we can talk. Sally will make us some breakfast." He began to gather our stuff. He must have seen the fear in our eyes. "It's ok, you're safe. We won't hurt you."

Shayla and I watched as he gathered our stuff. We followed him as he left the trees. Shayla was scared but as we approached the house she started to stare in amazement. I was limping a little. It hurt to put weight on my ankle.

"Are you ok?" The dad asked when he saw me limping.

"I fell yesterday," I said looking at Shayla.

"Can I look?" He asked as he put our stuff down. We were halfway to the house.

"Ok," I said.

He knelt down and pulled down my sock. "This is bad. I have a brace in the house but it might be too big. Here, Let me carry you."

He picked me up in his strong arms. I did not fight him. He had held me in my dreams and I liked his family. I trusted him. I hoped he would like me too. Shayla picked up our stuff and we continued on our way to the magic house.

"What is your name?" I asked.

"George," he said. "Is this your sister?"

"I'm Shayla. Do you really live here?" Shayla burst out before I could answer.

"Yes, I really live here," he chuckled. His chest jumped when he laughed.

"It looks like a castle," Shayla was so excited.

We were at the house now. Shayla held the door open as he carried me inside. He had us leave our stuff on the couch in the living room. He carried me into the kitchen and put me on a stool at the kitchen island. Shayla sat up on the stool beside me. Sally was there and he whispered to her at the sink for a minute. Then he turned to us.

"I am just going to get my bag. I will be back in a minute." He left the room quickly.

"Are you kids hungry?" Sally asked with a smile on her face.

"Yes," Shayla answered. Shayla was smiling ear to ear. I was worried.

Chapter 14

George came back in a few minutes with a brown bag. It turns out he was a doctor with a practice in town. He always kept some supplies at home just in case. He did not have a brace small enough to fit my ankle. He wrapped a bandage around the sprained ankle. Sally gave me a pill and said it would help with the pain. When they were finished with my ankle Sally started to make breakfasts. She was making pancakes and sausage. George went to put up the brown bag.

"Where are Brian and Lacy?" I asked Sally.

"They are still asleep. We were out late last night. They like to sleep in in the summer. They should be up soon," Sally was busily making breakfast but she smiled the whole time.

George reentered the room and sat beside me. Sally passed him a cup of coffee and he began to add sugar from the sugar bowl on the counter. Then he took a small sip.

"So, will you tell me what you need to keep safe from?" George asked looking at me.

"We can't," I said looking pointedly at Shayla.

"That is a bad sprain on your ankle," George looked at me kindly. Like he actually cared. "I also saw bruises on your upper arm and legs. If I were to look closer, would I find more bruises?"

"Maybe," I said looking down. Shayla and I were now holding hands under the counter.

"Is someone hurting you?" Sally asked as she paused in her cooking to look at me.

"Please, don't ask. We are fine. We should go now," I said starting to get up.

Now was the perfect time to ask for help but how could I. The recent bruises were not from Mom, they were from my vengeful sister. Besides, Krista was out there. I did not know if she was with Mom or not. If we told them we may never see Krista again. Mom would just disappear with her. We could not tell.

"No, it's ok. We won't ask any more questions for now. Please just stay for a little while. Besides you need to stay off that ankle," George said as he gently pushed me back onto the stool.

"Ok, for a little while," I agreed. Besides the smells from the food was making my mouth water.

"Can I have two pieces of sausage and four pancakes?" Shayla asked Sally, smiling again. I could tell that Shayla was glad we were not leaving and the serious talk was ending.

"You can have as much as you like," Sally answered with a sad smile on her face.

Sally continued to cook for everyone. Every once in a while she would look sadly at me and then look at her husband. I wondered what thoughts were being sent in those looks. Shayla was so excited that she was bouncing in her seat. George drank his coffee slowly. Soon I heard slow footsteps coming down the stairs.

"Good morning, sleepyheads." Sally said affectionately.

"Hey, kiddos. Nice to see you. I thought you were going to sleep all day," George got up and hugged his kids.

After hugging their dad each kid went over to Sally and hugged her as well. Brian stole a piece of sausage after hugging his

Mom. Then they sat down at the counter with Shayla and I. George had vacated his seat so Brian sat by me. Lacy sat by Shayla. George stood at the end of the counter by Brian. There were only four stools. Sally began making plates for everyone and we all ate around the table. I had forgotten that I did not eat last night so I was starving. The food tasted incredible. The pancakes were blueberry and the syrup was very sweet. The sausage mixed in the syrup and tasted funny to me so I gave my sausage to Shayla. I caught George and Sally eyeing me a lot during breakfast but I pretended not to notice. Instead I talked to Brian.

When breakfast was over George helped me move downstairs. Krista and I had not known there was a basement and therefore it was the first time I was seeing it. The floor was carpeted. The walls were a bright yellow color with framed pictures hanging on the wall. The room had a large table on one end and a couch and TV on the other. They had games sitting on shelves along one wall. In the middle of the room, separating the TV area from the board game area, was a ping pong table. This was their game room and family room. George sat me at the table and said we could play games while he was at work and he would check on me when he got home. There was a bathroom just off the game room and he told me if I needed anything to just ask Sally. Then he left as Brian started to get out a large stack of games.

I made sure to keep Shayla close by all day. I knew she might talk if she got the chance. We played board games for a while then I watched Brian play ping pong while Shayla and Lacy took turns playing against him. Brian was good and never lost. Sally brought down pizza for lunch. It was pepperoni. It was awesome. Shayla was having so much fun. My ankle was even starting to feel better. The bandage actually helped me walk a little.

After lunch we played some more games. We were playing our fourth board game when suddenly there was yelling upstairs. I immediately recognized the voice. Shayla recognized the voice as well because she came around the table and held my hand. She

looked terrified. Lacy and Brian were just staring towards the stairs in terror. I stood up and straightened my back. I took a deep breath. Our time here was over.

"I am sorry. We have to go. Thanks for playing with us," I said to Brian and Lacy as I took Shayla's hand and started towards the stairs.

"You can't go up there!" Brain grabbed my hand.

"We have to," I removed his hand from mine and walked up the stairs.

Brain said something else but I did not listen. I just walked as quickly as I could on my ankle. At the top of the stairs I could hear yelling coming from the front door. Shayla and I headed towards the front of the house. Shayla held my hand so tight it almost hurt. She looked so scared. Mom was standing in the doorway of the front door yelling at Sally. Sally was trying to calm her down and threatening to call the cops. Cops terrified me more than my mother. Sally wanted Mom to calm down so she could call George. Mom was having none of that and accused the woman of kidnapping. Mom saw us and pushed past Sally. She came over and yanked me up into her arms. Without a word she grabbed Shayla's arm. She carried me and dragged Shayla out to our car while Sally ran to the phone. Then Mom got into the car and we drove very fast down the driveway.

Chapter 15

Mom was furious. When the house came into view I saw Krista standing on the porch. It was then I knew she must have told Mom where we were. How did she know? Krista gave me a funny smile when Mom carried me into the house. Mom was practically running. Shayla and Krista followed us into the house. Shayla sat next to me on the couch when Mom put me down.

"You ungrateful little bitches!" Mom was red in the face, "I will punish you for the trouble you caused today but for now you will

listen to me. Do you understand?" We all nodded wide eyed at her. I don't know about the others but I was too terrified to speak. Mom looked crazy. "The police will be here soon. You will tell them that I gave you permission to camp on the other side of the hill and that you snuck away without permission. You will tell them you lied to that family. You will tell them that we are a perfect family. Do you understand me?" She grabbed my face and glared at me, "DO YOU UNDERSTAND ME?!?"

"But we didn't say anything," I mumbled. I could barely move my lips.

"You better not have. If you do not say what I told you to say then I will kill you all. Do I make myself clear?" Mom yelled.

"Yes, Mommy." The three of us said in unison.

Mom stood by the door looking down the drive. Shayla and I were still on the couch. Krista was standing by the couch.

"You told her where we were, didn't you?" I whispered to Krista.

"You left me here with her alone. What did you expect?" Krista whispered angrily.

"Did she hurt you?" I was immediately concerned.

"She didn't have to," Krista replied.

"Then why?" I asked again.

"Because you take everything that belongs to me. You deserve what Mom is going to do to you. I can't wait," Krista whispered with malice.

Shayla held my hand. She had heard everything and now was even more terrified. I let go of her hand and put my arm around her. I held her close to comfort her. Krista moved as far as she could away from me. I wished I could have made her forgive me. I felt so guilty. It was my fault that she hated me. We sat there for what seemed to be a long time. Mom began to smoke one cigarette after another. She would occasionally mutter about how ungrateful her daughters were.

"Here they come. Remember what I told you." Mom went out onto the porch to talk to the officers. We watched out the window while

they parked and approached Mom. They talked for a while. Then we saw a red car come down the drive. It parked behind the cop car and a woman got out. She had shoulder length blonde hair and was wearing a silky shirt with jeans. She approached my mother. Then my mom and the cops and the lady talked for what seemed like a long time. We could not hear what they were saying and we were all too scared to move closer. I kept picturing the last time I saw Stacy and then I would imagine her getting beaten over and over again. We waited to see what would happen. I was scared and confused.

Shayla was leaning against me with my arm around her. She was so scared. Krista looked angry as she stood on the other side of the living room. I wished I could fix everything. Finally, everyone came inside.

"Hello, kids, how are you today?" The lady with the blond hair said.

"Who are you?" I asked.

"My name is Jessica Poole. Would you mind if we talked for a while?" She smiled warmly at us.

"Are we in trouble?" I asked terrified. I looked at the cops. They looked so angry.

"No, sugar, you are not in trouble," She glanced at Mom then turned back to us, "We just need to clear up a little confusion."

"Ok, we will talk to you," I said, speaking for all of us.

"Could you please step outside? You can't be in here when I talk to them," Jessica said firmly to Mom.

"They're my kids and this is my home. You can't kick me out. You bastards should not even be here. I ought to press kidnapping charges on that fucking neighbor. You assholes have no right to be here," Mom yelled at Jessica and the cops.

"Ma'am, we already went over this. You need to calm down and cooperate or we will remove the children from your custody." One of the cops said firmly.

"Fucking pigs. You are violating my rights. You are abusing your power." Mom stormed out the front door. One of the cops, the one

that had not spoken, exchanged a nod with the first cop and followed her out.

Jessica turned back and looked at us again. Shayla was still in my arms. Krista was watching out the door.

"Are you kids ok?" Jessica asked.

We just stared at her. She had sounded nice before but when she talked to Mom she sounded cold and hard. What if we were in trouble and she was meaner than Mom? We just stared at her. Krista still looked mad and Shayla looked scared.

"Would you mind if I talked to you one at a time? I promise you are safe with me," she smiled at me.

"Who do you want first?" I replied.

I was scared but it was clear we did not have a choice so I took a deep breath and prepared for the worst. If you always prepare for the worst then you can only be pleasantly surprised when things are not that bad. It helps to see the world that way than to always be devastated by the cruelty of life.

"Well, who would like to be first?" Jessica asked all of us.

"I'll go," Krista spoke up.

She still sounded angry. She glared at me as she walked into the kitchen and sat at the table. Jessica followed her and sat beside her at the table. I saw them talking quietly at the table but could not make out what they were saying. The cop who had spoken to Mom earlier stayed in the room with Shayla and I. Shayla had sat up. We were just holding hands now.

"Remember what I told you not to tell the magic house family?" I whispered to Shayla.

"Yes, I did not tell them," Shayla whispered back to me.

"Well, we can't trust these people either. Don't say anything, ok? I don't want to lose you," I whispered urgently.

"I won't. I don't want to lose you either. I love you," Shayla whispered and then gave me a hug.

"I love you, too," I whispered into her messy hair.

"What are you two whispering about?" The cop said as he moved closer to us.

"Nothing," I answered, releasing Shayla.

"Nothing, huh? It seemed like something," he smiled but I was so scared of cops that it looked menacing to me. Shayla must have felt the same way because she took my hand again and held on tight.

"It was nothing," I said as confidently as I could. I felt like I was being attacked and wanted to protect Shayla as much as I could.

"What is your name, tiger?" The cop asked with a laugh.

"My name is Samantha. Not Tiger," I said, raising my chin a little.

The cop laughed, "Ok, Samantha. And what is your name?" He turned and smiled at Shayla.

Shayla looked at me terrified and hid her face in my shoulder.

"Her name is Shayla," I said, putting my hand on her head. "Why are you here?"

The cop sat across from me on the coffee table, "Well, your neighbors were concerned that you might not be safe. We just want to help protect you. That is our job."

He had to be lying because I knew cops had taken Stacy. Cops were always bad people. He must need new people to hurt. I was terrified he would take us.

"We are fine, please go," I said, feeling the terror overpowering me again and knowing that I had to be strong for Shayla. I didn't want to cry in front of Shayla.

The cop must have noticed my reaction because he stood up and crossed the room to stand again. He looked at me and Shayla on the couch with sadness in his eyes. He then looked at the kitchen table. Krista and Jessica were standing up. Krista sat back on the couch.

"Ok, Shayla, I will be right here. Don't be scared," I said as I gently pushed Shayla ahead.

"Well, Shayla, I guess we will talk now," Jessica said as she smiled at Shayla.

Shayla walked slowly to the table and sat so she could see me on the couch. I knew she was scared. I also knew that it would probably be best if I was last. I was the only one with visible injuries. I had to save my family from being tortured by the evil cops.

"What did you say to her? What does she want to know?" I whispered anxiously to Krista.

"Like I would tell you, bitch. This is all your fault." Krista turned as much of her back to me as she could while still sitting on the couch.

I turned from her. I watched the cop waiting to see if he would attack. I occasionally looked at Jessica and Shayla whispering at the table. I wondered what they were saying. The cop seemed to be very alert. He seemed to be watching someone outside the screen door and I wondered if it was Mom. He also kept watching Krista and I on the couch and Shayla and Jessica at the kitchen table. I wondered what he was thinking. Then Shayla and Jessica were standing up and Shayla came up to me quickly.

"Are you ok?" I asked Shayla as I stood up carefully to avoid putting weight on my ankle.

"Yes, I was good," Shayla answered.

"Ok, have a seat. I will be back soon." I said as I walked and limped to the kitchen.

"So, how are you today?" Jessica smiled.

"Fine," I answered suspiciously.

"All I want to do is make sure you are safe. So, we are just going to talk for a few minutes. You are not in any trouble." Jessica said reassuringly.

"Ok," I said in reply.

"Can you tell me how you hurt yourself? It looks pretty bad," Jessica said pointing to the bruises on my arms and my ankle.

"I fell," I answered quickly for fear she would hear my lie.

"How did you fall?" She persisted.

"It was an accident," I looked at Krista who was glaring at me. The cop was looking at Krista suspiciously.

"Was anyone with you when you fell?" Jessica asked, distracting me from Krista's glare.

"Yes," I said without thinking.

"Who was with you?" Jessica asked quicker.

"Why do you want to know?" I asked.

"Listen, if someone is hurting you then you can tell me. I will make sure that person can never hurt you again. See that cop over there," she said pointing at the cop, "Our job is to help you."

"Can I go?" I asked. I just wanted them to leave. I did not like these people.

"You need to tell me who hurt you," Jessica insisted.

"No one, No one," I lied.

"You just fell," Jessica said in a tone that indicated she did not believe me.

"Yes, I fell. That's all," I insisted. I was not going to let them take my sister away for hurting me. I loved Krista and was going to protect her.

"Fine, however, we also have to talk about last night," Jessica said.

"What about last night?" I asked, knowing the answer and knowing I would have to lie.

"The neighbors said they found you and your sister sleeping under some trees close to the road. Can you tell me why you were sleeping out there? The neighbor said you were afraid. You told the neighbor you were there because," she paused to look at the pad of yellow paper in front of her on the table, "you needed someplace safe to sleep. Were you not safe here?" Jessica finished.

"We...uh....had permission to sleep....uh....camp outside last night but we got scared....yeah....we got scared and we looked for a spot to hide.....uh.....to sleep and hide from.....uh......dogs. So, we looked and decided to sleep under those trees." I was really bad at lying.

"Do you have dogs here?" She asked.

"Uh.....no.......but uh....maybe ghost dogs," I responded

"Samantha, I don't think you are being honest with me. Are you being honest?" Jessica said gently.

"Can I go back to the couch now?" I said ignoring her question.

"Yeah, you can go back to the couch," Jessica said dejectedly.

I got up and went back to the couch and sat in the middle again. Jessica went and talked quietly with the officer. After a few minutes she turned to face us.

"Thank you for speaking to me today. If you ever need anything just call me," she put her business card on the coffee table and walked out the door with the officer. None of us reached for the card. We were all terrified. To me it was like a live snake sitting there. Whoever touched it would get bitten.

We watched as the officers and the lady talked to Mom outside again. Then the lady left followed by the officers. Mom watched them go. When they were out of sight Mom walked slowly back inside. We watched wondering what to expect. I don't know about my sisters but I expected horror.

Chapter 16

Mom came in the house but did not say a word. She walked into the kitchen and soon I heard the sounds of Mom making coffee. We sat on the couch. Krista still sat as far away from me as possible. Shayla was sitting so close that she was almost sitting on me. Shayla and I held hands.

Mom came into sight with her coffee cup but instead of coming into the living room she sat down at the table and stared out the window. The silence was terrifying to me because silence meant that a storm was coming. I sat and waited for the storm. Would I be able to save Shayla?

After what seemed to be forever, I heard a car approaching down the driveway. Mom looked towards the door but did not get up. Mom was wearing her angry face. Then we heard the car stop. Then a door shut. I watched Mom intently. Mom was glaring at the door. The look on her face was bone chilling. I then heard a second door shut. Mom looked at me and the look she gave me made my

heart stop. I could not breathe. I could not tear my eyes from hers. There was a loud knock on the door and Mom released me from her eyes and went to answer the door. I gasped for breath but could not quite catch my breath.

"I don't want you here," Mom said loudly.

I turned to the door to see who it was. George was standing there with his brown bag. I was so scared Mom would hurt him.

"You don't have a choice. The officers told you to let me see her. So, if you do not move out of my way I can always call them back here." George's voice was polite but firm.

"You asshole, who the hell do you think you are! These are my children not yours. You fucking bastard," Mom cussed at him.

"Lady, let me in or I will go get the officers," George was obviously annoyed.

"Asshole! Fine. She is on the couch," Mom turned and faced us.

"Thank you, can we have some privacy?" George entered the house.

"Samantha, you stay here. Krista and Shayla follow me," Mom headed to her room with my sisters. Shayla and Krista entered the room then Shayla turned to look at me. Mom turned and looked pointedly at me, "Samantha, I will be right in here with your sisters. You better be on your best behavior," Mom said threateningly. She went into the room and shut the door.

George came close, "Are you ok?" He whispered while sitting in front of me on the coffee table.

"No," I whispered back honestly.

"Who hurt you? If you tell me the truth, I can help you," George whispered urgently as he picked up my ankle gently and began to unwrap it.

"It would not help, trust me," I whispered back wincing from the pain.

"You won't know if it will help without telling me. Please just tell me," George whispered kindly. "Was it your Mom?"

"It was not my mom, honestly. I would tell you if it was her," I insisted quietly.

"You told Jessica that you were not alone when it happened. If your Mom was not there, who was? Was it your dad?" George puzzled.

"If I tell you, will you promise not to tell the cops?" I answered.

"I promise to do what is best for you," George answered.

"It would not be best for you to tell the cops. It was my sister, Krista. She was mad at me and tackled me from behind. She was mad because I betrayed her. Please don't let the cops take her away. I can't lose another sister," I tried to explain just to end the questions.

"You lost a sister?" George asked.

"Stacy, she is dead. Please, George, don't take Krista from me," I begged.

"No one will take your sister from you. But, does she hurt you often?" George looked at me intently.

"Krista loves me. She just got mad. Please, I hurt her worse. It was all my fault. It was all my fault. All of this is my fault," I started to cry.

"Shh, it's ok, just calm down. You're ok," George held me and comforted me as I cried on his shoulder.

I contemplated through my heartache if this is what having a father felt like. I eventually calmed down. It felt so warm and safe in his arms. But the tears stopped and he released me. He inspected the ankle and then rewrapped it. As he was finishing wrapping my ankle, Moms' door opened.

"What is taking so long?" Mom demanded.

"We are almost done. Can you come over here please?" George answered her.

"What?" Mom asked as she stomped over to the couch.

"I just want to give a few instructions for Samantha's ankle," George replied politely.

"Well, what the hell is it?" Mom asked rudely.

The contrast between Mom's communication and George's was striking. It was clear they were totally different.

"Her ankle is bad so it needs to be kept elevated. You should put an ice pack on it. Also, she should be kept off of it as much as possible.

I will need to do a follow up every day for a few weeks," George was clearly trying to keep me close.

"I am not driving her into town every day," Mom said rudely.

"No problem, I don't mind stopping by every day on my way home," George said politely yet with the obvious indication that no was not an option.

"Fine, jackass, go ahead and waste your time," Mom walked over to the table and took a drink of her coffee.

"I will be back in a few minutes, Samantha," George said.

"Ok," I said barely glancing at him as I watched my mom.

George went outside and I heard him getting stuff from his car. Mom just drank her coffee while staring out the window. She wasn't even sitting. I was worried. What was she thinking? Then I remembered my sisters. Why hadn't they come out of the room?" I looked at the door. Mom had not shut it all the way but the crack was impossible to see inside from this angle. I started to stand up so I could move closer.

"Sit the fuck down," Mom said harshly.

I sat back down and looked into the ice cold eyes of my mom. The front door opened and she turned back to the window. I looked at George with the fear still in my eyes. He saw and looked at my mom. He walked over to me and touched the top of my head.

"It might be best if she recuperates at my house. I don't mind if she stays with me for a while," George said hopefully while looking at my mom.

"Fine, it is up to her," Mom said looking at George.

"Ok, it is decided," George sighed.

"But her sisters stay here," Mom said looking at me coldly.

Mom knew I would not leave my sisters. Mom grinned an evil grin as she saw the fear on my face. She had won. She said the one thing that would always control me and she knew it.

"I'm sorry. I can't go with you," I said sadly to George.

"It's ok, I understand," he said, looking at me with sad eyes. Did he really understand? "I brought your stuff back and some other stuff

you can have. Sally also went ahead and washed all your clothes for you this morning while you were in the game room. So, if there is anything else you or your sisters need just tell me tomorrow and I will get it for you."

He put our stuff on the end of the couch and turned to me. He gave me a hug.

"Are you done now?" Mom said annoyed.

"Just finished. I will be back tomorrow evening, Samantha," George said before turning to face my mother. "Any chance I can assess her sisters. It is free of charge of course. I can give them physicals."

"After what you have already done you're lucky I even let you in this house. You can go now," Mom turned with her coffee cup in her hand and disappeared into the kitchen.

"I will be back tomorrow," George said then he hugged me and left.

I missed him already. Then before my mom could return, I got up and began walking to Mom's room. I just made it to the door and was pushing it open when someone grabbed me from behind.

"Where the hell do you think you are going, you ungrateful bitch?" Mom was behind me. "I may not be able to punish you right now because of your new friends, but I don't have to touch you to punish you. Shayla, Krista, get the hell out here. It is time to teach your sister a lesson."

Mom dragged me outside by my hair and down the porch steps. George's car was gone. Shayla and Krista followed us outside. Mom stopped about ten feet from the house. Krista came to stand beside me and I saw she had a smile on her face.

"Shayla come stand by me," Mom said and Shayla walked over and stood by Mom. "I will teach you to keep your mouth shut. What happens in our family stays in our family."

With that Mom threw me to the ground and began to beat Shayla. I tried to get up to help her but Krista held me down. I watched as Mom beat Shayla. I saw the blood. Eventually, Shayla stopped screaming and crying. The silence was worse. Mom stopped

hitting and kicking her. She walked over to me and grabbed my face hard. There was blood on her hand. Shayla's blood.

"What happens in this family stays in this family. Next time you open your mouth I won't stop." Mom turned and went into the house.

Krista smiled evilly at me and leaned down close to sneer "Not so perfect after all, now are you?" Then she turned and went inside.

Chapter 17

"Shayla, are you ok?" I asked anxiously.

"I'm....(cough).....I'm ok," Shayla said as she sat up.

"How bad is it?" I looked at my sister trying to assess the damage.

"It is ok, I only pretended to go to sleep. Mom does not hit hard if she forgets to use the belt," Shayla stood up to stand beside me.

There was blood on and around her lip. There were bruises on her cheek and arms.

"I'm sorry, Shayla." I hugged her the best I could.

"It is her fault you got hurt, you know," Krista said from the porch. "Mom says it is time to eat, Shayla. She said to get you and only you. Mom wants to talk to Samantha alone."

Shayla went inside but Mom did not come outside. I waited for a while then I walked slowly to the porch.

"What the hell are you doing?" Mom said startling me.

"I was coming to talk to you," I answered.

"Well, don't bother. You want to camp. Well, you can camp right here. Maybe a night outside will teach you some respect," Mom turned and went back inside.

I sat down on the porch steps. I did not know what to do. I sat staring at the house. It started to get dark and there were clouds in the sky. I turned and just watched the sun set behind the clouds. It was beautiful and I thought about how nice it would be to disappear with the sun. How easy that would be. It got dark but the stars never came. The night seemed so black. Shayla never came back outside

and I worried about her. I must have fallen asleep because the thunder woke me up. I looked around stunned. It took me a minute to remember where I was.

I could see the lightning flash in the distance. Then the thunder would rumble loud. I got up immediately. I curled up on a chair on the porch. I knew if I went inside Shayla would get my punishment, so I stayed on the porch.

The storm raged the rest of the night. The storm was beautiful but scary. The wind caused the leaves and rain to blow everywhere and it did not take long for me to be soaked. I was so cold that I was shaking. I wished Mom would wake and take me inside. I waited but she never came. The storm finally passed but the rain did not stop. The wind had slowed though so I stopped being drenched. I rubbed my arms trying to warm myself. I could not get warm. My clothes were almost dry when the sky started to get lighter. I sat up. It was still raining but the clouds were grey now not black.

"Did you learn your lesson?" Mom said as she stepped onto the porch.

"Yes, Mommy. I am so sorry, Mommy. Please forgive me," I said as I stood and limped over to hug her.

"Just do better today," Mom demanded. "You're drenched. Come here, I will help you get changed. You will get a cold if you are not careful."

Mom carried me inside and helped me get undressed. She ran me a warm bath and it felt like heaven. The shivering finally stopped as I felt the warmth of the water seep inside. I was so grateful to finally be warm. After my bath she helped me get dressed. She carried me to the couch and gently made sure my ankle was elevated. The bandage was still wet so she hung it up to dry.

"The cold must have helped because your ankle is not as big as yesterday," Mom said confidently.

"It feels a little sore," I said.

The reality is the ankle was still throbbing and hurt like crazy. However, I knew telling that to my mom might make her angrier. So I pretended it did not hurt that much.

"Well, it should be fine soon," Mom said.

Mom went into the kitchen to make coffee. As the coffee brewed she poured me a bowl of cereal. I was so hungry that I finished the cereal before Mom could even sit down with her coffee.

"Can I have some more, Mommy?" I asked as sweetly as I could.

"Not today. I don't want you to get fat, Sissy," Mom said and patted my hand.

She took my bowl to the sink and sat down to drink her coffee. I watched her drink while she smoked for a few minutes then I looked out the window. The rain did not look so cold in here. It was actually a little pretty. Soon everyone was awake and Mom served cereal to my siblings. Benny must have slept with Mom last night because he came out of her room. Krista and Shayla must have slept together as well because they both came out of that room. I watched them eat while still hungry. Shayla still had to eat on the floor even though my chair was empty.

After breakfast, Mom said I needed to stay inside so Shayla and I played dolls in our room. We were playing with our dolls on the bed when we started to talk.

"Mom is really mad," Shayla started.

"Did she hurt you last night?" I asked anxiously.

I looked toward the door but it was still shut. I hoped Mom was not listening.

"No," Shayla was looking down and spoke very quietly. "She did not touch us."

"Was she talking about me?" I was starting to worry.

"She said you were bad. She said that when this is all over she was going to break you." Shayla suddenly looked at me intensely, "Samantha, she says she is going to break us all. She was so mad she just kept talking. She is so mad at you and a little mad at me. She said.......she said..."

Shayla's turned to the window and I saw a tear roll down her cheek. I put my hand on her hand. I wanted to hug her but could not quite reach her.

"Shayla, Mom was just mad. I will fix it. Don't cry. Please," I tried to comfort her. "Besides, you know Mom loves me. She would never hurt me too much. I'm her baby. And you're my best friend. I will protect you."

"Krista was her favorite before you," Shayla answered.

I didn't know what to say. I had forgotten that. The words seemed to hang in the air. They echoed in my head. I changed the subject and we ended up coloring in our coloring books until lunch. I tried to smile and joke with Shayla but my mind was deep in thought. I had really messed up.

Mom called us in for lunch. It was cheeseburgers and french fries. It was delicious. I was so hungry that I ate every bite. After lunch Mom told us she was going into town later and would be back that evening.

"Is anyone going with you?" I asked with a lump in my throat.

I was terrified that Krista would be hurt. I was so scared it was happening again.

"No, I may have to go to several places and don't want to deal with any brats," Mom said, then she got up and left.

Chapter 18

I was stuck in the house so Shayla and I watched TV in the living room. It was nice. I barely saw Krista though. It was clear that she was avoiding me. When she did come inside she would glare at me. Then she would disappear back outside. How was I going to fix that? I did not know where to begin. Krista was my sister. I should have protected her. I failed. I messed up. I hurt her. It was my fault. Mom came home hours later. We heard her car pull up to the house. A few minutes later she came inside.

"Have you had dinner yet?" Mom asked.

"No, Mommy," I answered her.

"Ok, I will put something together. Did that asshole neighbor come by yet?" Mom turned to me.

"No, not yet," I responded, shivering just a little from the look she gave me.

"Good, I want to talk to him," She said, as she went to the kitchen.

I felt so much fear. What was she going to do? Would she hurt him? I put him in this situation. If he got hurt it would be all my fault. I also knew that I could not question Mom for a while because she was so mad. I wanted to see George but also wished he would forget about me and not come. Then he would be safe. I was so worried that I could not concentrate on what we were watching. I just kept listening for the sound of wheels on gravel. I could hear Mom in the kitchen and could smell her cooking something. Then I heard it. The sound of an approaching car.

"He is coming," I whispered to Shayla.

"Can I go say hi?" Shayla said excitedly. "Do you think he brought Lacy and Brian with him?"

"I don't know but probably not," I answered her. She was so innocent sometimes. It was like, with enough time, sometimes just a little bit of time, she was able to forget all the bad stuff in our lives. Her mind was so amazing. "Go say hi before Mom can stop you. I will tell her he is here."

Shayla sprang from the couch and raced out the door. I smiled after her. Then I slowly went into the kitchen. Mom was taking a dish out of the oven. I could not tell what it was but it was covered in cheese.

"Mommy, George is here. I think. I heard someone pull up and I think it is him." I said watching as her face hardened in anger.

"Fuck," Mom said in reply and then she sat the food on the stove.

As I returned to the living room I saw Krista and Shayla heading into the house with big bags of groceries. George was behind them with two more bags.

"What the hell is this?" Mom stood in the living room with her hands on her hips.

"Oh, I am so sorry for this. It was a miscommunication with my wife. I thought I was supposed to do the grocery shopping today but she actually already did it today. Since we don't need a double supply of food, I just thought with all these kids you could use it. Since I was coming here anyway," George smiled at me.

"We don't need your charity," Mom said, glaring at him.

"It is not charity. Actually, you are doing me a favor. This way the food does not go to waste," George turned and smiled at Mom.

Mom did not say anything. She just went and started to put the groceries away. I watched as George went back outside. Mom looked mad but as she unloaded the food she seemed to like some of it and her face softened. Just a little though. Would it be enough? George returned with two more bags. One of the bags contained a lot of clothes for me and my sisters. Mom just told Krista and Shayla to put the clothes up correctly in our bedroom. George then went outside for a third time. This time he came back with his brown bag and a stuffed cat. The cat was grey with a white tummy. It had a pink nose and clear whiskers.

"I saw this and thought of you. Do you like it?" George asked as he handed me the cat.

"Yes, thank you. I love it," I said as tears came to my eyes. I hugged that cat close and buried my tears inside. I decided right then and there that cats were the best animals in the world.

As Mom finished putting up the groceries George inspected my ankle. Even though he was clearly being careful, it hurt when he touched it. He picked it up and turned it slightly.

"What happened to the bandage I put on it?" He inquired.

"It got wet," I said looking towards Mom who had come into the living room.

"She went out in the rain without permission last night," Mom told him.

"Oh, I didn't think the rain started till around 3 am," George said politely but pointedly.

"I was asleep, so I don't know when it started," Mom said, then she went and dug through her purse. She took out a white piece of paper, "I made an appointment for Samantha with another doctor. So, we won't need your meddling anymore."

George looked at the card, "I don't mind coming out here. Really, it is a pleasure."

"I do mind. You need to keep your nose out of my business. We don't need you or your food. You are a son of a bitch who can't mind your own fucking business. I want you out of my house and away from my children. They belong to me." Mom turned to me, "SAMANTHA, TELL THIS BASTARD YOU WANT HIM TO LEAVE!"

"Please leave George," I said with tears in my eyes.

"It's ok, sweetie. I will go," George gave me another roll of bandage and then closed his brown bag. "May I rewrap her ankle before I go."

"You have one minute," Mom said.

Mom stood right there glaring at him until he finished. He looked at me and smiled before he left the house. I heard his car fade into the distance. I watched Mom. Would I be punished again?

"Good job, Samantha. Maybe now that bastard will leave us alone," Mom turned to the kitchen. "Tell your sisters that dinner is ready. Also, tell Shayla to go get your brother."

I hugged my cat close as I went to get my sisters. I told my sisters what Mom said and then went to the table. Mom was setting the table. When everyone got there we began to eat. I was sad that George was gone for good. I knew bringing it up would anger Mom so with my left hand I just patted my cat and I put a smile on my face. It was more important to act happy and normal than to show your true emotions. After all, truth in this family usually ends in pain.

Chapter 19

Things went back to normal for the next few weeks. Mom was home more than usual though. She liked to watch TV and drink coffee so my siblings and I avoided the living room. Mom seemed to calm down and I began to relax. Maybe she did not mean the things she said. Maybe it was just my fault for camping out. The peace did not last long. It started about two weeks later. Shayla and I were outside throwing our red ball back and forth. My ankle was healing and did not hurt as much. The swelling was almost gone too. Mom never took me to the doctors like she told George she would. George had not been back and I wondered if he even remembered me.

"Krista, Shayla, Samantha. Get in here now," Mom yelled from the doorway.

We quickly scrambled into the house. Krista had been making flower necklaces and had three of them around her neck. Shayla left our ball on the porch.

"Sit down on the couch. You girls are now old enough to start pulling your own weight around here. I have taken good care of you and you are not babies anymore. You are a young woman. You girls cost a lot of money so now you have to give it back. I have broken my back trying to pay for you. I can't afford to care for you so you have to get a job and there is only one thing you are good for. So your training starts now. I want you to watch these videos. Soon you will have to do what you see here." With that Mom pushed play on the VCR.

What I saw was disgusting. Men and women doing horrible things to each other. Men were putting their wee wee's into the women. Then they would pee white pee on and in the women. One scene a woman screamed as two men held her down and another man penetrated her with his wee wee. It was horrible. The man on top would hit the woman. The woman screamed and begged them to stop but they did not stop. When that man finished he switched places with his buddy and the friend hurt the women. They called the

woman horrible names like whore and bitch. When the second man finished they flipped the woman over so the third man could put his wee wee into the woman's butt. She screamed as he entered her. When she screamed the first man put his wee wee into her mouth and she began to choke. The men laughed when they saw that.

"If a man puts his dick in your ass that costs extra girls. So, if someone does that to you, you need to tell me so I know to charge them correctly," Mom said when we saw that part.

I looked at my mom in horror. Krista was right. How could Mom expect us to do these horrible things. These disgusting things. These painful things. These nightmarish things. Just then Mom noticed I was looking at her.

"Turn your eyes back to the screen or I will tear your eyes out," she yelled.

I quickly looked back at the screen. The scene had changed. Now there were five women kissing each other and putting their fingers inside each other. If there was a hole a finger or tongue would enter it. It was so gross that I grimaced. A few of the women were kissing one women's privates. Ewwww! I held Shayla's hand tight.

I could not take what I was seeing so I escaped the only way I could. I blocked out everything I was seeing and hearing. I imagined I was a little girl. I was sitting at the feet of a man on a stool. He said he had a present for me. He sang me a song. It was my song. I replayed that memory twice. Then I was in the yard of the magic house playing with Brian and Lacy. Sally came outside and offered us Kool-aid. It was cool and sweet.

"Ok, girls, we will watch the movie again tomorrow," I heard Mom say.

I looked around dazed for a minute. The movie must have been over because Mom was rewinding it in the VCR. She took the movie out of the VCR and put it in the case. She took it to her room. She returned a few seconds later without the movie.

"Go play until dinner is finished. Krista go to the kitchen and wash your hands. You will help me with dinner," Mom said.

Shayla and I jumped up and ran outside. There was a part of me that wished I could run forever. Just escape from this life. Shayla ran with me. I wondered what she was thinking. My ankle started to hurt bad so I laid down in the tall grass two hills from home and one hill from the magic house. I thought about going there but they had abandoned me. George never came back. They had probably forgotten about me. I still slept with the gray cat every night. I had named her Hope. But Hope was back at the house and I did not want to go back there. Shayla had sat down beside me.

"Are you ok?" I asked my sister.

"I don't know," Shayla said looking at the sky. "Do you think Mom is serious?"

"I think she is," I answered, watching a white cloud move lazily through the sky.

"Will it hurt?" Shayla said pitifully. She buried her head in her knees.

I did not have a reply. I knew based on what I saw that it must hurt bad. I could not imagine something going where the video showed the wee wee going. Krista was right all along. Why hadn't I listened? Now it was too late. We were trapped. If we went back to the magic house, Mom would kill us. If we stayed, Mom would hurt us. There was no hope. We stayed there like that until my fluffy cloud was far away.

"We have to go back before Mom thinks we ran away," I said as I stood up.

"Ok," Shayla said as she dried her tears on her shirt.

Shayla likes to wear shirts with shorts while I prefer dresses. We still liked the same things though. We just always wore the opposite outfits. We walked side by side towards home. I did not know what to say, so we said nothing. When we were standing at the top of the last hill and could see the house up ahead Shayla paused.

"Will I hate you …….after,………. like Krista does?" Shayla said looking at me intensely with tears in her eyes.

"I hope not," I answered, "You're my best friend."

"Promise we will be best friends forever," Shayla said.

"I promise," I said as I hugged her tightly.

We just held each other for a few minutes. I was crying. I had never even considered that she might hate me after. Was that what she had been thinking?

"Time for dinner, idiots," Krista said from a few steps away.

I had not even seen her approaching. We let go of each other and followed Krista into the house. Benny was already there. Shayla and I went to wash our hands before going to the table. Shayla sat on the floor by my chair. I sat in my chair. It was my favorite dinner, mashed potatoes, fried chicken, corn and gravy. Still I could barely choke down a few bites. Mom finished my food. I just could not eat. My stomach was in knots with dread.

After dinner, Krista was told to clean the kitchen as usual. Mom said she was going to town to make some phone calls. Benny went with Mom. Shayla and I played in our room. We had offered to help Krista clean up but she said that if I did not leave her alone she would stab me with a steak knife. So, I left the kitchen. Shayla refused to help if I did not have to. So there we were playing on our bed with our dolls. We did not talk about the video or its implications. We just distracted ourselves with dressing up our dolls.

Mom came home right before we got ready for bed. She had ice cream for all of us. It was chocolate. We ate the ice cream at the table. Then we all got ready for bed. Right before I fell asleep it occurred to me that Mom was acting funny. She so rarely made our favorite dinner and she never bought us ice cream. It was strange. I fell asleep wondering what that meant.

Chapter 20

I awoke from a nightmare I could not remember. The sky was just beginning to lighten outside the window. I hugged Hope close and looked out the window for a few minutes. Shayla was snoring softly beside me. I got up and went to the bathroom. When I was leaving the bathroom I noticed Mom's door open. Krista was still asleep on the couch so I peeked into the room. Mom and Benny were in bed together. They looked like they were naked. They were asleep so I shut the door quietly and went out to the back porch. I watched the sun rise above the hill in the distance. I like the colors of the sunrise. After a while, Benny came out the back door and headed to the shed. What did he do out there all day?

I went back inside. Mom was making coffee. I sat at the table. Mom came over with her first cup of coffee.

"Mommy, do you love us?" I asked, holding Hope tightly.

"Samantha, what do you want?" Mom sounded annoyed and cranky.

"I love you. Do you love us?" I asked again.

"Yes, I love you," Mom said clearly annoyed.

"If you love us, why do you want to hurt us like in the video. I don't want to be hurt like that," I said.

"Oh, shut up. You girls think that everything grows on trees. You are ungrateful, free loading, lazy, stupid bitches. You will do what I tell you to do or I will kill you myself. You belong to me. I own you. Now get out of my face. It is too early for your bullshit," Mom took a long sip of her coffee and looked out the window.

I got up and went to my room. Shayla was still asleep so I sat on the floor and played with Hope. I knew there was nothing that could be done. There was nothing to say to change Mom's mind. I wondered if I was being selfish. Was Mom right? I looked at Shayla. She was so sweet and good. No, Mom had to be wrong. But what could I do?

Soon it was time to get ready for the day. I woke up Shayla and we got ready together. I wore a pretty pink dress with blue flowers on it. It was cotton so it was very comfortable. I felt like a princess. Shayla wore green cut off shorts and a purple T-shirt. She

liked to be colorful. We went to the kitchen when we were done getting ready. Mom had made eggs and bacon with toast. I remembered that she had made our favorite dinner last night. Now she had made bacon knowing how much we liked bacon. I was suspicious and watched her closely. After breakfast Benny went back outside. Mom told Shayla and I to stay inside. Krista cleaned the kitchen. Shayla and I did not want to watch TV so we played in our room. I don't know about Shayla but I never wanted to watch TV again. When Krista was finished with the kitchen, Mom came and got Shayla and I. She made us sit on the couch again.

Mom made us watch the same video again. It was just as horrifying as the first time. I escaped as best as I could into my memories again. This time I remembered Stacy taking us to the park and pushing us on the swings. I remembered her reading to me and how she used to hold me at night.

"Why are you fucking crying?" Mom's yell ripped me out of my memories.

"I am sorry, I didn't mean to," I quickly replied as I wiped the tears from my face. I had not even realized I was crying.

"You are a baby, just go outside. We will finish the video without you," Mom said clearly frustrated.

"Can Shayla come with me?" I asked tentatively.

"Not if you don't want me to beat her senseless," Mom said matter-of-factly.

I went outside by myself. I hoped Shayla would not think I abandoned her. I just did not want to see that video ever again. I took the ball off the porch and kicked it in front of me as I walked. I went over the hill and walked until I could not see the house. My mind was so full. I could not concentrate. I just did not know what I could do. I felt lost and alone. I sat down in the grass. I don't know how long I sat there just lost in thought. I heard the footsteps first. I looked up and saw Shayla approaching.

"Mom told me to come get you," Shayla said with sad eyes.

"Are you ok?" I asked.

"No," Shayla answered.

I did not know what to say so I just gave her a hug. She hugged me so tight I almost could not breathe. So, I just hugged her tighter.

"You will be ok," I said when I felt her tears on my back. "We will be ok."

"Ok," Shayla said, releasing me.

We walked toward the house side by side. I did not know how things would be ok. I just remembered that Stacy had always told us that after one of Mom's punishments. I wished she was here. She would save us. I wanted to make her proud so I tried to be like her. I was starting to feel like I was failing. I couldn't seem to protect anyone. As we approached the house, Mom came out onto the porch.

"Hey, Sissy, where did you go?" Mom said warmly with a big smile on her face.

"I was playing with the ball on the other side of the hill, Mommy," I answered.

"Well, get over here and give your Mommy a hug," Mom said holding her arms out to me.

I smiled. I must be her favorite again. Maybe she does love us. I ran up and hugged her.

"I love you, Mommy," I said.

"I love you, too, Sissy," Mom said back.

Mom picked me up and carried me into the house. I smiled. I like it when Mom loves me. She went to the kitchen table where her coffee was. She sat down with me on her lap.

"So, what were you playing with the ball?" Mom asked as she drank her coffee.

"I was just kicking it around," I answered.

"Well, I am going to do some shopping this afternoon. Would you like a new ball?" Mom asked.

"Actually, can I have some bubbles and a new baby doll with extra clothes, Mommy," I said excitedly. Mom rarely bought us gifts.

"Maybe, you will just have to wait and see," Mom giggled.

"Oh, can I also have a stuffed doggy," I said, remembering that Shayla had wished she had a stuffed doggy to sleep with. I knew Shayla was a little jealous of my Hope.

"That sounds like it might be a possibility," Mom said with a kind smile on her face.

I sat on her lap watching her drink her coffee. I was so happy I was her favorite again. If I wait until tomorrow to talk to her she might listen to me. I just had to show her how good I can be.

"Do you want more coffee?" I asked when she finished her cup.

"No, Sissy, I need to get going," Mom said, putting me on the floor and standing up.

"I will put your cup in the sink, Mommy," I said quickly and reached for the cup.

"Thanks, Sissy. Can you also go get Krista?" Mom said.

"Ok," I said as I put her cup in the sink.

I passed Shayla sitting in the doorway to the kitchen. She had watched me and Mom the whole time. I found Krista on the porch just looking towards the hill. I wondered if she was thinking of the magic house. I told her Mom wanted her. We went inside. Mom was putting her shoes on in the living room.

"Krista, we are going shopping. Go get your shoes on," Mom told Krista.

"Can I go?" I asked excitedly.

"No, not this time. I only have room for three," Mom said smiling at me.

"Benny and Shayla are going?" I asked, confused.

Mom never took Shayla anywhere. It was odd.

"Yes. Shayla needs some new clothes and Benny needs some new shoes," Mom explained.

"I will be here alone," I said, a little scared. I was never alone.

"Just for the day. There is enough food in the refrigerator. You will be fine. We have to drive very far so we will be home late. Just go to bed without us," Mom said as she gathered her purse and keys.

Benny, Shayla, and Krista came into the living room. Shayla was excited to go shopping. She had seen how Mom was being nice and looked forward to Mom being nice to her. Krista had a strange look on her face. She still was not talking to me. She was still being mean to me. I told her bye and told her to have fun. She stuck her tongue out at me. Benny ran outside to get the front seat before Krista could. They were in the car and driving down the drive minutes later. I was excited. Mom was nice again. I was going to talk to her tomorrow and convince her not to do what she wanted to do to us. I could convince her. I felt happy and free. I looked at the house and realized there was only one thing I wanted to do. I ran into the house in a hurry.

Chapter 21

I practically flew over the hills in my haste. I had Hope in my hand and felt so excited. Mom was nice again. Maybe I would not have to be the mom. Maybe Mom was going to be a good Mom from now on. Maybe she would always be nice. She was even going to give me presents. I had the whole day and no one to see me. Now I could do whatever I wanted. There was only one thing I wanted to do. I ran over the last hill and heard laughter from below.

Brian and Lacy were in the yard playing tag. I ran as fast as I could to greet them. It felt like I was rising from the deep water and could finally breathe. The last few weeks were so stressful. I felt free.

"Can I play?" I said smiling ear to ear.

"Samantha," they both yelled in unison and hugged me.

"I was worried about you," Brian said.

"I prayed for you," Lacy added.

"I'm ok, Mom was just mad. I messed up. Lacy, what does prayed mean?" I asked, confused.

"Praying is when you talk to God. Mommy and Daddy taught us how. Don't you pray?" Lacy said.

"Oh, we don't know any God," I answered, still confused.

"Samantha," Sally said, running off the porch and hugging me tightly.

I cried. They had not forgotten about me. They still loved me. Sally held me as I cried on her shoulder. I felt Brian hug me from behind. I felt safe. I dropped Hope and Lacy picked her up. Sally dried my tears when I finally stopped crying.

"Are you ok? We missed you so much," Sally said, looking at me all over.

"I'm ok. I thought you had forgotten about me," I said looking down.

Sally put her hand under my chin and had me look at her, "We will never forget you."

"Promise?" I asked hopefully.

"We promise," Brian said beside me.

"Does your Mom know you are here?" Sally said worriedly.

"No, she went to town with my sisters and brother. She is nice again. I'm sorry she scared you," I added.

"That was not your fault sweetie. Come inside, I made some cookies earlier," She took us inside for milk and chocolate chip cookies.

Brian and Lacy told me stories and chatted the whole time. They laughed and joked with me as we ate our cookies. Then we all went down to the game room. My ankle was better so we all took turns playing ping pong. We were having so much fun. Brian even showed me some techniques and I won a few games of ping pong.

"Hey, Kiddos," we turned and saw George coming down the stairs.

I picked up Hope and ran and hugged him. He hugged me back.

"Sally called and told me you were here. I took the rest of the day off. I am glad you are here," he said.

"I am sorry I sent you away. Are you mad at me?" I asked with tears in my eyes.

"No, sweetie. You are perfect. I knew you did not want me to go. You are more than forgiven," George enveloped me in a big hug. I looked over his shoulder and Brian was standing there smiling at us.

I wished in that moment that I had been born into this family. They seemed perfect to me. They were my miracle. My safe haven. My only safe haven.

"Ok, Kiddos, I got some good news," George began as he pulled back and dried my face, "I brought home pizzas. Who is hungry?"

"Me, me, me," Brian, Lacy and I said in unison.

It was just so easy to be happy in this family. It was so easy to feel safe and loved. It was like a sanctuary.

We all ate pizza at the table in the kitchen and no one had to sit on the floor. After lunch George asked if he could look at my ankle. He turned it this way and that. I told him it did not hurt too much. He said it looked pretty good and I was a fast healer. Then Lacy and Brian wanted to play in the sprinkler outside. Lacy let me borrow one of her bathing suits. It was pink with white flowers on it. It also had a little skirt on it. Brian met us downstairs in swim shorts that had crocodiles on them.

We spent the afternoon playing outside. We were soaked as we ran through the sprinkler. When we were tired of that we played tag and hide and seek. It was so nice just to play and be free. I felt like I was in heaven. George and Sally watched us from the porch with Sandra who played on a small blanket with a few toys before taking a nap. For just a little bit it felt like this was my family. I laughed more that day then I had in months. I had more fun than you can imagine. It is one of those memories that help you survive the rest of life.

At some point Sally must have gone inside because what seemed like just a short while later Sally was calling us all in for dinner. We didn't even have to change. We just went in and washed our hands and sat at the table. Brian and I were teasing each other and laughing when Sally put the food on the table. She sat down and then they did a weird thing. Everyone bowed their heads and folded

their hands. Brian nudged me and I did it too. Then George started composing some sort of letter out loud. I think it was a letter because it started with dear God. I had never heard a prayer or gone to church so this was strange. He said he wanted this person to protect us all, even me, he specifically said my name. I felt special even if I did not know who this person was. He asked that the meal be blessed and I wondered what that meant. Then he said amen and everyone looked up. George smiled at me.

"Help yourself to whatever you want, Samantha," George said.

"Thank you," I said.

Eating at their table was different than I was used to. Everyone was laughing and joking. They were all smiling and having fun. There was more than enough food for everyone. Eating at their table was entertaining and loud. I loved it. I think in that moment I truly felt envy. I was not envious of what they had, I was envious of the life they had. Their happiness, their relationship, their peace. To me I would have given anything for their peace. Life at home on its best day was full of worry. I wondered if Brian and Lacy had ever gone to bed hungry, or walked barefoot in the snow because they did not have shoes. I was envious of that moment. I wanted the life they got. Why did my life have to be so hard? I felt tears sting my eyes.

"May I go to the bathroom?" I asked abruptly interrupting Brian who was telling his dad a story I was not listening to.

"Sure, Samantha, just wash your hands before you return," Sally said without looking at me. She was feeding Sandra some kind of orange goo.

I went to the restroom before the tears could fall. I decided I could not return to the table. I wiped my face and stepped out of the restroom. I could hear them still at the table. I had left Hope in the front hall. I tiptoed over and picked her up. They did not hear me as I quietly snuck out the front door. As soon as I quietly shut the door behind me I turned and ran as fast as I could home. It was not until I was home that I realized I was still in Lacy's bathing suit. I was

relieved when I did not see Mom's car. I had time to change. I ran inside and grabbed my bed clothes. I decided to take a shower just in case Mom could smell the magic house on me. I took a shower and put my nightgown on. I hung the almost dry bathing suit in the closet behind a lot of other clothes. I hoped that when Mom did see it she would not suspect where it came from.

I had not eaten much for dinner at the magic house. So I went into the kitchen to find some food. I grabbed a slice of cheese and some crackers and sat down at the table to eat. I was looking out the window when I saw him. There was George walking over the hill. He paused and looked around before coming down the hill. I quickly cleared my table. I ran and grabbed Hope from my bed. Then I hid with Hope in my closet. I heard George knock on the door several times. Then I heard the door open.
"Samantha, are you here?" George yelled, "It's ok, I just want to make sure you are alright."

How could I tell him that I had ran away because the love in his house broke my heart? I was sad, embarrassed, envious, and lonely. I could not tell him how sad I was so I just hid. Soon I heard the front door open and shut. I waited a few minutes before creeping out of the closet. I peeked out my bedroom door but did not see him so I moved to the living room window. I saw him disappear over the hill. I walked to the door. Just outside the door on the porch was my clothes neatly folded. I had not even noticed that he had been carrying them. I opened the door and picked them up. I took them and hung them in the closet. Then I crawled into bed. I hugged Hope and cried. I felt lost. When the light began to fade I got up and washed my face. I brushed my teeth. Mom still was not back. I went to bed hugging Hope.

Chapter 22

Here is the thing about little kids, they actually want to trust and love their parents. They want to believe what their parents say.

Kids have an innate love for their parents. It is automatic, like imprinting in birds. That is why they take so long to see evil in their parents. After all, their first instinct is to love these beings who brought them into this world.

I awoke in the middle of the night startled. It took me a minute to pin-point what had woke me up. Then I heard it again. Someone was crying and others were talking. It took me a few minutes to wake up fully. I was groggy and thirsty. I sat up slowly and looked around. Shayla was not beside me. I tiptoed across the floor and looked around the house. I could see well because the moon shone bright through the curtainless windows. Krista was sitting on the couch with tears running down her cheeks. She did not make a noise as she gripped her stomach. She was wearing the white dress again. I peeked down the hall. The bathroom door was open and Mom was telling Shayla to clean herself up. Shayla was in the bath crying.

"Mommy, it hurts. Please, Mommy," her whimpering broke my heart.

"Shut up, whore. Clean yourself up or I will and if I have to do it I will really give you something to cry about. I swear, you are such a filthy ugly mutt. I should have aborted your ass," Mom sounded really annoyed.

I looked at Krista again. She must have sensed my presence because she looked up at me. She put a finger to her lips and quietly said shhh. I looked back at the bathroom. Mom gave Shayla a towel. "Get to bed now. And do not wake up my baby. She may love you but I don't. Now get, you beast." Mom said angrily at Shayla.

I snuck back into my room and quietly got Shayla some pajamas and underwear. I then crawled into bed and pretended to be asleep in case Mom peeked inside. Shayla came in alone. I sat up and without a word helped her get dressed. Shayla seemed to be hurt and stiff in a few areas. I saw a few new bruises but could not see how bad in the dim light. She had tears running down her cheeks. The tears shimmered in the moonlight. I helped her into bed and

tucked her in. I crept back to the door. I peeked out. Mom was gone but the bathroom door was shut. Krista saw me from the couch and ran over to me. She pushed me into the bedroom and shut the door. "What are you doing?" She asked hastily in a whisper, "If Mom sees you she will blame us for waking you up."

"What is going on?" I whispered back.

"She sold us again, you idiot. What did you think she was doing?" Krista replied. "Just get in bed and pretend to be asleep. Mom is going to check on her *perfect angel* before she goes to bed."

Then she was out the door and back on the couch. I walked quickly back to bed. I laid there with my eyes closed. I kept thinking about how nastily Krista had said "perfect angel" and what she had said about Mom selling them. What did it all mean? Should I have known? I felt so sad. I felt guilty for going to the magic house and having fun while my sisters were being hurt.

I heard the door open wide and heavy footsteps across the floor. I kept my eyes closed and tried not to move. Someone brushed the hair back from my forehead. Then I felt a kiss on my forehead. "I love you, my perfect baby," I heard my mom whisper.

I listened to the retreating footsteps. I opened my eyes just a little and saw Mom close my door until it was just barely cracked. "Krista, get cleaned up and then get some sleep. Don't wake up your sisters," I heard Mom tell Krista.

A few seconds later I heard a door close only to be followed by another door closing. I turned over and looked at Shayla. "Are you ok?" I whispered.

"No, it hurts. Samantha, they tried to kill me," Shayla whispered through her tears.

"I thought she was taking you shopping. What really happened?" I whispered insistently.

"We did but then she took us somewhere else," Shayla said.

"Where? Tell me everything that happened?" I whispered in a panic.

What had I allowed my sister to walk into? I was supposed to protect her. What had happened? I flashed back to two weeks ago

when Krista came home in pain and hating me. I still don't know exactly what happened but I do know that what happened was bad. Very bad.

"She bought me a white dress like Krista's and pretty underwear that was see-through. Then she took us to this big building where people can rent rooms. She rented two rooms. The rooms opened up to the parking lot. She took Krista in one and me in the other. I did not see Krista after that until time to leave. Mom sent men in to me, Samantha. I tried to fight but they were stronger than me. One of the men complained to Mom and Benny came in and hurt me. He kept hitting me and then Mom told him to stop. Mom told me to stop fighting or she would let Benny beat me to death," Shayla was crying as she told me. I just listened in horror as she continued, "When I did not stop fighting, Mom told the men they could handle me anyway they wanted. I kept fighting because it hurt so much. It was man after man. They just kept coming. Some of them laughed at my tears. They were so much stronger. They did the things in the video over and over. Mom would call one out just to send another one in. It was terrible. They called me names. Samantha, I am bleeding down there and it won't stop. Mom is mad that I got blood on the new white dress. Samantha, she says I have to get used to it. What if she does it again?"

Shayla broke into sobs. I held her as tight as I could. I wished I could help her. I was shocked and did not know what to say or what to do. I hated myself for allowing my mom to take Shayla and do this. Why didn't I do something? I was so selfish and stupid. I knew this was all my fault. Krista had said so when she returned last time. It was all my fault and there was nothing I could do.

It did not take long for Shayla to cry herself to sleep. I crept out of the room to see Krista. I opened my door slowly. The door to Mom's room was shut. I listened at the door for a minute. There were noises coming from inside. Grunting noises and heavy breathing. I was curious so I turned the knob slowly and cracked the door. Mom and Benny were naked. Benny was on top of Mom and

they were moving like the people in the video. Disgusted and embarrassed, I closed the door. I looked around the room. Krista was laying on the couch with her back to me. I walked over to her and knelt beside her.

"Krista, are you awake?" I whispered.

"What do you want?" Krista said, sounding funny.

"Are you ok?" I asked.

"What do you care?" Krista said.

"I love you, please, I love you and I am sorry," I found myself tearing up.

Krista rolled over. She had been crying. She looked at me intensely for a minute then she hugged me. She did not say anything. She just hugged me and cried quietly on my shoulder. I hugged her as tightly as I could. I whispered "I'm sorry," over and over knowing it was not enough. I felt so guilty. I knew that Stacy would be so ashamed of me. I held my sister until she also fell asleep. I pushed her gently back onto the couch. I was tired but did not deserve to get to sleep. While I was happy, my sisters were tortured. Mom said that they did not matter and that they were nothing, but the reality was that I was nothing and did not matter. I walked outside and looked at the stars. I stood there just looking up not finding answers. Lost in my own failures. I was an awful person.

I replayed everything that Krista had said after her first time. Then I replayed everything that Shayla had said. I tried to make sense of it. It made no sense. Why? I couldn't even picture it, I couldn't believe it. Yet I had seen some of the video. I imagined the horror of what my sister went through. What both my sisters went through. Suddenly, I ran to the side of the porch and threw up. I threw up until I was just dry heaving. Then I cried. I could not stop. When the tears finally stopped I sat back. The stars were gone. The sky was pink and purple with blue on the horizon. It was morning. I felt so sad that I almost felt numb to anything else.

I went inside and went to the restroom. I washed my face. I looked at the face in the mirror. Mom always said I was beautiful

and perfect. I had straight brown hair that curled at the ends, I had dimples on my cheeks that showed when I smiled, I had hazel eyes that sparkled. Yet when I looked in that mirror I only saw sadness. I saw a nobody who could not protect the ones she loved. At that moment, I hated Stacy for leaving us. I hated her for leaving me. I hated her for not being here to protect us. But most of all, I hated myself for my failure. I was to blame for everything.

Chapter 23

     I left the bathroom and went into my room. Shayla was still asleep. I covered her where the blanket had slid off. I got dressed for the day quietly. Before I left the room, I took Hope and put her under Shayla's arm. Krista was still asleep but someone was in the bathroom. I looked towards Mom's door. Benny was just coming out wearing a t-shirt and cut-offs. He headed toward the backdoor. Then he was gone. I walked toward the bathroom and heard the shower running. I walked back to the living room and out to the porch. I sat on the top step and watched some ants walking back and forth. I heard the door open behind me but did not look up.
"Samantha, I did not know you were awake," Mom said behind me.
     I knew how to act from years of practice. Yet this morning it seemed almost impossible.
"Mommy, you're home. I missed you," I said as I put a smile on my face and hugged the mother I was born to.
"I got you some surprises. Do you want to see?" She smiled at me.
"Yes," I said, pretending enthusiasm.
"Ok, grab my purse from the car and I will put your presents on the table," Mom said before going back inside.
     I walked slowly to the car. I had forgotten to put my shoes on so the gravel hurt my feet. However, I welcomed the pain. I deserved the pain. I got Mom's purse and walked back to the house. When I stepped inside it took a minute for my eyes to adjust to the dimness.

Mom was at the table with a stack of wrapped gifts. I sighed and put a smile on my face. I ran over and handed Mom the purse.

"Are these for all of us?" I asked.

"No, of course not. These are just for you," Mom said smiling at me. "These are for my perfect angel."

"Thank you, Mommy," I said around the lump in my throat.

"You're welcome, baby. Why don't you open them while I make some coffee," Mom gave me a hug then handed me one of the gifts.

I sat down at the table. I put a smile on my face and opened the gifts one at a time. There were two new dresses and one headband. There was a box of bubbles. There was a little girl baby doll and five outfits for her. There was a stuffed dog that was white with black spots. There was a jump rope and a yo-yo. In the last present there was a new coloring book with a big box of crayons. The presents made me ill. I looked towards Krista. She was watching me with a look of pure hatred on her face. I looked back at the presents. I still had that fake smile on my face. Mom was sitting at the table again just watching me. I walked over to her.

"Thank you, Mommy. I got everything I wanted and more," I said hugging her.

"You're welcome, Sissy," Mom said before looking out the window and drinking her coffee.

I began to pick up all the wrapping paper. I wondered when Mom had time to wrap all this. It did not matter to me. The truth was that I hated the very sight of the gifts. They made me feel dirty somehow. Mom looked at me picking up the wrapping paper. "Samantha, leave those there. You don't need to clean those up. You are too special and perfect to do chores. Krista, get over here and clean this mess up. Then help your sister carry her new treasures into her room," Mom smiled warmly at me.

I handed the wrapping paper that I had in my hands to Krista. She aggressively took it from me. She quickly gathered the rest of the paper. I started stacking the gifts to make them easier to carry. I grabbed as much as I could and went to my room. I put the gifts I

was carrying on my side of the bed. Shayla was awake but still in bed. She had been crying. I grabbed the black and white stuffed dog and took it to her.

"I did not know this would happen. I am so sorry," I said softly. "Please forgive me. Before you left yesterday Mom asked me what gifts I wanted. I did not know how she would get the money. I am sorry. I asked her for this because I knew you wanted one. You can have it and all the other gifts you want. I don't want them anymore anyway. They're yours, just please don't hate me."

"I don't hate you," Shayla said, taking the stuffed dog.

"Don't tell me you bought that," Krista said, putting a pile of gifts on the bed. "She knew what would happen just like she knew what would happen to me my first time. She is the selfish one."

"No, I swear, I did not know!" I argued.

"You knew. You are a liar. You may have everyone else fooled but I see who you really are. You are not as perfect as you think you are, *princess*," Krista nastily accused.

"You knew, didn't you? Why didn't you warn us?" I said piecing it together.

"Of course I knew, I am not an *idiot*. You knew too, you just don't want to admit it," Krista angrily said moving around the bed.

"You could have warned us. I could have saved you and Shayla. Krista, why didn't you tell us?" I said, confused and hurt.

Krista slapped me across the face.

"Like you saved me?!?" Krista glared down at me before storming out of the room.

I stared after her in shock. Krista had known and let it happen. She had not warned us. Mom had tricked me into a false sense of security. Shayla and I were on our own. Even if we went for help, Krista would not go along. I would have to abandon her. I could not abandon her. I could not question Mom because it could make everything worse. We were trapped. I would not abandon my sister like Stacy abandoned us. Mom would take Krista and I would

never see her again. Things would get worse for Krista. I looked at Shayla as the realization that we were trapped sunk in.

"Are you ok?" Shayla asked me, getting up out of bed.

"I am fine, just fine. Let's get you cleaned up," I replied.

Shayla was covered in bruises. I put her in a dress because the bruises between her legs looked really bad and I was worried that shorts would hurt her. Shayla was also moving funny. She said she felt stiff. I helped her get dressed.

"Try not to cry in front of Mom. It will make her mad. We will talk later about everything. Also, don't tell Mom I gave you my gifts. Tell her I said you could play with them. Stay as close to me as you can. I will try to protect you," I instructed Shayla before walking back to the kitchen.

Shayla followed me to the table. Mom was making pancakes for breakfast. Krista was helping her and did not see us enter.

"Mommy, can Shayla and I eat on the porch?" I asked.

"Sure, Sissy, anything my baby wants. Go get the porch ready," Mom answered smiling at me warmly.

I took Shayla's hand and we walked to the front porch. There were two chairs and a small table out there. Shayla sat down in a chair while I put the table in front of the chair and pushed the other chair across from her. I went inside and Mom gave me a wet dishcloth to wipe the table. Then I put our breakfast on the table. I knew how stiff Shayla was and did not want her to have to sit on the floor in the kitchen. This way she had a chair. Shayla and I ate our pancakes outside. Shayla must have been really hungry because she ate her pancakes before I could even eat a third of mine. I gave her the rest of mine even though I was still hungry. Shayla deserved it and I didn't. After Krista cleaned up everything from Breakfast, Mom called us all inside.

"Krista and Shayla sit down on the couch. It is time to watch the video again. It was clear to me from your behavior last night that you need to see it again. Samantha, go to the table. I need your help with something," Mom dictated and we obeyed.

I sat down at the table in my spot which just happened to face away from the living room. I tried not to think about the things my sisters were about to see. Mom came in. She poured herself a cup of coffee. On the way to the table she grabbed a pack of cigarettes, a lighter and an ashtray.

"What do you need my help with?" I asked.

"You're going to help me count all the money I made last night," Mom answered me. "Go grab my purse."

I went into the living room. Mom's purse was on the floor by the couch. I gently ran my hand on Shayla's hand as I grabbed the purse and returned to the kitchen.

"Thank you, Sissy. Now sit down. I want you to help me count and organize the money," Mom said as she started digging in her purse.

Mom started pulling bills out of her purse. I started organizing them by denomination. Mom was smiling. Mom liked money. I began to count as soon as she gave me the last of the money. Mom wrote down the numbers as I counted them. I counted twelve one hundred dollar bills, twenty-eight twenty dollar bills, sixty-nine ten dollar bills, and forty-eight one dollar bills.

"This is great. Once they get used to it I can probably double this," Mom said after she counted up the money.

"Mommy, doesn't it hurt them?" I asked softly.

"Oh, they're just being babies. It does not hurt that much if they would just relax and stop being spoiled brats," Mom said glaring towards the couch.

I wondered which daughter she was angry at. I did not believe her. I had seen the bruises on Shayla. What happened hurt. Yet I also knew if I angered Mom she might take it out on one of them. I could not risk it.

"Mommy, I just want to thank you for the gifts. They are beautiful," I said to distract Mom.

"You're welcome, Sissy," Mom said smiling at me. "I just realized that maybe you needed to get a little bigger before you grew up.

Anyway, a few more nights like last night we might be able to move to town. That would be fun."

"Yes, that would be fun," I said to appease her.

"So, what did you do yesterday, Sissy?" Mom asked, sipping her coffee.

"Oh, I just played all day. I did some exploring. Just played," I said.

"That sounds like fun. You are so lucky, you know that? You are a perfect angel," Mom said looking at me.

"Um, do you need anything else? Can I go play please?" I said quickly. Mom was looking at me funny and it made me nervous but I did not know why.

"Sure, go play. Just stay out of the living room," Mom said.

I got up and ran to my room. I looked at the gifts on the bed and felt sad. Shayla and Krista were destroyed for my selfishness. I will never be selfish again. I walked over and started to put away the toys and clothes. I wanted them out of sight. The dresses were beautiful and I hated them for what they represented. I put them in the back of the closet and vowed to never wear them. When I had finished putting the gifts away, I smoothed the blanket out on our bed. There was a dark reddish brown stain on Shayla's side of the bed but it was dry so I made sure the cover covered it. I then put the stuffed dog and Hope at the top of the bed. I liked how nice that looked. Somehow cleaning up the room was making me feel better. I could not control what was happening to my family but this I could control. This I could do. Just as I was finished, Shayla returned to the room.

"Is the movie over?" I asked.

"Yes," Shayla said.

"Do you want to play?" I asked. I hated the sadness I saw in her face.

"No," She answered and sat on the bed. She reached for her stuffed dog and hugged it close.

"Would you like to color?" I asked.

"Ok, could you get it?" She asked.

"Sure," I said and quickly grabbed what we needed.

I purposely left the new coloring book and crayons behind. We colored on the bed. Shayla stayed sitting while I laid on my belly. I could see the door and after a while I saw the door open a little. Krista was looking into the room. I watched her as she watched us. I felt bad for her. Shayla and I were best friends. I was Mom's favorite. Before me Krista was all those things. I knew that because Krista had told me over and over again how I had ruined her life. Krista saw me looking at her and she glared at me. If looks could have killed, I would have been dead.

"Samantha," I heard Mom yell.

I jumped up and ran to find Mom. I went past Krista who hit me with her elbow as I passed her. It was just in the arm and did not hurt too bad. I found Mom in the kitchen. She was putting her coffee cup on the counter by the sink.

"Yes, Mom," I said.

"Samantha, I am going into town today. I will be home later. Can you call Benny in?" Mom said as she headed into the living room.

"Is Shayla and Krista going with you?" I asked, terrified of the answer.

"No, not tonight," Mom answered.

I ran outside and approached the shed. Benny was rifling through some old box of dirty junk. I told him Mom wanted to see him. He ran past me into the house. I was close behind him. Mom told him to sleep in the shed tonight. Then she left. I ran into the bedroom to tell Shayla Mom had left.

Chapter 24

I entered the bedroom and saw Krista and Shayla talking together. They did not see me so I just stood there quietly listening. "She is the reason this even happened to us. She told Mom to do this to us. She just wants pretty toys and dresses and does not care where the money comes from," I overheard Krista say to Shayla.

"She didn't know what Mom was goin to do. You did. That means it's your fault," Shayla said.

"She knew two weeks ago, I told her," Krista argued.

"I don't believe you," Shayla said, sticking up for me.

"It is true," Krista insisted.

"Is not, you lie," Shayla said, crossing her arms.

"Listen, I am not lying. You have to listen. You and me, we can unite and fight her together. We can go for help. We will leave her here and then she can make Mom money. You just have to side with me," Krista pleaded.

"No, I love her and you are mean," Shayla said.

"Fine, it is your funeral. You are on your own from now on," Krista said.

Krista turned and saw me in the doorway. She walked over and pushed me down hard.

"What are you doing, bitch? Are you spying on me? Fuck, you're such a noisy little bitch," Krista yelled. She kicked me in the leg before stomping outside. I stood up and rubbed the spot she kicked. It was red. I then walked over to the bed.

"Thanks for defending me," I said.

"Krista is mean," Shayla said in reply.

"Well, Mom said she is gone for the day. Do you want to go outside?" I said changing the subject. I wanted to distract her. She was still in so much pain.

"I am too stiff," Shayla replied.

"You can sit on the porch. We can play catch," I said smiling.

"Yeah, ok. Can I bring Cookie?" Shayla asked.

"Is that the name you gave the puppy?" I asked.

"Yes, I like cookies and I like Cookie," Shayla explained.

"I like it. Let's take Cookie outside," I said.

Shayla sat on the steps to the porch. I ran to the side of the house to retrieve the ball. When I returned I looked around. I did not see anyone. I wondered where Krista had gone off to. I walked over to Shayla and we played catch. Shayla liked to throw the ball so I

would have to run to retrieve it. I played along but it was not too long before I got too tired. Then I picked a lot of flowers and Shayla and I made little crowns and necklaces. It was fun. I slowly saw her smile reach her eyes. The more we played the happier she got. However, I was hungry so we decided to go back inside.

Shayla must have been feeling better because she actually ran back into the house with me. We went to the kitchen and got the last of the lunch meat, cheese and chips. We took it all to the table and ate. Shayla was already putting last night out of her mind. I wondered where Krista was and why I had not seen her. Shayla wanted to watch TV after lunch. I still did not want to watch it so I told her to watch it without me. I told her I wanted to take a walk. I did want to take a walk. I wanted to find Krista.

I went outside and decided to start at the magic house. This time I approached it from the back. When I was there yesterday I saw there was an old barn that they did not use far back from their house on the top of a hill. George told me that it was unsafe and to stay away. That meant that they would not be there. If I climbed to the second story I would be able to see a great distance. Because it was on the top of a hill, I would not be in view to anyone in or around the house. That was perfect because I was a little embarrassed that I ran from them yesterday. I also felt guilty for feeling so envious. It was not their fault they had more than me. That was just the life they were born into.

I went into the barn. It was dusty and smelled funny. There was a ladder leading up to the second story. The ladder was missing a few rungs but I could still climb up. The ladder creaked and groaned as I climbed. It sounded like a spirit was complaining. It scared me a little. The barn had rocks, dirt, and old hay on the floor. There were cracks in the walls that let in light. There was a hole in the roof on one side. The doors were off their hinges. One door was just laying on the floor. The other set of doors seemed to be missing. The whole place seemed like the perfect place for a ghost to live. It was a little creepy. I tried not to think about how creepy. I made it to

the loft. I saw that there was some stuff piled in the corner. Dust and cobwebs covered the boxes and old chairs. I wondered what was inside but was afraid that I would see a spider or a mouse. I had seen a few mice downstairs. I walked over to the big door. That door laid on the ground about a dozen feet below.

I looked out. The sun was blinding and it took my eyes a minute to adjust. The sun had just passed the magic house and it was very bright. I looked towards the house but did not see anyone. I scanned the area around the house. I did not see anything out of place. I stared at the wooded area in the distance for a long time looking for movement or anything that did not belong. Then I remember the day Krista had hurt my ankle. She had watched me playing with Brian and Lacy, but she had not watched me from the trees. She must have another hiding place. I began to look all around the area looking for a hiding spot. At first I saw nothing, then I noticed a tree. It was about half up the hill on the side of the house that was closer to our house. I did not see anyone around the tree. The tree was too leafy to really see much. I decided to check it out. I turned around and paused. The barn was not as bright inside as outside. Once I could see well I retraced my steps. I almost fell when I broke one of the rungs on the ladder. I made it out of the barn. I circled around to the tree. I approached slowly and quietly. I did not see anyone behind the tree. I looked up and saw it was a perfect tree for climbing because the branches grew in a way that made it easy. I kept looking up and saw that almost to the top Krista was sitting looking toward the magic house. She did not see me.

"Hello, Krista," I said in greeting.

"What are you doing here?" Krista said startled.

"I was worried about you," I said.

"You scared me," Krista said.

"Why are you here?" I asked, confused.

"What, I can't even look at your precious second family?" Krista said sarcastically as she began to climb down.

"That is not what I meant," I said.

"Oh, so you do think they are your family," Krista snared.

"You're my family. Can't we just be friends?" I pleaded.

"Oh, I thought I was not good enough for Mom's precious little angel," Krista was almost to the ground so I backed up about eight feet just in case I had to run.

"I never said that, I love you," I insisted.

"You did not have to," Krista said as she jumped to the ground.

"Why are you so mad at me? I didn't do anything," I begged.

"Why am I so mad at you?!? Why am I so mad! You told Mom to sell me. Men hurt me over and over and it was your idea, your plan, your fault! You planned it all. You even kept me from getting help. Now, I am going to destroy you. I am going to take everything you have and I will make sure you are hurt ten times as much as me. You are nothing. You are not perfect. You are not an angel. I hate you!" Krista advanced towards me as she yelled.

As she advanced I backed away. When she started to yell I turned and ran. The last sentence she yelled as I was running and she was chasing me. I should have stayed home. Krista chased me halfway home but I was too fast and she gave up and turned around. I ran back to the house. I took a deep breath and put a smile on my face before going inside.

Shayla and I played the rest of the day in our room. There was less food in the kitchen because Mom had not done any shopping since George had brought his groceries. We ate the last of the leftovers for dinner. We did not know how to reheat them so we ate them cold. Krista returned home while we were eating supper. She grabbed a box of cereal and ate it dry while watching TV. She seemed to be ignoring us. Shayla and I went to bed early because Shayla said she was too tired. I was afraid to sleep while Krista was awake so I laid next to Shayla and watched the door. Shayla fell asleep quickly. I listened to the TV. Finally it turned off. I heard Krista getting ready for bed. Then it was quiet.

I listened to the quiet for what seemed like a long time. I was thinking about what Mom had told Benny. Why did Benny have to

sleep in the shed? Where did Mom go? It took me a while but then I remembered Stacy waking me up and making me hide in the closet with my sisters. Mom was fighting with some man and they were getting physical. I remember falling asleep in Stacy's arms while we were hiding. What if it was happening again? Did Mom have a boyfriend? I had to warn Krista. I got out of bed and went to the living room.

"Krista, wake up, it is important," I said when I was beside her.

"What?" Krista said groggily.

"You need to come sleep with us," I said.

"No," Krista rolled over so her back was towards me.

"Krista, I know I did not protect you the first time. I am sorry, but Mom is up to something. You have to trust me, we are not safe," I pleaded.

"What do you mean?" Krista said sitting up and looking around with fear in her eyes.

"I don't know. Just come to our room. We will protect each other. Please," I said.

"Ok, but just for tonight," Krista said, rising and walking toward our room. "But this does not mean I forgive you." She added.

Krista slept on the other side of Shayla. She stole a lot of the blanket but that was fine. For tonight we were safe. I hugged Hope. I fell asleep listening to my sisters breathing.

Chapter 25

I awoke suddenly. I felt alert but did not know why. I heard a noise and realized what must have woken me. I moved to the door and peeked out. I heard someone laugh. I did not recognize the voice and could not quite make out what was said. I watched the shadow coming closer to the door. I watched as a man practically carried my mom through our front door. I shut the bedroom door and locked it. We were not supposed to lock the door but I would just tell Mom it was an accident or something. I went back to the bed. Shayla and

Krista were still asleep. I sat on the bed and listened. I heard some more banging but then it ended abruptly.

"Fuck," I heard a man's voice yell.

I tiptoed back to the door to listen. The man was trying to wake up someone. I figured Mom must have fallen asleep. I listened some more. I heard footsteps across the floor. I heard the footsteps go down the hall and figured he was going to the bathroom. I returned to the bed. This time I laid down. I was listening to the noises. I was still tired but was afraid to sleep. I was looking at the door when I saw the door knob move. It moved back and forth a few times. The lock held. Then someone banged against the door. I sat up terrified. He banged against the door several times with increasing noise. I just sat there terrified. What if he gets inside? What will he do? How could Krista and Shayla sleep through the noise? I looked at them for a second. Krista had rolled over. Shayla was still snoring softly. I looked at the door. There was one last loud thud. Then it was quiet. I sat there staring at the door. I expected another noise but only heard silence. I got out of bed and walked to the door. I laid down on the floor and peeked under the door. I did not see anything or anyone. I sat up and looked around. I walked over to the window and looked out. There was a breeze blowing through the window. I reached up and shut the window. I locked it and returned to bed. I laid there tired but unable to sleep. I just stared at the door.

I jumped when I felt movement. I was groggy and confused. I must have fallen back to sleep. Shayla was getting out of bed. I looked quickly at the door which now stood wide open. The room was bright with the early morning light. Krista was gone. I jumped up and ran out of the room. Krista was coming out of the bathroom. I sighed with relief. I looked around. I did not see anyone but Krista and Shayla. I walked to the front door. Mom's car was outside. The car was parked at a weird angle and was more in the front yard than the driveway. I walked to Mom's bedroom door. It was cracked but not opened. I pushed it open a little and looked inside. Mom and the

man from last night were in bed asleep. Mom was missing her shirt and bra but still wore her pants. She also still had one of her shoes on. The man was naked.

"What are you doing?" Krista whispered right behind me. I jumped.

"Shh," I said as I quickly and quietly shut the door.

"Why are you being weird?" Krista demanded.

"That man tried to come into our room last night. I locked the door," I said in response as I walked towards the bathroom.

"Why?" Shayla said. She was standing in our bedroom doorway listening.

"I don't know. He tried to break in but then just stopped," I turned and answered her.

"You're making that up," Krista said.

"No, I am not," I said crankily.

"Yes, you are. She is just trying to scare us," Krista said, turning to Shayla.

"I don't lie. It happened. Whether you believe me or not," I started to walk to the bathroom again.

"I know you are lying because it would have woken us up if it did happen. You are just trying to scare us so you can keep Mom's boyfriend all to yourself," Krista said.

I turned to face her, "Krista, believe what you want. I am NOT lying. You slept through it. I was terrified." I then stepped into the bathroom and closed the door.

Shayla was waiting outside the bathroom door when I came out.

"I believe you," Shayla said as she went to the bathroom.

I went into the room and got out clothes for Shayla and myself. Shayla returned and we got dressed for the day. We raided the kitchen for breakfast. Krista was already there.

"There is nothing to eat," Shayla complained.

"Maybe there is something in the freezer," I said as I tried to see the top shelf of the cabinet.

I was not tall enough but there looked to be a bag or something. I went to the table and dragged over a chair. Shayla was on her tiptoes trying to see into the freezer. Krista was looking into the cabinets over the counter. I climbed onto the chair. In the back corner of the pantry cabinet was two bags of muffin mix. One was chocolate chips and the other was blueberry.

"I found something," I said, putting the bags on the counter and climbing down.

"We can't eat this. We can't cook," Krista said grimacing at the package.

"You help Mom cook all the time," I countered.

"No, Mom cooks and tells me what to do. I don't cook," Krista insisted.

"It can't be hard. Aren't there instructions?" I asked.

"I don't know," Krista sounded doubtful.

"There is nothing else to eat," I pointed out.

"Ok, I will try. You two have to help," Krista turned the package over.

Krista sent Shayla to find a special pan. I was sent to find two big bowls and two big spoons. We carried our finds to the table. Krista started the oven and gathered the ingredients. We were out of milk so she used Mom's creamer mixed with water. Then she put them in the oven. We cleaned the kitchen while they cooked. Krista kept looking in the oven to check on the muffins. They smelled good. We were done cleaning so we just sat at the table waiting. Krista took them out of the oven but said we still had to wait a few minutes. We had made eleven muffins.

Krista was putting the muffins on a plate when Mom walked into the kitchen. We had been so focused on the muffins that we had not realized she was awake.

"That's great, girls. I was worried we would not have anything to offer him for breakfast. How do they taste?" Mom said as she took the plate from Krista and took a bite out of a muffin. "They are not

too bad. Thanks, girls." Mom started to put the last few muffins on the plate.

"Mom, those were for us. There isn't any other food. We're hungry," I begged.

"Just stop complaining and get outside before he comes in here and you annoy him too," Mom said as she took one hand and pushed me away.

I started to push Shayla to the back door. I saw Mom set the plate down and turn to the coffee maker. I quickly grabbed a muffin in each hand and ran outside. I gave one muffin to Krista and broke the other in half. I gave Shayla the biggest half and we ate our breakfast.

"I'm still hungry," Shayla whined.

"I know," I patted her shoulder.

"It's not fair. We made them," Shayla sounded angry, "I'm hungry."

"If you can keep a secret, I have an idea," I said to them both.

"What?" Krista said, suspicious.

"I know a place that always has food. A magical place....." I hinted and saw the realization hit Krista.

"Ok, let's go," Krista said.

"We can't let Mom find out," I said.

"I know," Krista said as she started walking.

Shayla and I followed Krista. I was a little worried about returning after the last time but I was hungry. We did not have much food yesterday. We were all hungry and Mom was feeding her new boyfriend our food. I hated that man so much. That was our food, not his. Krista headed to her tree when we got there.

"No, just follow me," I said.

I walked up to the door and knocked. I did not see their car but just figured that George was at work. I knocked again when no one answered the door. I looked in the window. The playpen for Sandra was not in the living room. I did not see anyone. I tried the door. It was locked. Where were they? I looked around. I walked around to the back. We all looked in the windows. I tried the back

door but it was locked. Krista and Shayla checked the windows while I looked for a hidden key. Under the third flower pot on the left side of the door was a little silver key. I tried it in the back door and the door unlocked. I called my sisters over.

The house was cool when we entered. I went upstairs and downstairs. No one was home. There were no clothes in the hamper. There wasn't even trash in the trash cans. I returned to the kitchen. "I think they moved," I said.

"They did not move. This is all their stuff," Krista said rolling her eyes at me.

"We leave stuff when we move," I said standing my ground.

"We are not normal. We don't move, we run," Krista said.

"We don't run," Shayla giggled, " Mom drives."

I couldn't help but laugh. Krista just rolled her eyes and kept looking in the refrigerator.

"There is no milk but they have pudding and jell-o. Come get what you want for breakfast," Krista said as she carried two things of pudding and two of jell-O to the table.

Shayla and I went to the refrigerator and got some too. We all sat at the table and ate. It was really good.

"If they did not move, where are they?" I asked Krista.

"They probably went on vacation," Krista said wisely.

"What's a vacation?" Shayla asked. I was wondering the same thing.

"A vacation is when you go somewhere to have fun," Krista said.

"But they have fun here all the time. Why do they have to go somewhere else?" I asked, confused.

"Maybe they want to have fun with friends far away," Krista speculated. "Or maybe they were just tired of you annoying them all the time." She added.

I did not know what to say. Krista always seemed like she was on the edge of being mad at me anymore. Everything I did or said she argued with. I was frustrated that I could not repair our relationship. She was my sister and I loved her. We were never close but I wanted us to be. I had to fix us.

We decided to spend the morning at the magic house. Krista spent a lot of time in Sally's room. Shayla and I played games downstairs in the game room. We knew we had to go home before Mom came looking for us. We ate lunch before we went. We cleaned up so that they might not know we were there. Krista even emptied the trash. I locked the door before we left and put the key back under the third planter. We walked home together.

Chapter 26

Mom's car was gone when we got home. Shayla went to see if Benny was home. Benny was gone. No one was home. I was relieved. Mom always brought home men who were too touchy with us. Plus, I was afraid to meet her new boyfriend because of last night. It was too hot to stay inside so Shayla and I brought our dolls outside and played in the shade of a tree. Krista brought out her toys and played in the shade about ten feet away. I felt sad for her.

We heard Mom's car before we saw it. Mom had bought groceries. Mom had Krista, Benny, and Shayla carry in the groceries. Mom and I put the groceries away. When all the groceries were inside, Mom had me put up the groceries while she talked to Shayla and Krista in her room. I was a little worried that Shayla or Krista would tell Mom where we were this morning. I hoped they would not tell her. I put up the groceries carefully. Mom returned a few minutes later but did not say anything. I sighed with relief. When we were done, Mom told me to go take a shower. She said I smelled. I quickly went to my room and grabbed some clean clothes. The shower felt nice.

After I got dressed and brushed my hair, I went to find Shayla. She was gone. No one was home. Mom's car was gone. I could not find Shayla, Krista or Benny. They were all gone. I looked in the closets and everything. Mom had left me home alone. Mom had tricked me. Mom had taken my sisters again. I sat down on the porch steps and cried. I had allowed Mom to take my sisters again. I

could not save them. I had failed again. Krista was right to hate me. I deserved to be hated. I missed Stacy but I was also starting to hate her for leaving me here to fail over and over again.

I don't know how long I sat there just crying. Eventually, I got up. I looked to where I had been playing with Shayla. I walked over and carried in our toys. I put them up in our room. I then went outside and picked up Krista's toys. I put them in the corner of the living room where she kept her stuff. I then went into my room. I pulled the books from under the bed. I looked through the books several times. I made up stories to match the pictures. I wished I could read. I was really good at counting. Why couldn't I read? I eventually got hungry. I went to the kitchen to find food. I made a sandwich and got some chips. I ate by myself at the table. It was already sunset and so after I ate I just went to bed. I hugged Hope as the room got darker. I could not sleep. I just listened for Mom's car.

I hate silence. Silence means something bad is coming. Silence is the calm before the storm. I like noise. The dark does not scare me. It is silence that scares me. I lay there listening to the silence. I heard the noise outside as the bugs came alive. The owls hooted. The coyotes howled. Yet the sound I wanted to hear was the sound of my sister snoring softly beside me. I listened and just felt sad. I was in a world full of life yet I was all alone. I lay there as silent tears flowed down my face.

I finally heard an engine. I jumped up and ran to the door. The engine got closer. I saw the headlights first and I ducked down and hid. Mom would be mad if I was awake this late. I peeked through the living room window as Mom parked. I was grateful that it was so dark. I was hidden from view. I watched them exit the car then I ran to my room. I got out a nightgown for Shayla. I laid back down with Hope and pretended to be asleep. I heard them move around the house. I heard footsteps in my room. I felt someone pick up the nightgown at the foot of the bed. I peeped through my lashes and saw Mom exiting the room. I waited patiently for my sister. Shayla was crying softly as she came in with Mom. Mom told her to

shut up and get in bed before she woke me up. I felt a kiss on my forehead. I peeked and saw Mom softly close our bedroom door behind her.

I rolled over and touched Shayla's face with my hand. I then hugged her. She cried on my shoulder as I whispered that I was sorry over and over. I did not ask her what happened. I just held her. There was nothing else I could do. After a while, I heard our door open softly. I looked up startled and saw Krista there.

"Mom went to bed," Krista said holding her stomach.

"Come on," I said, motioning for her to join us.

Krista shut the door and joined us in bed. She slept on the other side of Shayla. We fell asleep hugging each other because that was the only thing we could do. I woke up first. The sky was just starting to lighten beyond the window. Shayla was sleeping on one of my arms. Krista was holding my other hand. I felt uncomfortable and stiff. I slowly freed my hand then I freed my arm. I went out of the room. The house was quiet. I opened Mom's door a crack. Benny was in bed with Mom. They were both naked. I closed the door and went to the restroom. I returned to the room and went back to bed. I was hoping to go back to sleep. I felt tired. After a few minutes however I felt movement and turned to see Krista sitting up.

"Are you okay?" I asked.

"Why do you ask that all the time?" Krista said grumpily.

"I worry. I don't know what else to ask," I replied.

"Ok," Krista said after a minute. She really thought about it before responding.

"Why do you hate me so much? We're sisters. We should work together. We should be friends," I pleaded.

"When I see you all I see is what you took from me. You stole Mom's love, everyone loves you. There is nothing left for anyone else. You walk around like you are some kind of princess but in reality you are just stupid white trash like the rest of us. You destroyed my life even before you were born. You destroyed my life again when you stole the magic family from me. You destroyed my

life when you allowed Mom to sell me. You are the devil. So, no, you are not my sister. You are just the bitch that ruined my life," Krista started out speaking calmly but by the end she was whispering angrily.

For a second I just stared at her. What she said was heartbreaking. I kept hoping that one day she would forgive me and we could be friends. I did not just see anger in her eyes. I saw pain. She really did blame me. To her I was evil. To her I was to blame. I felt guilty and sad. Krista just stood there glaring at me. I could think of only one thing to say.

"I'm sorry," I whispered with tears in my eyes.

Krista left the room. I was crying. Krista had never liked me but I always thought she loved me. She was right. Mom did love me. Benny and I were Mom's favorites. Mom treated Krista like a servant and she treated Shayla like an annoying animal that she was forced to care for. I did not think I was a princess. I was not sure what white trash was but I did not think I was stupid. None of us were stupid. I didn't mean to take the magic family from her. Why couldn't we share them? After all, they seemed to have so much love. I was to blame for Mom selling us but I did not know how to make it stop. If we told, Mom would kill us. Besides, who would we tell? I wanted Krista to be my sister. I loved her. I had to do whatever I had to to make her love me. I just had to.

Shayla was half awake and half asleep. I got out of bed and got dressed. I put out a dress for Shayla and left it on the bed. I gently closed the door behind me. I hoped Shayla went back to sleep. I knew she was tired.

I went to the kitchen. I opened some cereal and got out the milk. I poured my own cereal and sat down to eat. I heard Krista moving around the living room but did not say a word. Krista came in and poured some cereal for herself. She did not even look at me. "It looks like a nice day," I said. When she did not even acknowledge me I added, "I brought in your toys from outside yesterday."

"Shut up," Krista said.

I finished my cereal and put my bowl and spoon in the sink. I went to check on Shayla. She was still asleep so I grabbed a coloring book and crayons. I went outside to the porch. It really was a beautiful morning. I wondered who painted the sky. It seemed to me that every time something really bad happened someone came along and painted the sky extra pretty. I always loved the sunrise. It represented another day, another chance, it brought hope on wings.

I was lost just staring at the sky daydreaming until I heard voices inside. I went inside and found Mom yelling at Krista. Someone was coming and Mom wanted to get everything cleaned up before he came. Mom gave Krista a long list of chores. Apparently at the hotel last night Mom had washed our laundry and Krista had to put it away, sweep, dust, sweep the porches, clean the bathroom, and wash the windows. Benny was sent outside to mow the grass. "Samantha, I am glad you're up. I need to go to town and pick up a grill. Before I go I need you to help me count the money," Mom said as she retrieved her purse from the living room.

I sat at the table and counted the money. There were sixteen hundreds, five fifty's, five twenties, twenty-seven tens, twenty-six fives, and seventeen one's. Mom seemed satisfied. She went to put some of the money in her room. Then Mom got ready and left. She told me that if her friend came while she was gone that I should entertain him until she returned. She told Krista that all the chores should be done before he arrived. She left and I went to wake up Shayla. I was surprised when Shayla was not in bed. I looked in the bathroom but she was not there. I had not seen her in Mom's car. Where was she? I looked for her and called her name. She came out of the closet.

"Why were you in the closet?" I asked, curious.

"I did not want to go with Mom. I was hiding," Shayla said as she began to get dressed.

"Mom went to town. The man is coming back though so we need to get dressed," I said to warn her.

After she was dressed, we went to the kitchen. Shayla had cereal while I tried to help Krista with the chores. Shayla helped after she finished eating. We ended up having to sweep the porches twice because Benny mowed grass all over the newly swept porches. However, we got everything done. Krista moved her stuff into our room so we could lock our door again tonight. We had a plan. When we were done we all went to the front porch to wait. I colored while Shayla and Krista played with the Barbie dolls.

I knew Krista was still angry with me. She had been angry with me my whole life. It just did not make sense to me. Grudges only hurt the people holding them. It is so much better to just let things go. I liked the way Shayla handled things. She just accepted what reality was and did not think. She just lived in the moment. I wanted to be more like her. She seemed so happy and I was always so worried. Krista always seemed angry. Krista was like Mom, a fuse that is constantly ready to explode. I don't think Krista was ever happy. No, I wanted to learn to be like Shayla and live only in the moment. I just did not know how to stop worrying. I had to try to protect my sisters anyway I could. I remembered Shayla hiding this morning. What if I could predict when Mom would take them. Then I could hide them so Mom can't take them. I started to think of the different hiding places I could hide them.

Chapter 26

We heard a loud vehicle approaching. Krista told Shayla and me to carry the toys and coloring stuff inside. We quickly gathered everything up. We were just going inside when a red pickup truck came into view. Shayla and I hurried to put the stuff up in our room. I was worried about leaving Krista alone with him but was also scared to go outside to see the man who tried to break into our room. I sent Shayla on outside as I finished putting stuff up. I went to the living room window and looked out at the stranger. I had only seen him in the dark for a short time.

He was a tall, thin, brown haired man. He was not ugly but not quite handsome either. He wore jeans and a flannel shirt over a white t-shirt. He was wearing brown cowboy boots. I did not like how he looked at Krista. He looked like he was about to eat her. I could not hear what they were saying so I went outside. He did not see me at first. He had his arm around Krista's shoulder holding her close to his side.

"You must be such a heartbreaker. I bet you have a lot of boyfriends," He said to Krista.

"No, I've never had a boyfriend," Krista said looking embarrassed.

"Hello," I said, interrupting.

"Well, who do we have here," He said, taking his arm off of Krista and leaning down to look me in the eye. "Well, you are absolutely gorgeous. I can't wait to be your daddy. My name is Eric Donner. What is your name, baby?"

"I am not a baby. My name is Samantha, this is Shayla, and I guess you met Krista," I said trying to stand taller.

In the absence of courage it is sometimes best to pretend courage. It does not matter how scared you are. You still have to stand strong.

"Well, aren't you a spitfire. I like that in my girls. I am going to have so much fun with you," he said as he smiled weirdly at me.

The look that he had given Krista was now directed at me. I could not help but feel the shiver run down my back. It was a hot day but I felt cold. I was terrified that he would turn into a wolf and eat me up.

"Mom, will be back in a little bit. Would you like me to show you around?" Krista said, trying to get his attention back on her.

"Well, I think I'd rather have this little lass show me around," Eric said, not even glancing at Krista.

Krista crossed her arms on her chest and glared at me. Shayla walked over and took my hand. Did she see how scared I was?

"Um, Ok. This is the front yard and the backyard is in the back. Mom is getting a grill. Do you want to go inside?" I said, turning away from his terrifying eyes.

"Well, pretty lady, I would love to go inside," He said, snaring my other hand.

He practically pulled Shayla and me inside. I was holding on to her with a death grip. Krista stomped up to the porch following us and sat on one of the chairs with her arms crossed. The man led us into the house and looked around.

"Well, I was here the other day but you were not home. Why don't you show me around?" Eric said walking to our bedroom where he had tried to break in the other day.

"Mom, will be back soon. Let me get you a drink," I said as I finally pulled my hand free.

Still holding Shayla's hand, I ran to the kitchen. Mom had made lemonade. I got a glass and Shayla helped me pour the big pitcher. I carried the glass with two hands into the living room. Eric was on the couch. He grinned at me.

"Well, thank you, little lady. Why don't you come up here and sit on my lap? We can watch some cartoons," Eric said as he patted his lap.

"I will turn on the TV," I said quickly.

I ran over to the TV and turned it on. I stood there turning the channel knob until he told me to stop. It was a cartoon. He patted his lap again and told me to come on over. I told him I had to go potty. I went to the restroom and shut the door. I wish Mom was here. Eric was scary. He kept looking at me like he wanted to eat me. I flushed the potty I did not use and washed my face and hands. I opened the door. Eric was there. He blocked the door and came in. He shut the door behind him. He picked me up and put me on the counter by the sink.

"Please, let me go," I whimpered as he played with my hair.

"You are so beautiful. You know that right?" Eric said as he began to kiss my face and hair.

"Stop, No, HELP," I yelled as his rough hands rubbed me aggressively.

He tried to put his hand on my mouth but I bit him as hard as I could.

"FUCK!" He exclaimed as he stepped back and held his hand. "You bitch!"

I used his momentary shock to jump down and open the door. I fell onto Shayla. Shayla must have heard my cries for help. We looked back at Eric. He was coming at us. We scrambled to untangle ourselves. Eric leaned down and grabbed my arm hard.

"If you tell, I will kill you and your whole family. Do you understand?" Eric hissed at me. I nodded my head. "This is not over." Eric added before releasing my arm and walking away.

I just froze in terror. Even if I told Mom she would just be jealous and mad at me. I just had to avoid Eric.

"Did he hurt you?" Shayla asked.

"He tried," I responded in shock. I rubbed my arm where he had grabbed me.

"Krista is jealous," Shayla added.

"Why?" I asked bewildered.

"She wants him to be her daddy," Shayla answered.

Why would anyone want him as a daddy? He seemed so evil. So mean. I shuddered and stood up. I straightened my clothes. I sighed and left the hall. Eric was on the couch watching something on TV. It was no longer on the cartoon channel. He watched me as I went outside to the porch. Shayla followed me outside. Krista was still on the porch. I sat on the floor so Shayla could have the last chair. For a few minutes no one said anything. I was thinking about what had happened and something occurred to me.

"Did you hear me yell?" I asked looking at Krista.

"Yeah, so," Krista said, not looking at me.

"Shayla came to help. Why didn't you?" I asked meekly.

"Because you asked for it. You came out here and stole him all for yourself. You acted like such a perfect princess. You asked for it. Why should I waste my time?" Krista said, glaring at me.

"I didn't ask for anything," I said hurt.

"Oh, yes you did, you came out here all flirty and prissy. Of course he went for you. You don't even have to try. I hope he rips you apart so I don't have to look at your loser face ever again," with that Krista stood up and went inside. She slammed the door behind her.

I sat there stunned. What did flirty mean? What is prissy? Can he really turn into a wolf and rip me apart? Was he a monster? Was I the evil one? Was I asking for it? Was it my fault? I sat there just staring at the door. I saw from the corner of my eye that Shayla had made two dolls out of flowers and was playing with them. I just looked at the door and wondered how it was my fault. After a while I turned my head and looked down the drive. I was not really looking at anything. I was just lost in my own head.

Eventually we heard Mom's car coming. I got up to tell Krista and Eric. Shayla went to help Mom when she parked the car. I went into the house and found Krista giggling on the couch beside Eric. She was very close to him and he had his hand on her upper leg. It was creepy watching them. A part of me wanted to run over and try to protect Krista. However, Krista seemed to be having fun. She was touching his arms. Was that flirting? I never did that with anyone. I saw Eric's hand move closer to Krista's bathing suit area and got nervous.

"Mom is here," I said and hastily went outside to meet Mom.

I ran out to greet Mom. She had just parked and was opening her door.

"Mom, Eric is here. Shayla and I poured him some lemonade. We were nice," I said immediately.

"Eric's here, damn, I wanted to set everything up before he got here. Help me unload the car," Mom said.

"Well, there is my sexy mama," Eric said, as he came out of the house.

Shayla and I started to take bags out of the trunk while Eric and Mom embraced. We tried not to see the kissing. Eww. Although, I was more than a little relieved to have him kissing Mom and not me. I went towards the porch. Krista was on the porch looking at Mom and Eric kissing. She looked jealous.

"He likes me better," she whispered as we walked past.

"Krista, don't make Mom mad. Don't look at them like that," I admonished Krista in a whisper.

"I know. I am not stupid," Krista said hopping off the porch and heading towards car.

Shayla and I put the bags on the table and went outside for the rest. Mom was talking to Eric as Eric unloaded a charcoal grill from the back seat. Shayla and I got the rest of the bags as Krista followed Eric to the back porch with a big bag of charcoal in her arms. Mom followed Shayla and I into the house carrying a 24 pack of beer and a 12 pack of cream soda. We all unloaded the bags of food. Mom even bought cake and pie. There was a large tub of vanilla ice cream. I looked at all the food and got excited. This might be a fun day after all. Mom called Krista inside to help her in the kitchen. Mom sent Shayla and I to play in the backyard so Eric could see what good kids we were. I had hoped to avoid him.

Shayla and I took our bag of Barbie dolls and clothes to the backyard. We were in the middle of the backyard about fifteen feet from where Eric was starting the grill. The grill was black with some kind of silver decoration on the top in the shape of a circle. It looked nice though. Mom brought out a beer for Eric and he cupped her butt as he kissed her. Shayla and I just turned away. I wished Mom would not drink. Mom drank to get drunk. When Mom was drunk she either got really sleepy or really mean. I hoped mean Mom would not show up but sleepy Mom scared me more. Eric was mean and I worried what he would do if he could. Mom went back inside. Eric sat down near the grill. He just watched us. The way he watched us was a little too intense and it made me feel scared. I pictured him turning into a wolf and eating us. Or maybe he would turn into a

giant bear and gobble us up. I straightened my back and tried to ignore him. I just had to pretend to be strong and confident.

I moved so my back was to Eric. Out of sight out of mind. After a little while I actually did half forget about him. Shayla and I were playing house with our Barbie dolls. Shayla was a good distraction. Everything was a game to her. It was fun. We were laughing and having fun. Then it was time to eat. Mom made Krista and Shayla eat on the porch. Benny, Mom, Eric and I ate at the kitchen table. It was not too bad. Whenever Mom was around Eric, he would concentrate all his attention on her. Mom loved it. However, Eric kept giving Mom more to drink. I did not like how funny the alcohol made Mom. She was slurring her words and making silly mistakes. After dinner, Krista cleaned up while Mom and Eric went to the living room. Benny went back to the shed. Shayla and I picked up our toys outside. We decided to play hide and seek. Shayla went to hide while I ran inside to put our toys in our room.

Mom and Eric were on the couch. Mom was laughing too loud. They were touching each other in the bathing suit areas. I quickly ran and put up the toys.

"SSSSammmmanha, cccomm herrreeee," Mom giggled. "ISssnnn't ssshee predddy."

I came close and Mom started to pet my head.

"Ssssshhheeessss mmmmyy bbbbaabbbeee," Mom said.

Eric picked me up and put me on his lap.

"Well, she certainly is beautiful," Eric said.

Mom and Eric started to kiss with me on his lap. I felt Eric's hand under my dress. I started to squirm. Mom was touching Eric but Eric was touching me. I felt something hard on my bottom. I finally managed to squirm free. Eric laughed as Mom tried to call me back. I ran outside. I ran around the side of the house and stopped to catch my breath. I was terrified of them both. I also felt sick to my stomach. I took a minute to recover. I needed a minute. Then I took a deep breath, I put a smile on my face and went to find Shayla.

I played hide and seek with Shayla but my mind was a million miles away. I avoided the house. I even went potty behind a tree to avoid going inside. We got tired when the sun was sitting. I could not avoid the house any longer. I went inside holding Shayla's hand tightly. Mom and Eric were not on the couch so we quickly got ready for bed. Krista got ready for bed with us.

"Come on, let's get inside the room so we can lock the door," I said to Krista when we were all ready.

"No, I am going to sleep out here," Krista said as she headed to the couch.

"We made a deal. We agreed. It is not safe," I insisted. Shayla was already in the room.

"I like him, he is nice. He likes me better than you or Mom," Krista said.

Krista always tried to make Mom's boyfriends like her. She always thought they would save her. She wanted them to love her more. I had to do something. I had to protect her anyway I could. I had to save her this time. I had to.

"Ok..........but maybe you should wear your other nightgown. It is prettier," I had a plan.

"Really?" Krista said looking down at her nightgown.

"Oh, yes, much prettier," I said, knowing I was tricking her.

"Alright," Krista said, walking into our room for her other nightgown.

The door to Mom's room was shut. I followed Krista into our room. I shut and locked the door behind me.

"I am sorry, Krista. I lied. If you hit me I will scream for Mom and she will hurt you. I can't let him hurt you," I said, pushing my back against the locked door.

"You bitch," Krista hissed, whirling around to face me.

"I'm sorry," I said again.

"You're just jealous that he likes me more than you. Move out of my way or I will kill you," Krista said, trying to push me aside.

I did not say anything. I was just trying to stand my ground and keep the door locked. Shayla came over to help me block the door. We were all panting by the time Krista stepped back to glare at us. We had prevented her escape.

"You're siding with her! She just wants someone else to fawn all over her," Krista hissed.

"Eric is bad," Shayla said. I wondered if she was remembering how he talked to us in the hall.

"Krista, Eric is not nice. He will hurt you. I am not moving. You can't go out there. We have to stay together. PLEASE," I said.

"Fine, whatever, you can't stay there all night," Krista said and went to her side of the bed.

She lay there glaring at me. Shayla went to bed too. I stood there waiting for my sisters to go to sleep. Shayla was blocking Krista's view so Krista rose up on one elbow. She stayed like that just glaring at me. Finally, she began to close her eyes more and more. She laid down. I still stood there. I tried not to be tired but I was. When I was sure Krista had fallen asleep, I tiptoed to the bed and grabbed Hope. I returned to the door and laid down in front of it. I watched the bed for any movement. The floor was cold and hard. It took me a long time to get comfortable.

Just as I was dozing off I heard the doorknob turn. I sat up and scrambled away from the door. Someone turned the knob and pushed the door hard. I jumped up and backed away from the door. The knob turned over and over again. Someone was pushing on the door as they turned the knob. I looked at my sisters. They were still asleep. I stood there just a few feet from the door hugging Hope. The door knob stopped turning. A few seconds later someone knocked lightly on the door.

"Sugars, your Mom wanted me to come check on you. Are you awake?" I heard Eric say through the door in a loud whisper.

I glanced at my sisters. If he woke Krista up we may not be able to prevent her from opening the door. I took a deep breath, I hugged Hope tighter, and I moved towards the door.

"We are fine. We are sleeping," I whispered through the door.

"Well, you don't sound like you are sleeping. Why don't you unlock the door and I will tell you a bedtime story," Eric whispered.

"No, we are asleep. Please just go," I whispered back.

"If you don't open up I might think you don't like me. You don't want me to tell your Mom you were mean to me, do you?" Eric threatened.

I backed away from the door. I did not know what to say. I could not find the words to say. I was terrified. I bumped into the bed before I realized I was still backing up.

"Open this door!" Eric said louder and meaner.

Eric started trying to push the door open again. It got louder and I wondered why Mom did not wake up.

"What's happening?" Shayla asked sitting up.

"Is it Mom?" Krista said terrified.

"It's Eric. He wants in," I said terrified that Krista would let him in.

Eric was cussing as he tried to break down the door. Krista surprised me. She came over and huddled with Shayla and I. We stared terrified at the door.

"God Damn it. You stupid fucking bitches. Open this mother fucking door right now or I will really hurt you," Eric ranted on the other side of the door. "FUCK!"

Suddenly it got really quiet. We backed up to the wall on the opposite side of the room. We were by the open window. We kept staring at the door but we didn't hear anything. I started to think that he had given up.

"Well, hello, ladies," Eric snarled from the window.

Eric reached up to take the screen off. I turned around and quickly shut and locked the window. Eric slammed his hand against the side of the house and stomped off. We turned around. We heard footsteps approach the door. The doorknob turned and someone pushed against the door. Then it was quiet again. After a while we got back into bed. We left the window locked.

"Promise you won't open the door?" I asked Krista.

"I promise," she said.

We fell asleep huddled in each other's arms. I tossed and turned all night.

Chapter 27

Morning came way too soon. I was exhausted. Shayla and Krista were still asleep. I had to use the restroom. I got out of bed and tucked Hope into bed. I walked quietly to the door. I listened. I did not hear anything. I got down on my hands and knees and looked under the door. I did not see anything. I got up and looked towards the bed. I really had to go potty. I slowly opened the door and stuck my head out. I did not see anyone. Mom's door was shut. I quickly shut the door and locked it. If I went out there and he was awake he could hurt my sisters while I was in the bathroom. I really had to use the bathroom. There was only one solution. I got clothes for the day. I opened the door and stepped out. I quickly locked the door behind me before I could change my mind. At least my sisters would be safe. I ran down the hall and locked myself in the bathroom. I got ready for the day in the bathroom.

I quietly peeked out of the bathroom. I still did not see anyone. I tiptoed down the hall. The door to Mom's room was still shut. I went to the kitchen and got a drink of water. I put the glass beside the sink and went outside to the front porch. I wished I had remembered to bring some toys. I picked some flowers and made some dolls. The sunrise was beautiful. Eric's truck was still in the driveway so I knew he was still here. I tried to listen for any noises in the house. I wanted to stay outside so I could run if I needed to.

I enjoyed playing on the porch in the quiet of the early morning. It was peaceful. I really got into playing with my flower dolls. They were fairies who were building rainbows so the unicorns could cross the big river. After all, everyone knows that unicorns can't swim. I was having so much fun that I forgot to listen for noises. I did not hear the screen door open and shut. I did not hear

stealthy footsteps behind me. I was rescuing unicorns. I did not know he was there until he was less than a foot behind me.

"Well, what do we have here?" Eric said as he leaned down and put his hands on my shoulders.

I yelped, startled and looked behind me. Mom was in the doorway. Eric was right behind me.

"Ha, ha, ha. We scared her. Isn't she adorable?" Mom laughed at my fear.

"She certainly is adorable," Eric said sitting in the chair beside me. He still had one hand on my shoulder.

"I will start some breakfast as soon as I finish my cigarette. I have to work today so you will need to leave after breakfast. What are you in the mood for?" Mom said as she smoked her cigarette.

"How about pancakes? Do you like pancakes, honey?" Eric said as he looked at me.

"Oh, she loves pancakes," Mom said as she came to sit on Eric's lap.

I felt paralyzed. Mom would be mad if I fought Eric's hand on my shoulder. Mom wanted Eric to like her. Mom threw her cigarette in the grass and started to kiss Eric. Eric was gripping my shoulder in one hand and Mom with the other. Why wasn't he letting go? His grip was actually painful and I tried to free myself but he just gripped me tighter. Mom got up and went inside. Eric watched her go to the kitchen through the window. He then turned to me.

"Well, sugar, there is no locked door between us now, is there," Eric said barely above a whisper.

"I will yell," I threatened weakly.

"Well, you certainly are a spitfire," Eric reached down and picked me up like I weighed nothing.

I tried to get free but my efforts were useless.

"Please, let me go," I begged.

"Well, princess, stop squirming. I just want to be your daddy. Don't you want a daddy?" Eric said as he refused to let me go.

"I don't want you," I said loudly as I tried to kick him.

The pain was sudden. He had slapped me hard in the face. My mouth and cheek stung.

"Now, you listen here, missy. I am an adult and you will respect me. If you don't start being nice to me right now I will make you regret it. Do you understand?" Eric snarled.

I nodded that I understood through the tears. He pushed me onto his lap. I had been hit a lot in my life yet the blows still shocked me. I wondered if I would ever get used to them. My cheek stung and I tasted the rusty taste of blood in my mouth. I was seated facing away from Eric with my butt on his wee wee. I had to get down but fighting did not work. Mom was busy and I did not know if my sisters were awake. I had to be smart. What could I do? His wee wee was poking me and one hand was moving my hair away from my neck so he could kiss my neck. He was breathing funny. His breath was coming fast and hot against my neck. He finally moved the arm that was around my waist and I immediately jumped down. He still had my hair in one hand and I screamed as I tripped and my hair was pulled. He released my hair and I tumbled off the porch. He quickly zipped his pants as Mom ran outside. There was blood on the base of my neck where some hair had been ripped out. There was a cut on my arm. Mom ran to me. I saw Krista and Shayla at the front door in their pajamas. Mom looked up at Eric.

"What happened?" Mom asked Eric.

"She was showing me a dance and she fell off the porch. I tried to catch her but only grabbed some of her hair," Eric said quickly holding up a small clump of hair with a little blood on the ends.

"Ok, accidents happen. She will be fine," Mom said.

"But, Mom, that is not what happened," I cried.

"Of course it is. Eric would not lie," Mom said helping me up.

Mom took me into the bathroom. I followed and allowed her to lift me up on the counter. She put a band-aid on my neck and three band-aids on the cut on my arm. Then she took my face roughly in her hands.

"You listen here. I like Eric far more than I like you brats. You be nice to him or I will hurt you. Do not push him away," Mom said.

Mom released my face and left the room. I turned and looked in the mirror. I had a hand shaped red mark on my face. You could barely tell that I had my hair ripped out. One side of my mouth was a little swollen but it did not look too bad. The arm did not get blood on my clothes so I did not need to change. I climbed down off the counter and fixed my clothes. I left the bathroom. Mom was putting pancakes on the table. Benny and Shayla were taking their pancakes to the porch. Mom and Krista were getting everyone drinks.

I was not hungry anymore. I was sad. Really sad. And hurt. It was not fair. I wished that I belonged to any other family. Surely that would be better than this. I saw Shayla come back in to get drinks for Benny and her. If I belonged to another family I would not know Shayla. I loved Shayla. At least I had her. I took a deep breath and straightened my back. I walked into the kitchen and sat down in my chair. Mom sat across from me. Krista sat on one side and Eric sat on the other. They all started to eat. The food stung the sore side of my mouth. I did not eat much. I did slowly drink all my juice. I caught Krista looking at me a lot during breakfast. She was not glaring but she was looking at me funny. Eric and Mom were laughing and talking a lot. As soon as breakfast was over I asked to go outside. I ran to the trees and hid behind one to cry.

I leaned against the tree crying. I felt so alone. I heard Shayla calling my name. I was worried about how I looked. I did not want to return to the house. I wanted to move deeper into the trees and disappear forever. Shayla was still calling me. I had a responsibility to try to protect my sisters. I could not abandon them. I took a deep breath and straightened my back. I walked out of the trees.

"Shayla," I yelled loudly.

"Samantha," I heard her yell again.

I could not see her but her voice was coming from the other side of the house. I ran around the house and saw her at the top of the hill.

"Shayla, I'm over here," I yelled again hurting my sore mouth.

"Where were you?" Shayla asked as she came close.

"Nowhere. What are you doing?" I asked.

"Mom says Eric is leaving and wants you to say good-bye to him," Shayla said.

"I don't like him," I said.

"Krista says you do. She said that he told her that you wanted him all to yourself," Shayla said.

"Krista lied. I hate him. He hurt me," I touched my face. My cheek still hurt.

"Why did you leave the room?" Shayla questioned. "Krista said you left the room to be with him."

"No, I woke up and had to go potty. You were asleep. I had to lock the door behind me so you would be safe. That meant I was locked out. I was playing outside when he and Mom snuck up on me. I swear I did not leave the room to be with him. I only locked the door behind me so you would be safe. I had to go potty. Please believe me," I explained.

"For real?" She asked.

"I promise," I said.

"Ok, I believe you. Come on, Mom sent me to get you," Shayla said, taking my hand as we walked to the house.

Mom and Eric were in the living room. They were saying good-bye.

"Here is my baby. Come say good-bye to Eric," Mom said giving me a look that made sure I knew I did not have a choice.

"Well, here is my princess," Eric smiled as he picked me up and spun in a circle before stopping in front of Mom. "She looks just like you. We would make a pretty good family." Eric said as he smiled at Mom.

Mom beamed. She looked so happy. I wanted down but was afraid to fight Eric in front of Mom.

"Good-bye, Eric," I said.

"Well, I ought to be going," Eric said hugging my mom with one arm.

"When will you be back?" Mom asked.

"How late do you work tonight?" Eric asked.

"Oh, we can't do it tonight. I work very late," Mom said hastily.

"Well, alrighty then, I will just have to see you tomorrow. How about I pick you up at 5?" Eric said squeezing me a little too hard.

"Sounds great. I will see you tomorrow at 5," Mom said kissing Eric again.

"Well, sugar, I guess I have to go. I can't wait to see you again," Eric said kissing my mouth before putting me down.

As soon as he turned I wiped his slobber off my face. Yuck! I did not like him. At least tomorrow he would be taking Mom somewhere else. Mom walked Eric out to the car. Krista, Shayla and I stayed inside. I did not see Benny. Krista was glaring at me.

"I told you she wanted him all to herself. She is so selfish," Krista hissed.

"What?" I said.

"He told me how you were outside dancing for him. You were so afraid that he would like me more. He told me how he only wanted to read us a story last night but you lied to us and made us scared of him. He is a nice guy. You are just selfish. Everyone has to worship the almighty Samantha," Krista said angrily and sarcastically.

"No, he lied. I never danced. He picked me up and I could not get free. He slapped me and I tried to get free and I fell," I tried to explain. "Please, Krista. He tried to hurt me. I swear!"

"You would say anything to get your way. Well, I'm not buying it," Krista said walking towards the door.

"Krista, wait. Please just listen. Believe what you want but there is something else we have to do now," I said quickly putting my hurt aside. We had pressing business.

"What?" Krista said whirling around.

I saw Eric pulling away and Mom heading back to the house.

"Not here. Quick follow me as fast as you can," I turned and ran for the back door.

I heard my sisters behind me. I ran until I was over the first hill and could not see the house. I hoped this would work.

"Ok, thanks for following me," I began.

"Just tell me what you want," Krista sounded annoyed and winded.

"Mom wants you to work today," I said.

"Are you sure?" Shayla asked.

"Yes, I'm sure. She mentioned it to Eric. She said she was going to work. Lately that means you," I answered.

"Why are you telling us this?" Krista said suspiciously.

"I want to help. If Mom can't find you then you can't go to work with her. I want to hide you," I explained.

"That will never work. Mom will find us," Krista said.

"We have to try," I plead, "Please."

"Ok, where do you hide us and when," Krista agreed.

We returned to the house to hide. Mom was smoking on the couch. Krista hid under the front porch with a book. Shayla hid in an empty cabinet in the kitchen. The cabinet was under the counter and Mom did not use it because she did not like to bend over. I got our Barbie dolls for Shayla to play with. I went out to see Mom. If I kept her happy she might not notice my sisters were gone. I emptied her ashtray and got her a drink. Mom got up to get ready to go. She sent me to find my sisters. She went into her room and shut the door. I went to see my sisters. I told them that Mom was getting ready to go and they should be very quiet. Krista said she needed a drink. Mom was coming into the living room when I entered the house.

"Where are your sisters?" Mom demanded.

"I could not find them," I lied.

"What do you mean you could not find them?" She said angrily.

"They must be playing somewhere, Mommy. I don't know where," I lied again.

"Fuck, I will find them. Damn it, those brats are just wasting my time," she said stomping outside.

I heard her yelling their names over and over again. I went to the kitchen to get a juice box for Krista. I came outside just as Mom was coming back to the porch.

"Are you sure they aren't in their room?" Mom asked.

"Maybe," I said holding the juice box.

Mom went inside so I quickly went to give Krista the juice box.

"You little liar!" Mom roared from the open door.

She must have seen me from the window. I forgot about that. Mom came over and pushed me into the dirt. She looked down and saw Krista cowering under the porch spilling her juice box. Mom turned to me and kicked me before I could get up. She then straddled me and kept hitting me. Finally she stopped.

"Get the hell out from under there or I will come get you and you will regret it!" Mom threatened Krista.

Krista dropped her juice box and came out quickly. She was shaking. I felt so bad for her. Mom knelt back down and hit me twice more.

"Tell me where that bitch Shayla is or I will do far worse to you," Mom yelled at Krista.

Krista immediately told Mom where Shayla was. I tried to stop her but Mom slapped me where Eric had slapped me. I tasted fresh blood in my mouth. I watched helpless as Mom got my sisters ready and left. Benny went with them laughing as Mom dragged my sisters by their hair to the car. She kept hitting me when I got close. She drove away nearly running me over when I begged her not to go.

Chapter 28

They were gone. I stood in the driveway just staring at the spot where the car disappeared. I tried. I failed. Again. There was blood running down my cheek. My side hurt. The pain must be coming. Right? I felt numb. Shocked. I froze in that spot. I could not feel anything. My sister's faces flashed before my eyes. The look on

Krista's dirt smeared face as Mom ordered her out from under the porch. The look of terror on Shayla's face when Mom yanked open the cabinet and dragged her out by her hair. The horror on their faces as Mom made them put on the white dresses and see-through underwear. The pain and terror as Mom dragged them to the car by their hair. The tears that ran down their cheeks as Mom drove away. I felt rain falling from the clear sky. I looked up confused. I realized that it was not raining. It was my own tears. The problem was not that I felt nothing. The problem was I felt everything. The blows I received paled in comparison to the blows my sisters would take tonight. Their pain was my pain. Yet, here I was. Paralyzed by the pain I could not prevent. I was useless. I was nothing. I was useless. I could not even protect the only people I loved.

I don't know how long I stood there. Eventually, I turned and returned to the house. I retrieved the spilled juice box under the porch. Krista didn't have a chance to drink it because when Mom discovered her she squeezed it so hard that it burst open. I felt so sorry for letting Mom discover her. Ants were crawling all over it so I brushed off as many as I could. I took it inside and put it in the trash. I picked up the Barbie dolls that had fallen out of the cabinet when Mom dragged Shayla out. I put them back in our room. Mom had Benny put the dirty clothes in the trunk when my sisters were changing. He had missed some socks and underwear so I picked them up and put them in a pile in our closet. Somehow cleaning seemed to help me. I had no control over anything but when I cleaned or straightened up I was in control. When I finished all I could do, I went to the bathroom.

I looked in the mirror. There was a small cut above my right eye. There was a lot of bruising on my cheek. I did not know if the bruising was from the blow Eric gave me or the one Mom gave me. It did not matter. My clothes were covered in dirt and blood. I peeled my clothes off. It hurt to raise my arm and my legs were sore. I had a lot of bruises on both sides of my body. I looked like I was turning blue. I put my clothes in the bathtub and stepped inside. I turned the

water on. The water stung in a few areas but it also felt good. I had made the shower cold and it made my body shiver but it also numbed the pain. I washed off then I sat down and began to wash my clothes by hand. I could not get all the blood out but the dirt came off. I rinsed myself and the clothes. I hung the clothes over the side of the tub and went to my room. I put on my nightgown before returning to the bathroom. I wrung out the clothes and left them on the side of the tub to dry.

I was too tired to eat. I hurt all over. I did not want to think anymore. I turned out all the lights and went to bed. I did not think I could fall asleep but I did. I did not wake up all night. In the morning I found Shayla and Krista in bed asleep beside me. I was a light sleeper and was surprised to find I had not woken up when they came home. I tried to get up to look at them but I hurt all over. I managed to sit up and look at their sleeping faces. Krista looked okay but Shayla had a cut on her swollen mouth. Did a man do that or Mom? I did not know. Krista and Shayla both had dry tears on their faces. I felt so sad for them. Why couldn't I protect them?

I slowly got out of bed. I felt slow and heavy. My side was killing me. I went to the bathroom and looked in the mirror. My side was back and blue. It hurt to raise my arm. I returned to the bedroom. I found a light airy dress and put it on. I felt tired and laid back down. I fell back asleep beside my sister.

I awoke alone. It was really bright outside. I missed the sunrise and felt sad that I had missed it. I looked around the room. I was not ready to try to move yet. I heard noises and voices coming from the living room. I saw that someone had tucked the blanket tightly around me. Hope and Cookies were beside me. Was it Mom or one of my sisters? I un-tucked the blanket and got up slowly. I was still stiff and sore, but it could be worse. I made the bed before going to the door. I opened it just a little. Mom was in the living room watching TV on the couch. She was smoking a cigarette and drinking coffee. The voices and noises were coming from the TV. I did not see my sisters. I opened our bedroom door and stepped out.

"Hi, Mommy," I said softly not knowing how she would react.
"Well, there is my little sleepy head. I thought you were going to sleep all day. Come here and give your Mommy a hug," Mom said lovingly.

I walked over and gave her a hug. She picked me up making me wince and sat me on her lap.
"Krista, KRISTA! Get in here," Mom yelled loudly.

Krista came running inside.
"What do you need, Mommy?" Krista said coming to a stop a few feet away from us.
"Go and make your sister some soup," Mom said to Krista.

Krista quickly ran to the kitchen. She was acting weirdly obedient. I wondered what had happened last night.
"So how is my perfect little angel?" Mom asked me.
"I'm fine. Are you still mad at me, Mommy?" I asked timidly.
"Oh, I can't stay mad at my little princess. I do hope you learned your lesson yesterday though. You need to stop fighting me or I will have to break you. You do understand that, don't you?" Mom said.

I felt terrified. I just nodded. That seemed to appease her. She turned her attention to the TV. I couldn't stop trying to help my sisters. I had to at least try or I would not be able to survive. I just had to keep trying. Mom let me go to the table to eat. I hurt everywhere but the chicken noodle tasted great. I ate the whole bowl while Krista just sat there watching me.
"Are you okay?" I asked in a whisper.
"Are you?" she replied.
"I don't know," I answered honestly.
"Same here," Krista replied looking down at her hands.
"Where's Shayla?" I asked.
"She's on the porch. She got hurt by one of the men last night but she is fine," Krista said.
"I'm sorry she found you," I said as a tear rolled down my cheek.
"I'm sorry, too," Krista said before she stood up and took my dirty dishes to the sink.

I don't know what changed but Krista was nice to me all day. We avoided Mom all day. I was too sore to play. I was also still tired. We played in the valley making flower necklaces, bracelets, earrings, and crowns. We even made some fairy dolls. We did not talk about what had happened. We did not have any answers. We just had reality. We heard a loud vehicle coming up the driveway. Krista and Shayla laid on the grass at the top of the hill to see what was happening.

"It's Eric. He must be here to pick up Mom," Krista said excitedly.

Shayla came back to sit with me again.

"I'm going to go say hi. How do I look?" Krista said.

"Please don't go," I whispered.

"Oh, don't be jealous. I will be back in a minute and I will tell you everything that happens," Krista giggled as she ran quickly over the hill.

I stood up and walked towards the top of the hill. I gently sat down in the grass. I could just barely see over the hill. I saw Krista run up to Eric and give him a hug. He picked her up as he walked over to the porch. He gripped her bottom firmly in his big hand. She smiled so big. I wondered what they were saying. Please don't let him hurt her. Mom came to the door and talked with Eric for a few minutes before going back inside. Eric sat down with Krista on his lap. I saw him put one hand up her skirt and the other hand he used to take one of Krista's hands and put in his own lap. I could not see what was really happening but it looked bad. What was Mom doing? What was Krista doing? She was not smiling but she was not fighting him either. After a few minutes he made a funny face and released Krista's hand. He took his hand out of Krista's skirt and put Krista down. Krista walked off the porch and rubbed her hand on the grass. Why was she doing that? Eric went inside while Krista returned and sat on the porch chair. She brought her knees up to her chest and hugged her legs tight. She looked sad. Eric returned without Mom. He picked Krista up and sat down with her in his lap again. Was it all going to happen again? They were talking about

something and I wished I could hear. Krista began to smile and laugh while sitting on his lap. Mom came out about ten minutes later. Eric and Mom left in Eric's truck.

Krista turned and headed up the hill. I stood up and headed down the hill to the house and Krista. Shayla followed silently behind me.

"Hey, Krista," I said when we were close.

"Hey," Krista said looking down.

"What took so long?" I asked.

"Oh, Eric was early so Mom had to shower real quick. Then they left," Krista said, not quite looking at me.

"So, did you get to spend time with Eric while Mom was in the shower?" I asked wishing she would tell me the truth but also kind of scared that she would.

"Not much, we just talked. He told me a few jokes. That's all," Krista said looking away from me.

"Ok. Do you want to watch TV?" I asked.

"Yeah," She replied.

We spent the rest of the evening watching TV. We did not talk about what happened on the porch. We just watched cartoons. We ate leftovers and popcorn for dinner. We all went to bed before the sun went down. I was so tired I forgot to lock the door.

Chapter 29

I awoke in the dark. I was confused. I looked out the window. The fireflies were lighting up beyond the window. The stars shone bright against a dark blue sky. It looked like a magical fairy kingdom. I looked down at my two sisters. They were both asleep. What woke me up? I looked toward the door. I did not see anything. The house was really dark. I got up and walked to the door. I looked around. I liked the night. Everything was quiet and peaceful. I felt drowsy and wondered if I was dreaming. I returned to bed and laid down.

I listened to the night. At first I heard nothing. Then I heard a noise. I looked toward the door. I was not fully awake which was what took me so long to recognize the noise. It was the sound of a door closing. Then I was awake as the realization that our door was wide open hit me. I had not shut it. I had not locked it. I heard footsteps approaching. I hoped it was Mom. I pretended to be asleep. I heard footsteps approach my side of the bed. The footsteps stopped. I kept my eyes closed and tried to breathe normal. I was so scared. What was happening? I peeked.

Eric was standing above me. He only had on underwear. He smiled when he saw my eyes open. It was a weird smile. I thought he would turn into a wolf and eat me. He looked hungry. I was frozen in terror. He tossed the cover off of me and reached to pick me up. "AHHHHHHHHHH!" I screamed as I propelled myself backwards to escape.

I landed on Shayla and Krista who also woke up yelling and screaming. It was loud and Eric grabbed my ankle and pulled me to him. He had my leg. Krista fell off the bed and was standing there screaming. Shayla grabbed my arm and chest and pulled. I kicked him with my other foot but that was the hurt ankle so it hurt me more than him I think. Where was Mom? Why didn't she respond to our screams? I screamed as loud as I could as Eric yanked me out of Shayla's arms. He hugged me to his chest and carried me as he grabbed Shayla with one arm and threw her out of the room. I kicked and screamed. I hit him over and over. He pulled me away from him and threw me on the bed. I jumped up to try and run but he slapped me hard and I fell back in tears. He walked around the bed where Krista was crying and screaming and grabbed her by the arm. She kicked him as he dragged her to the door. Just as he was holding back Shayla and about to throw Krista out of the room, Benny came charging in. Benny tackled Eric and they all went falling to the floor.

I jumped up and ran to Krista who was sprawled face down on the floor. I helped her up as Benny and Eric fought each other. I grabbed her hand and ran to where Shayla was getting up in the hall.

I grabbed Shayla's hand with my other hand and ran out of the house. I pulled my sisters with me. I was not letting them go. I did not think, I just ran. I hoped Benny would be ok but I knew that Eric would keep fighting if we were there. Where was Mom and why wasn't she helping us? Krista kept pulling back and trying to get me to release her but I held on and dragged her with me. I did not realize where I was going until I topped the last hill. There was the magic house. It was dark but their car was there. We were safe, they would help. Then it hit me. We could not go to them. Mom would kill us. I had bruises everywhere. They may call the cops and we would be tortured. I stopped about halfway down the final hill. We were trapped with nowhere to go.

"We can't go to them, can we?" I asked, suddenly realizing what would happen if we did.

"We can't go back," Shayla said looking behind her like she expected Eric to be there.

"He must have thought you were me.....He loves me....me...He loves me....I'm special," Krista said in a daze. "He must have thought you were me....He said he loved me.......I was special.......me.......He must have thought you were me........"

I rolled my eyes. Krista was not going to be any help.

"We will have to camp. Stay here. If Krista tries to go back, tackle her," I told Shayla.

I walked quietly up to the house. I tried the backdoor. It was locked. I retrieved the key from the third planter. I unlocked the door and tiptoed inside. I went to the hall closet. I had seen some blankets in there when Krista and I had first found the house. I found five thick blankets that were rolled up and had zippers to lock you in. I grabbed three. I took them out the backdoor and put them on the porch. I went to the living room and took three pillows off the couch. I then went outside. I relocked the door and put the key back. I picked up the pillows and ran to Krista and Shayla. Krista was on the ground muttering to herself. Shayla was standing over her with her hands on her hips. She looked funny and I had to smile as I dropped

the pillows and ran back for the blankets. When I returned we decided to move away from the magic house so the family would not see us.

We went halfway back to the house and slept halfway up a hill. The incline was nice. We all tucked ourselves into the blankets and zipped them up. Krista was in the middle and I moved my sleeping bag so it was slightly over hers. I looked up at the night sky. I listened in fear of hearing footsteps. Krista kept muttering to herself until she finally fell back asleep. Krista had tears running down her face. I listened in the moonlight. Shayla was restless and kept tossing and turning. I watched as the moon slowly made its way across the sky. I was thankful that it was not raining.

I could not sleep. I was so tired before but after everything that happened I was wide awake. I wished I had Hope. I felt so scared and alone. I wanted to hug Hope close and cry into her soft fur. I was terrified to close my eyes. All the noises that used to feel so comforting to me were now somehow terrifying. The sound of the owl hooting. The sound of crickets singing. I knew what Eric wanted from me but it scared me. I remembered the video Mom made me watch. I remembered the look on Eric's face as he looked down on me. I remembered Eric shoving his way into the bathroom and picking me up. I remembered the feel of his rough hands on my body. I remembered his threat as he loomed over Shayla and I in the hall. My mind was an endless loop of terrifying images and voices. I watched as the sky began to lighten just slightly and I zipped myself out of my blanket. I stood up and looked toward the sunrise.

I decided to see what was happening at the house. I left my sisters sleeping on the hill and walked back to the house. I laid on the ground when I reached the last hill and looked over the top. I could not see anyone. Eric's truck was still here. I moved closer and ran to the shed. Benny was not there. I looked towards the house in terror. I moved quickly to the side of the house. I heard silence inside. I peeked in the window. Eric was on the couch drinking a beer less than three feet away. He was looking towards my room. I

ran to the other side of the house keeping low so I would not be spotted. I slowly looked in Mom's bedroom window. She was face down on the bed passed out. She was still wearing all her clothes. I ducked down and went to my bedroom window. I looked into the window. Benny was on the ground with blood on his nose and mouth. He was half on his side and half on his belly. He looked to be asleep. One of his eyes was swollen and blue. There were four empty beer cans laying on and around Benny. I felt confused. I jumped when a beer can came flying out of the living room and hit Benny in the back. I tripped and fell down.

I scrambled to my feet and ran to the back of the house. I hid behind the shed. My heart slowly calmed down. I peeked around the corner. I did not see anyone so I ran as fast as I could over the hill and back to my sisters. I was short of breath when I got back. I looked in amazement that they were still asleep. I looked at the sky and realized that the sun had just started to rise. I realized that only a little while had passed. I returned to my blanket. I put the pillow in the bottom and rolled the blanket up the best I could. I then sat on the rolled up blanket and watched the sunrise as I waited for my sisters to wake.

Chapter 30

We walked to the house slowly not knowing what to expect. When we were at the last hill we decided to hide our rolled up blankets in a small clump of trees behind the shed. We could hear yelling inside the house. We went to the back door and quietly went into the house. Mom was yelling and so was Eric. We peeked around the corner into the living room and saw Mom and Eric in a huge argument. Mom was hitting Eric and cursing. Eric was shoving her and telling her to shut the fuck up. They were screaming. I looked towards our doorway to our room for Benny. I did not see him. I yanked myself out of my sister's arms. I quickly ran out of the

kitchen, through the living room, around Mom and Eric and into our bedroom. Benny was sitting up and leaning against the bed. He was holding his t-shirt to his head and he was now topless. I went to him. "Are you ok?" I asked sitting down next to him and taking the t-shirt out of his hands.

"My head hurts," Benny said.

"You're ok, it is not bleeding. Come on we have to get you out of here in case Mom can't get Eric out," I said as I inspected his head then helped him to his feet.

Mom and Eric were still fighting in the living room when we exited the bedroom. Benny and I walked along the wall to stay out of the way of the fight. Shayla and Krista were still in the doorway of the kitchen watching the fight. I told them to take Benny out to the shed and to lock themselves in if Eric comes for them. They took Benny. I turned around and looked at the fight. Mom and Eric were really going at it and Mom had a handprint on her face where Eric must have slapped her. I ran into Mom's room and grabbed all of Eric's clothes. I felt his wallet in his pocket and got an idea. I took out his wallet and found a handful of bills. I took them all and hid them under Mom's dresser since I did not have pockets. I then returned the wallet to his pants and ran to the living room. I went around the fight and ran out the front door. I threw his clothes into the open window of his truck. I opened the door and saw his keys in the ignition. I sat in the driver's seat not even knowing what I was doing. I turned the key and the engine roared to life. I put my hand on the horn and started to push it like crazy. Mom and Eric came running out of the house. I pulled on the stick thingy but it would not budge so I just jumped out of the truck before Eric could catch me. Eric got to his truck a few seconds after I had gotten out. Mom was right behind him yelling and screaming at him. Eric must have seen the clothes in the truck because he got in and shoved Mom out of the way so he could shut the door. Mom landed on her butt.

"Screw you, whore. I don't need this shit. Go to hell, skank. I was only with you so I could screw your bitches anyway. You are

nothing," Eric yelled then he turned his truck around and sped down the drive.

I ran to my mom as she sat where she had fallen. She had tears in her eyes. I helped her up and inside. She sat at the table. I went to get her a juice box because there was no coffee and I did not know how to make coffee. I brought the juice to the table.

"Thank you for all your help, Sissy. Where is Benny? Did you know that son of a bitch kicked Benny's ass last night. I ought to kill that bastard," Mom said as she pushed the juice box to her bruised cheek.

"Benny, Krista and Shayla are in the shed ready to lock themselves in if they need to. Are you ok?" I asked.

"I'm hurt. Eric hit me a few times. It was my fault. I overreacted. I saw Benny groaning and hurt and I was furious. Benny is my boy. I probably should have given him the chance to explain. Do you know why Benny was in your room last night? Does Benny come to your room a lot? Did Krista try to seduce him?" Mom speculated.

"No, Eric came to our room last night. Benny tried to save us," I explained.

"Don't tell me that whoring bitch Krista seduced my man!" Mom yelled.

"No. No. I swear, no one seduced him. Eric tried to hurt me. I said no. I promise I did not seduce him, Mommy. I didn't want him to hurt me," I plead.

What in the world was seduce?

"You! That asshole. Trying to get a freebie," Mom said as she hugged me.

"Mommy, is he going to come back," I asked.

"Do you want him back?" Mom asked, looking intensely at me.

"No, he was mean. I don't like him at all," I said.

"Well, sometimes in life you don't always get what you want. Mommy is getting older and can't earn enough to support you kids. Eric was well off. He comes from an upstanding family in town. Besides, you know a woman is nothing without a man," Mom explained.

"But Mom, he wanted to hurt me like the girls in that video," I said.
"Well, if it gives us a good life would that be so bad?" Mom said, looking me in the eye.
"But it will hurt, Mommy. Please don't bring him back," I begged with tears in my eyes.
"It will only hurt if you fight him. Next time don't fight," Mom said.
"I don't want him to hurt me so I have to fight," I said.
"Stop being such a selfish, spoiled, little brat. You will do what is necessary for this family or I will hurt you worse. Is that understood?" Mom said angrily.

I just looked away. I vowed I would never stop fighting Mom and every man who wants to hurt me. I don't want to be hurt.
"Go get your sisters and brothers. We need to get breakfast started," Mom said getting up abruptly and heading for the coffee maker.

I went outside to the shed. I told everyone that Eric was gone. We all went into the house to get some breakfast. I retrieved the money from under Mom's dresser and hid it in my room. Mom went into town to meet with Eric later that afternoon but came back angrier. She beat Krista, Shayla, and I for not being nicer to Eric. She said he dumped her because of us. Mom continued to take Shayla and Krista to town every other day to work. I tried hiding them but it never worked and only made Mom angrier. Eric never returned. We moved two months later. I don't know where we moved but I do know it took us several hours to drive to the small town we moved to.

Chapter 31

Our new place was in town. It was bigger than the farm house. It also had lots of neighbors. There were two bedrooms but also a glassed in porch in back that was divided in half by a doorway. There were no doors but it was still cool. It was right off the kitchen. I think it used to be the laundry room because it had a sink in the back half of the porch. I took the front half for my room

while Shayla took the second half of the porch. I felt that it was pretty cool. We were close but for the first time in my life I had my own room. It was a very small space but Mom was able to put one dresser and one twin bed in each room.

Mom introduced us to Aunt Penny Borden. She was married for ten years before her husband divorced her for a younger woman. Now she raised her three sons on her own. Their dad only saw them a few times a month. Her sons were Ramon Borden who was 19 years old, Gregory Borden who preferred to be called Greg and was 17 years old, and Brien Borden who was 16 years old. Brien was cute and all three of us had an instant crush on this brown haired, green eyed, handsome boy. He looked like a fairy tale prince from a movie. Aunt Penny and her family lived two blocks away from us.

We were still moving into the house and Aunt Penny was helping us unpack. The next day Mom took me to Aunt Penny's. Mom said she needed to go get the last of our stuff from the old house and Aunt Penny was going to babysit me. That scared me because I worried that Mom would never return or that she was really trying to sell my sisters again. I was scared. I did not want them to go but I watched them drive away without me. I ran to the corner to watch but they disappeared so quickly. I stared down the road where they disappeared, hoping that they would be back. Aunt Penny insisted that I go into her house. Her sons offered to play games with me, watch TV with me, play ball with me or even take me to the park. I knew that they were trying to be nice and distract me. I said no to every offer and kept trying to sneak off to the corner to watch for my sisters.

I was worried about what was happening to them without me to protect them. Aunt Penny kept getting mad that I was going to the corner. She said she worried someone would take me. That made me think that someone might take me to my mom and sisters. Aunt Penny just kept insisting I stay inside. That evening Aunt Penny made a dish I had never seen before. It was called goulash. It had meat, noodles and spaghetti sauce. It was really good but I could

only eat a few bites. I was so worried about my sisters. The nicer Aunt Penny and her family were the sadder I got. I wanted my sisters to experience this kindness. Not me. I was not a good enough girl. I could not even protect my sisters. For all I knew my sisters were being hurt this minute.

Aunt Penny urged me to eat more but I said I had a tummy ache. She also offered apple pie. I said no. My sisters were not having apple pie so I would not either. After dinner, Brien and Greg played catch in the front yard so they could keep me from going to the corner. I sat on the front porch with my head in my hands just waiting. Just before dark Mom returned with my beloved sisters. I ran to give Mom a hug first so she would not get mad or jealous. Then I ran and hugged my sisters. I cried as I hugged them both in a big bear hug. Shayla cried too. We stayed to enjoy apple pie and ice cream with Aunt Penny. I ate it all and thanked Aunt Penny for being so nice to me all day. Aunt Penny was happy and gave me extra hugs. I liked Aunt Penny and told her so. She laughed and said she liked me to.

Then we went home. We started school soon after that. My memories of that short period were happy. However, about two weeks later Mom started sending me to Aunt Penny's house after school every day. Mom said she was helping my sister's with their homework. I did not mind because Aunt Penny and I had become close. She told me more than once that I was the daughter she always wished for. We loved each other. We would play games together. She also showed me how to bake. She loved to bake pies. She told me stories of her childhood and would read to me every time I asked. So every day after school I would walk to Aunt Penny's while my sisters went home.

During this time I made new friends and Shayla and I kind of drifted apart. She was still my best friend but we did not spend much time together. However, we both loved the Teenage Mutant Ninja Turtles and the Power Rangers. We would watch movies together often. Krista avoided me altogether. She would glare at me all the

time. She would push and shove me when Mom was not watching. Still she never said a word. Shayla and I talked late at night but the conversations were different. I always felt she was keeping a secret from me. However, I was happy and never questioned it. I just thought she was busy with her own friends. Brien and Greg would hang out at my house while I was at Aunt Penny's. It was not long until Shayla told me that Greg was her boyfriend and Brien was Krista's boyfriend.

I admit I was jealous. I had a crush on Brien. However, I also liked having Aunt Penny all to myself. She always listened and was willing to play with me. I even liked it when I helped her clean her house. She would turn the radio up loud and we would dance as we dusted and swept. She made everything a game. She was even better than Stacy. She made me laugh every day. She told me that I was her favorite niece and that she loved me. One day when Aunt Penny was working at the table I got permission to explore. There was an abandoned church not far from her house that I wanted to see inside. I was not allowed to go that far but Aunt Penny was busy and would never know. I told her I would be in the back yard and instead went to the church.

I entered the front doors that were damaged and no longer closed. I heard some noises and was quiet so I would not be found. It seemed like a magic place. Like what Aurora's castle must have looked like when she was asleep. I half expected to find fairies flitting around planting flowers. The noises were coming from the big room. I stayed low and peeked around the door. The room was massive. There was colored glass on a big window at the front of the room. There were big benches throughout the room. Some benches were turned over and others were stacked in crazy piles and still others were pushed in weird directions. I stared at the massive colorful window. I forgot about the noises and stared at the picture. Two men were in the water. One man was in a dark yellow dress and the other was in a white dress. The man who was in white was half in front of the other man. Both men had brown hair and big brown

beards. However, that was not what caught my eye. Above the two men was a white bird flying and holding some small leaves. It captivated me for some reason and without realizing it I began to move closer.

I tripped and fell. That is when I saw them. I was so distracted by the window that I had not seen them before. There was Brien, Krista, Shayla, and Greg. Brien and Krista were doing the thing in that video while Shayla and Greg were doing the same thing just a few feet away. I jumped up. I ran all the way back to Aunt Penny's house. I ran inside and found Aunt Penny at the table. I ran to her and hugged her tightly. I don't know why but I cried. Aunt Penny comforted me until I calmed down. Aunt Penny asked me what had happened but I was afraid she would judge my sisters and send me away. I told her I fell and got scared. That was mostly true. I asked to go home. She said that was fine and walked me home. That evening I confronted my sister Shayla in her room.

"I saw you at the old church," I began.

"What did you see?" she questioned.

"I thought it hurt to do that. You said it hurt," I accused.

"It does hurt. But Greg loves me. He is my boyfriend. That is what you have to do to have a boyfriend," Shayla said.

"Well, I never want to do that. I don't want to be hurt. You should not do it either," I argued.

"I'm not pretty. Greg will only be my boyfriend if we do it," Shayla said.

"Well, I do not need a boyfriend," I said matter-of-factly.

"Are you going to tell Mom?" Shayla said.

"No, she would be upset. Besides, I am always at Aunt Penny's. Weren't you supposed to be doing homework with Mom?" I stated.

"We never have homework. Mom gave us the day off," Shayla said.

"What do you mean? You always have homework. What do you mean, day off?" I said as a dread started in my heart.

"We are not supposed to tell you," Shayla said looking away.

"Tell me what?" I said, suddenly uncertain if I wanted the answer.

"Mom has been selling us here in the afternoons. The men come here so she does not have to rent hotel rooms. Every day after school when you are at Aunt Penny's Mom is here selling us. If we yell she lets Benny, Brien and Greg hurt us. So we are quiet," Shayla admitted as tears fell down her face.

I had nothing to say. I had abandoned my sister for my own selfish happiness. I hugged her as she cried. I was guilty. However, something did not make sense. I was curious.

"Why is Greg you're boyfriend if he hurts you?" I said.

"What do you mean?" Shayla said, confused.

"You said Mom lets him hurt you if you make noise. So, why is he your boyfriend?" I asked.

"Oh, that is just his job. He does not like to hurt me. He loves me. It is just his job. Mom pays him," Shayla insisted.

"Oh," I felt very confused, it didn't make any sense.

That night after Shayla fell asleep I laid in bed and could not sleep. For the last few months I was happy. Really happy. I like where we were and loved the school. I had many friends and Aunt Penny was like a fairy tale Mom. I was happy. However, my happiness hurt my sisters. No wonder Krista would not talk to me. While I was off being happy she was being hurt over and over again. I heard Mom come home late and peeked into the rest of the house. She was alone. I waited until she went to her room. I tiptoed to her bedroom door. It was shut so I opened it a crack. Mom got undressed and woke up Benny who was asleep in the bed. Benny and Mom began to do the things in the video. I looked away and waited for the noises to stop. When they were done Mom got ready for bed. Mom and Benny soon fell asleep. I shut their door and crept to the living room where Mom kept her purse. I dug through her purse and finally found it. It was the notebook Mom wrote down the amounts of money in when we were at the farmhouse. I pulled it out and went to the bathroom. I shut the door and turned on the light. I sat on the edge of the bathtub. I looked through the notebook. There in Mom's handwriting were amounts for almost every day. Shayla had told the

truth. I cried quietly. I was a fool. I should have known. I was selfish. I was the worst sister in the world.

After that I started trying to stay close to home. Mom started getting mad when I refused to go to Aunt Penny. She forced me to go. I did not want to leave my sisters alone with Mom. So I got smart. I insisted to Aunt Penny that Shayla and Krista should play with us. Soon my sisters and I would spend every afternoon at Aunt Penny's. Mom was furious and started staying out late every night. She was so angry she stopped speaking to me. Yet it was worth it to save my sisters. We all had such fun at Aunt Penny's. This went on for about two weeks. However, happiness and safety never last, do they? We were safe at Aunt Penny's but we could not stay forever.

It was a Saturday. Aunt Penny had to go out of town and left her sons home alone. Mom brought home a new movie on VHS. I was really happy because it was a movie we all wanted to see. Teenage Mutant Ninja Turtles III. It was not even strange when Brien and Greg showed up after dinner to watch it with us. Mom popped the popcorn. Then the strange began. Mom said it was late and insisted that Shayla, Krista and Benny go to bed. However, Mom insisted that they all go to bed in her room and that I stay up to watch the movie with Brien and Greg. Mom escorted my siblings into her room and shut the door. Greg started the movie while Brien picked me up and put me on his lap. I felt special because I liked Brien. I thought he was cute and wanted him to be my boyfriend. I thought that Shayla was wrong. You don't have to be hurt to have a boyfriend. Besides, everyone said that I was cuter than Krista.

Greg sat close beside us as the movie began. Soon Brien started to rub his hands on my arms and legs. I just pushed my dress down further and pushed his hands off my lap.

"Hey, do you want to do something fun?" Brien asked me.

"We are doing something fun. We are watching Teenage Mutant Ninja Turtles," I replied.

"Something even funner?" Brien said.

"Like what?" I said finally looking at him.

Greg opened the dresser and grabbed a pair of socks. I tried to scream but he shoved the socks in my mouth. Greg held my hands as Brien climbed on top of me. I tried to fight. I kicked but it did not stop Brien. He pulled my legs apart. Brien shoved his wee wee into me. The pain was horribly. I thought they were going to rip me apart. I screamed as loud as I could but the socks muffled my voice. The socks got wetter the more I screamed. When the socks were too wet to work well Greg took them out and put some new ones in. That happened five times. I fought as they took turns on top of me. My fighting made them laugh. They seemed to be excited by me fighting.

I hoped I would pass out but I did not. I remember every excruciating detail. I remember the sound of Brien panting on top of me. I remember Greg licking the tears off my face and laughing at me. I remember Brien biting my shoulder and calling me his little whore. I remember Greg asking me if I liked him best. They each took four turns. I thought it would never end. When it did finally end I wished I could end. The pain I felt on every inch of my body felt like I was going to die. Brien took me to the bathroom. I could barely walk. Greg cleaned up the blood on the bed as Brien cleaned me. I felt dirty and did not want to be touched but Brien did not give me a choice. I did not like them anymore. I wanted to hurt them. Brien took me back to my room. Greg was done cleaning and had returned to the living room. The movie was over so he was rewinding it. Brien put me in a long sleep shirt nightgown. Brien refused to let me wear any underwear. I crawled up on my bed and reached for Hope.

"What do you think you are doing?" Brien said picking me up before I could reach Hope.

"I want to go to bed," I said weakly.

My voice was hearse from trying to scream through the socks.

"Your Mom said if we broke you we could have you all night. You are going to sleep with us in case we decide to have some more fun," Brien said as he carried me into the living room.

Brien and Greg laughed when he sat me down. I stood there terrified. Greg and Brien took the cushions off the couch and made a bed on the floor. Greg laid down first. I was forced to lay beside him and Brien laid on my other side. Greg got up and turned out the lights. He laid back down. Brien put his arm around me and held me close to his side. I cried for a long time but I was in pain and soon fell asleep.

Chapter 32

I awoke sore and stiff. There was a weight around my waist. I remembered what had happened the night before. I remembered everything. The tears flowed down my face. Tears that had a life of their own. I could not stop the tears flowing from my eyes. I heard voices coming from the kitchen area. I listened with my eyes closed and hoped they would not see the tears that would not stop.

"You were supposed to break her in, not make her love you" I heard my mom say.

"We did break her in. We rode her good," I heard Greg respond as he chuckled.

"What kind of fool do you take me for? That high horse bitch would not have slept with you if you did break her in. You were supposed to get her used to it not make her love you. Now she will end up falling in love with every dick. I don't need that shit," Mom sounded annoyed.

"Relax, Aunt Stacy, she did not want to sleep with us. We forced her to in case we got a little frisky in the night. Like I said, we did break her. You should have heard her cries," Greg said.

"Well, you better be right. I have lost too much business because of her lately," Mom said.

"It's not polite to eavesdrop, Samantha," Brien said as he squeezed me tighter and nibbled at my ear.

I was startled. I did not know he was awake. I struggled to pull away from him. My body hurt but he pulled me tighter. "Please let me go, Please," I begged as my tears fell harder.

I hated begging him but was not strong enough to escape. I groaned when he squeezed me too tight and my body hurt.

"Let her go, Brien. You only got her last night," Mom said loudly.

Brien laughed and let me go. I got up and put my back to the wall facing everyone. I looked for escape routes. I was ready to run if they came at me. Mom stood there with a huge evil smile on her face. Greg stood beside my mom grinning at me. Brien sat up and looked at my mom.

"What can I say? I thought I could play a little, that's all," Brien said to Mom.

"Fuck, What the hell, assholes? You weren't supposed to bruise her. Fuck, now I have to wait for the bruises to heal before I can use that bitch," Mom said turning to Greg.

"You said to break her. We broke her," Greg said, shrugging.

"Fuck, Fuck, Fuck," Mom said turning towards the stove. "Go get yourself cleaned up, Samantha." Mom said over her shoulder to me.

I went into the bathroom and locked the door behind me. I felt stiff and sore. I looked at myself in the mirror on the back of the bathroom door. I had big hand shaped bruises on my arms and legs. I had deep purple and blue bruises between my legs all the way up to my private place. I looked red and swollen in my private place and I worried it would always be red and swollen. I had to go potty. It hurt when I peed and I saw some blood in the potty before I flushed. I felt dirty so I turned on the shower. I took a long cool shower and washed myself several times. I still felt so dirty. I thought about everything that my mom, Greg, and Brien had said. They wanted to break me. NO! I would not let them win. I had to keep fighting. I made a promise to myself that if anyone wanted to break me they would not be able to. I would not stop fighting. I refused to give up.

Even if I was not strong enough to fight them off at least I was strong enough to try. I vowed to always fight.

I got out of the shower feeling a little empowered. I was better than them or they would not be trying to break me. I wrapped a towel tightly around me and tried not to look at the bruises. I unlocked the door and opened it. I walked through the house and to my room with my head held high. I purposely ignored Mom, Greg, and Brien when they watched me pass them. I got out two pairs of underwear and put them both on. I then put on a pair of shorts and a sky blue sundress. I usually did not wear shorts under my dresses but now I thought it would be best. I had also never worn two pairs of underwear but I wanted to protect myself and make it harder for anyone to undress me. I was dressed to fight if I had to.

Here is the reality of how I felt at that moment. I was hurt but there was a stronger emotion. I was angry. I was angry at Mom for doing this to me. I was angry at Greg for hurting me and laughing about it. I was angry at Brien for being cruel and breaking my heart. However, more than anything else, I was angry at myself. I trusted Greg and Brien. I trusted them because I trusted their Mom and I had a secret crush on Brien before last night. I felt safe with them when I should not have. I was angry I could not fight them off. I was angry no one came to help me. I was angry to have survived. I was HURT! I climbed on my bed and hugged Hope close. I was hurt and angry. I knew I would fight anyone who would try to hurt me like they did but I also knew I was too small to fight anyone off. I felt lost and hopeless. I was trapped and alone. I was cursed.

I was powerless and I hated myself for it. Shayla came in to get dressed for the day and saw me on my bed. She did not say anything. She got dressed and left. She looked at me when she left the room. I just watched her go. I will learn later that Mom told her not to talk to me. At the time I just felt abandoned by my sister. I laid down on my bed and covered myself up. My stomach hurt and I felt sore. I cried until I fell asleep. I would wake, cry, and sleep over and over again. I stayed in bed all day. No one checked on me.

It was early morning when I woke up. I sat up. The sky was beginning to lighten so I got up. I wanted to watch the sunrise. My room only had windows that faced west. I carried Hope with me as I walked quietly through the house. I opened the front door and stepped outside into the cool morning air. I walked over to the chairs on the porch. I was still wearing the blue dress I put on yesterday morning. I sat down and hugged Hope to my chest. I watched the colors explode in the sky. It was perfect. I drew strength from the sunrise. After all, the world can't be all bad if it was so beautiful. I heard movement inside the house. Soon the front door opened and Mom came out. I looked at her. She came over and sat in the seat beside me.

"You know you brought it upon yourself, right?" Mom said.

"No," I said as I hugged Hope tighter.

"I was willing to let you grow up without working but you kept butting your nose where it did not belong. Shit, you actually thought you could just move into Penny's house with your sisters and I would just let you all go. You and your sisters belong to me. I am your Mom. I created you. You belong to me. You all need to learn some respect and do what I say. Fuck! I have been taking care of you and your sisters a long time and now your bill is due. You have to pay me back for all the things I do for you. Fuck, I should have just aborted all of you. You brats have ruined my life. If I had aborted you bitches I would be living a much nicer life. But, no, I gave birth to ungrateful bitches who can't even be bothered to lift a finger to help their mother out. If I could go back I would abort everyone of you. So, you brought this on yourself. You have no one to blame but yourself. You don't have a choice," Mom ranted.

"Mommy, what does abort mean?" I asked.

"It means I should have killed you all before you could ruin my life. Killed you before you are even born," Mom almost yelled at me.

"Mommy, I am sorry you hate us," I said, feeling really sad.

"Oh, Sissy, I don't hate you. Actually, you're one of my favorite children. You and Benny are my favorites, you know that. I do love you. Here, come here," Mom said patting her lap.

I hesitantly went to sit on her lap. I knew it was an order not a request. I climbed on her lap and only hurt myself once. My whole body felt sore and broken.

"Sissy, I love you. I know you think that what happens here is wrong but it is actually normal. This happens everywhere in every home with a daughter. This is how girls are raised. It is a child's job to make life easier for their parents. I raised you, now you need to help me survive because if you don't your fate could be worse. At least I provide you a safe place to live, food to eat and clothes to wear. None of those things are cheap. You need to accept the reality of life," Mom said as she hugged me and stroked my hair.

I listened quietly but did not answer. I did not want to believe what she said. I did not like what she said. However, maybe she was right. Maybe it was normal. I just refused to stop fighting. Mom pushed me gently off her lap and went inside. I sat down in my previous chair and hugged Hope even tighter. I refused to give up. I would never accept my mother's reality.

Chapter 33

That afternoon Mom made me go to my room after lunch. She told me to stay there and not move or make a sound. She made Brien sit in the doorway to guard me. I heard men coming and going and I heard crying but nothing was too loud. Brien sat in the doorway grinning at me. I was afraid to go near him so I stayed on my bed. I knew what was happening. I also knew if I tried to escape Brien would delight in hurting me again. I hugged Hope and stayed on my bed. I pretended I was a princess locked in a tower guarded by a fire breathing dragon with bad breath. I was not aware how much time had passed but suddenly Mom came into my room.

"I brought you and Brien a sandwich and some chips. You can eat in your room. There are customers in the living room," Mom said to Brien and me.

"Mommy, can't you make the men leave?" I asked pitifully.

"I made myself clear this morning. Fuck, you never listen. Shut up or I will start sending the men in to see you," Mom yelled and turned to leave.

"If the men came here would that mean Shayla and Krista would not be hurt?" I asked.

Mom stopped and turned to look at me in surprise. Brien paused with his sandwich half to his mouth. Brien just looked at me with his mouth still open. Mom came over, moved my plate aside and sat on the bed beside me.

"I love you, Sissy. You are perfect. You are my favorite child," Mom said as she hugged me and kissed the top of my head. "Now eat your dinner and stay here."

Mom stood up and left the room without saying another word. Brien put his sandwich back on his plate. He stood up and moved closer to the bed. I was terrified. He put his plate on the bed and then turned and moved his chair close to the bed. I worried because that blocked the way out of the room. He sat down and smiled at me but it was a kind smile not the mean smiles he had been giving me since last night.

"I think I saw some soda in the refrigerator. Would you like one?" Brien asked nicely.

I just cowered in the corner confused about why he was being nice and feeling cornered.

"I will go get you one," Brien said as he went to the door.

I watched him closely. When he reached the door he turned to look at me with a worried look.

"Just stay in the room. I will be right back," Brien said before leaving the room.

I just looked after him for a minute, not moving. Then I realized I could escape out the back door. I started to get off the bed.

I walked to the door and opened it. I looked into the backyard and realized I had nowhere to go. I ran outside anyway. I climbed the fence and wished I had shoes on. I heard Brien cuss behind me and hoped I could escape. I hopped off the fence and ran as fast as I could. I headed to Aunt Penny's house but knew I could not go there. I did not hear anything but the pounding of my heart in my ears. I turned and headed to the old church. The place with the colored window that was so pretty. I ran inside and ducked under a broken table by the door. I stopped to catch my breath and listen.

Eventually my breathing slowed and my heartbeat stopped drumming in my ears. I listened but did not hear anyone coming. I crept out of my hiding spot and quietly went to the big room with the fancy window. It was a little scary in the evening light but not too scary. It was better than at home. I started to think that maybe if I convinced Shayla and Krista then we could live here and Mom might not find us. I walked to the front and sat on a bench in front of the window. I looked up at the window. The window was broken in a few places and it was dirty. However, it looked so pretty to me. I liked how it looked like there was light coming from the clouds above to shine on the white bird and the two men in the water. It looked almost magical. I could see because of the evening light shining through the window. I looked around this magical place. I could see how pretty it used to be. I decided to explore.

I left the big room and took the hall to some stairs. The rooms I passed along the way were empty of everything but some trash. I went upstairs. I found a room with some old, dusty boxes and started to open the boxes to see what was inside. Most was just filled with paper that was old and crumbling. There was a stack of three boxes. I tried to move the top box onto the floor but it fell with a loud crash and spilled its contents. In the bottom of that box I found an old picture book that was filled with stories. I took the book and moved to the window and sat down. The corners of the book looked like they had been eaten and the book smelled yucky. When I opened the book it seemed to show the life of a little boy whose

family lived in a barn when he was born. I was so engrossed in the book that I did not hear footsteps on the stairs. I did not hear or sense that someone was approaching until suddenly strong arms were picking me up.

"AAAAHHHHHH!" I screamed before a hand promptly covered my mouth.

"Shh, it's me. It's Brien," Brien said in my ear.

I screamed against his hand. I tried to fight him as he dragged me into a windowless room and shut the door.

"I am going to remove my hand but only if you promise not to scream," Brien said.

I stopped screaming and nodded. Brien removed his hand and put me down. I ran a few steps away and turned around. Brien was blocking the door. The room was very dark. I could barely see Brien standing there.

"Are you ok?" Brien asked.

"What do you want?" I asked back ignoring his question for now.

"I have to take you back before your Mom sees you are gone. I am not going to hurt you," Brien said, raising his hands in the air like he was surrendering.

"You hurt me last night," I accused angrily.

"I know. Listen if your Mom sees you left then she will get angry. Please just let me take you back," Brien said.

"You won't hurt me?" I asked, realizing I did not have a choice.

"No, I won't," Brien said as he held out his hand.

I took his hand and he opened the door. I was scared but went with him anyway. He took me downstairs.

"How did you know I was here?" I asked.

"I didn't. I thought you would go to my mom's but when you were not there I remembered that I saw you when you caught me and Krista in here. So, I came here. I did not see you but then I heard a thump upstairs and found you by that window," Brien said.

"I spilled a box," I replied.

"What was in the box?" Brien asked as we left the church.

"Just some old papers and a picture book," I said as I remembered that I had dropped the book when Brien picked me up.

"What was the book about?" Brien asked as we crossed into an alley.

"Some boy who lived in a barn when he was a baby," I answered.

"Jesus," Brien answered.

"What?" I asked, confused.

"The baby's name was Jesus," he explained.

I didn't say anything else as we walked the rest of the way home. I tried to get Brien to release my hand but he held it tight. I did not like him touching me. We entered the house by the same way we exited. I asked to go to the restroom and Brien escorted me. There were men in the living room and they stared at me like they were hungry as I passed. I went potty and washed my hands. Brien came inside and had me hide in the shower while he pottied and washed his hands. He said he did not want to send me to my room alone just in case. We then returned to my room together. Brien moved his chair and sat on the other end of my bed. I drank my soda and ate my sandwich. Brien watched me closely.

"So do you want to play with some toys?" Brien asked.

"No," I said as I handed him my almost empty plate.

Brien put the plates on his chair which was now back in the doorway. He came back to the bed.

"I could read you a story?" Brien said.

"Ok," I said as I showed him where my few books were.

Brien read me the books one by one. At first he stayed away but then he moved closer. I was nervous but I liked to look at the pictures so I let him come closer. I got drowsy and dozed off. I woke up a little before dawn. I was still wearing yesterday's clothes. I was tucked into bed. I sat up and checked. It did not appear that my clothes had been removed. I breathed a sigh of relief. I got up and straightened my bed. I went to Shayla's bed but she was not there. I went into the living room and found Shayla asleep on the couch. The living room was dirty. There was trash and cans everywhere. I went to Krista's room. Krista was asleep. She had tear marks down her

face. I went in and pulled the blanket up to her shoulder. I then went to Mom's bedroom door. It was shut so I opened it slowly. Mom and Benny were sleeping in the bed. Mom had her arm around Benny. I shut the door quietly. I walked out to the porch. I sat on the chair to watch the sunrise. It was beautiful. I wondered who painted the sunrise every morning.

Chapter 34

Life returned to normal. I went to school during the day. In the afternoons I was made to stay in my room or in the backyard. Mom made me wear long sleeve dresses and tights to school so no one would see the bruises. It was late fall so it was not too hot. I felt horrible that my sisters were being hurt but Mom would not change her mind and she would not talk about it with me. She said I was too young to understand the realities of life. Brien was with me most afternoons and he actually was nice to me but I did not trust him anymore. Greg watched me the other afternoons. He was cruel and would try to touch me or kiss me. I had to be very alert when he was watching me. I would actually stay awake until he left because as soon as I laid down he would try to climb into my bed and touch me. I was scared of him and would imagine him with fangs.

Thanksgiving was coming up and everyone at school was excited about it. I knew we would probably have to work so I was not very excited. I felt isolated from my classmates. They seemed to have such a happy life. They were allowed to just be kids. They did not have to worry about everything I did. I withdrew from my school friends. I stopped answering in class and just played by myself. I felt sad and lonely.

Shayla and Krista were mad because they said I made their boyfriends cheat on them with me. I told them what really happened but Krista said that if I was not always prancing around like a perfect little princess Brien and Greg never would have done what Mom told them to do. Shayla was willing to forgive me but then Krista

told her that I was flirting with the boys when they were not watching. So, neither one of my sisters would talk to me. I was isolated at home and school. I was alone and I hated it.

Mom kept me away from Aunt Penny. She refused to let me go there and Aunt Penny never came to our house. Every afternoon until late in the evening men would come. Mom liked working my sisters every day.

On Thanksgiving Mom decided to leave us at home alone. She gave Krista and Shayla a list of chores to get done before she returned. She gave Benny permission to go to a friend's house for a few nights. Shayla, Krista and I were supposed to stay home. Mom left in the late morning and Krista and Shayla started getting the chores done because we did not know when Mom would return.
"Can I help?" I asked Shayla.
"Sure," Shayla said.

Shayla and I gathered all the trash and took it out to the trash cans. We dusted and wiped down the table and kitchen. Krista vacuumed all the rooms and swept and mopped the floors. When we finished those chores we gathered all the dirty clothes. Krista started the washer with the first load of clothes.
"That's it until the washer is done. Let's go find some lunch," Krista said.

We went to the kitchen. The refrigerator was full of beer, soda and ice tea. There was one piece of lunchmeat and some condiments. Krista immediately ate the last slice of lunch meat. The cabinets were empty. There was no food. Krista was mad.
"What are we supposed to eat?" Krista said as she slammed a cabinet closed.
"Maybe Mom is going to bring home food," Shayla said.
"That bitch is not going to get us food. Shit she left us here with nothing because she doesn't care about us," Krista fumed.

Krista stomped into the living room and turned on the TV. Shayla went to sit on the floor and watch TV with her. I had an idea. I went to my room. I retrieved the money I had taken from Eric's

wallet. I emptied my backpack onto my bed and put the money in the small zipper compartment. I put on my shoes and went out the back door. There was a grocery store four blocks away. I climbed the fence and ran down the alley to the street. I walked on the sidewalk to the store. I went inside. I bought two boxes of cereal, a loaf of bread, peanut butter, jelly, bananas, and a quart of milk. I went to pay for it and grabbed three candy bars at the register. I put everything but the milk and bananas into my backpack. I carried the milk and bag of bananas to the house. I could not climb the fence with the milk so I knocked on the door. Krista came to the door and let me in.

"Where did you get this stuff?" Krista exclaimed as I emptied my backpack.

"I took it from a house a few blocks away," I lied because I did not want her to take my money away.

"Did anyone see you?" Shayla asked.

"No, they were playing outside so they never saw me," I answered.

"Next time let me know before you take off. I didn't even know you were gone," Krista said.

"I'm sorry," I said.

"It's ok, let's eat," Krista said.

For that day it appeared my sisters forgave me. We all ate lunch and watched TV together. I had already hid my money back in my room. There was some left and I knew we may need more food. After we ate dinner I showed my sisters the candy bars I got. We were all excited about the rare dessert. We laughed and joked as we ate the candy. We all fell asleep on the couch watching TV that night. It was a perfect Thanksgiving.

Mom was not home the next morning so we finished the laundry and put all the clothes away correctly. We spent the day playing with toys and watching TV. It was fun. Some men showed up and knocked on the door in the afternoon but we just hid and pretended no one was home. We were afraid of the men. Mom stayed gone all day and we finished the food I had bought. I knew I

would need to get more the next morning. A few more men banged on the door that night. They saw the lights and demanded to be let in. We screamed at them to leave us alone. They eventually left. We decided to sleep in the back bedrooms. Shayla and I slept in my bed while Krista slept in Shayla's bed.

The next morning I awoke early and grabbed my backpack. I took the money from my dresser and slipped out the back door. It was dark so I walked around and through the gate to the front yard. I went to the sidewalk and walked to the store. The sun was just beginning to rise and the sky exploded in pink, purple, orange, yellow and blue. It was breathtaking. I picked up a leaf and pretended I was painting the sunrise. After a few minutes I continued to the store. It had just opened so I went inside. I bought apples, two boxes of cereal, a loaf of bread and a gallon of milk. I also grabbed six candy bars and a bunch of tootsie pops. There were ten tootsie pops in a bunch. I paid for my purchases but noted I was almost out of money. I put everything but the milk and bread into my backpack and carried the bag with the loaf of bread on my arm like a purse and carried the milk in my other hand. It was heavy so I walked home slowly. I went around the side of the house. I opened the unlocked backdoor and went inside. Shayla and Krista were still asleep so I took the food into the kitchen and put it up. I hoped we would have enough food for a few days. I left the candy in my backpack and went to the living room to wait for my sisters. I turned on the TV to watch some TV. I heard a knock on the front door. I went to look outside and saw Brien standing there.

"What do you want?" I said from the window by the door.

"Open the door," Brien said.

"No," I replied.

"Come on, we're friends, right?" Brien asked moving closer to the window until he was just on the other side of the glass.

"What do you want?" I asked again.

"I just want to make sure you guys are ok," Brien said.

"We're fine," I said.

I heard a sound at the back of the house and turned to look. Coming in the unlocked backdoor was Greg. He glanced into the bedroom back there and then turned and grinned evilly at me. He began to walk toward me with his hungry grin. I realized in that second that I did not have much of a choice but with Brien I might have a chance. I ran to the door and threw it open and ran onto the porch. I ducked under Brien's arms and ran to the chairs. I sat down and grabbed the chair with my arms and legs. Greg came running out the door. He and Brien stood there smiling at me.

"If you touch me I will scream and the neighbors will hear," I said loudly and determinedly.

"We could just cover your mouth," Greg said, obviously amused.

"The neighbors will see," I said a little scared.

"And what prevents you from running for the neighbors as soon as we go inside," Greg said, stepping toward me menacingly.

"I won't, I promise," I said with a tremble in my voice.

"And why should we trust you," Greg said as he leaned close to me.

I was too scared to reply. I tightened my grip on the chair and prepared to scream. I was so scared.

"I will stay outside and watch her," Brien said.

"Fine, but that whore better not cause any problems or I get to punish her," Greg said as he stepped back and headed for the front door.

"If I hear my sisters fighting you I will scream!" I said to Greg's back.

Greg turned quickly and stomped back to me. The slap was swift and hard. I almost flew off the chair. Then Greg grabbed my chin hard and yanked my head around to look at him.

"You even think of screaming and I guarantee you will not like the amount of punishment I put you through. I have a lot of friends who would like to have some fun with a sweet young thing like you. We will tear you up so bad you will be praying for just me," Greg said and then he shoved his tongue into my mouth. "Watch her closely."

Greg said to Brien when he stopped kissing me. Greg licked the tears off my cheek before he let me go and went inside.

I wiped the slobber off my cheek and tasted blood in my mouth. Greg slaps hard and involuntary tears fell from my eyes. I turned and looked into the window. I watched Greg go to the backroom. A few minutes later Greg and Shayla came out of the backroom arm and arm. Shayla was beaming at Greg. They went to the couch and began to kiss. I shuddered and looked away. Tears were still falling and I touched the cheek he hit.

"Are you ok?" Brien said, coming close and kneeling in front of me.

"He is mean," I answered.

"Come inside and I will get you some ice?" Brien said.

"He will hurt me," I fretted.

"I will protect you," Brien said comfortingly.

"Promise?" I said looking at him.

"I promise, Samantha," he promised.

"Ok," I said.

Suddenly Brien just scooped me up and carried me into the house. He carried me past the living room where Greg and Shayla were kissing. He took me to the kitchen and sat me down on the kitchen counter. Brien opened a kitchen drawer and took out a washcloth. He opened the freezer and took out some ice and put it on the washcloth. He picked up the washcloth and put it on my cheek.

"Brien, please go lock the doors. Men keep coming and trying to get inside," I said as I took his hand off the washcloth and pushed him away.

While Brien had been nice to me for several weeks and had not hurt me I still did not like him touching me. I did not trust him. I knew he still wanted to hurt me. I know he enjoyed hurting me that night. I did not want him to touch me. Brien went to lock the doors. Greg told Shayla to go into Mom's room and he would be there soon. Shayla ran into Mom's room and I cringed. I knew Shayla loved him but he was evil and just using her. I could not do anything though because Shayla was just now talking to me again. I needed

my sister. Greg came into the kitchen. He took a beer out of the refrigerator. He turned to me and stepped closer. I scooted back and leaned away from him. He tucked a loose strand of hair behind my ear.

"It's a shame that you are so feisty. We could have fun, you know?" He suggested.

"I don't want to have fun with you," I said pathetically.

"You better start being nice to me or I might just have to show you who is the boss," Greg said angrily.

"Hey, what's going on in here?" Brien said as he came back into the room and came in between Greg and me.

"I was just leaving," Greg said as he left the kitchen and went into Mom's room.

"Good morning, Brien," I heard Krista say from behind Brien.

"Oh, good morning," Brien said absently as he turned back to me while Krista glared at me, "Are you alright?"

"I'm fine," I said looking at Krista.

"Have you had breakfast?" he asked me.

"Not yet," I replied looking back at Brien who was smiling at me.

"I haven't eaten," Krista interjected.

"What do you want to eat?" Brien asked me.

"Cereal," I answered.

"We're out of cereal," Krista said angrily.

"I got more. It is in that cabinet," I said pointing to the cabinet I put it in.

Brien got out two bowls, two spoons, milk and some cereal. He picked me up and put me on a stool at the counter. He served me and him some cereal as Krista glared at me.

"I wanted some, too," Krista said loudly.

"Oh, I did not know. Well, grab a bowl and join us," Brien said as he took another bite.

Krista grabbed a bowl and spoon and sat beside Brien. Krista kept trying to get Brien's attention but he just kept ignoring her. I

was feeling uncomfortable so I stopped eating after only finishing half my cereal. I got down and went to my room.

"Where are you going?" Brien said as I left.

I did not reply. I grabbed Hope and some Barbie dolls and went in the backyard. I sat in the grass with my back to the house and played quietly. That day Greg and Brien were there all day so I stayed outside. I was angry they were eating all the food I just bought. I was angry that I could not stop them. I was angry because I knew I did not have money for more food. It was chilly and my jacket did not keep me warm. I finally went inside. I saw that Greg, Brien, Krista and Shayla were watching TV. I went to the bathroom. I then got ready for bed. I went to my room and laid down in bed. I pulled the blankets up to my chin. The sun had sat a while ago so I decided to stay in bed. I was hungry but the food was gone. I ate two of the candy bars. Then I went to brush my teeth again. When I was finished I went back to bed. I dozed off.

I awoke in a panic. Brien was standing by my bed with just his underwear on. He pulled them off and threw back the blankets. I started to yell but he put his hand on my mouth.

"Shh, don't scream or Greg will hear you. It is just me. Don't scream. You will like it this time. I am not going to hurt you," Brien hissed into my ear as he held me close.

I felt his wee wee hardened against my leg as he came closer. He slowly took his hand off my mouth and covered us up quickly.

"Please, just leave me alone, please," I begged him pitifully.

He was right if I screamed Greg would come in and hurt me bad. However, if I did nothing Brien would hurt me. I was trapped without a way to escape.

"Please, just go away. Brien, please don't hurt me," I begged him.

"I love the way you say my name. I love you. You are so beautiful. I don't want to hurt you but you tease me. You are irresistible," Brien said as he began to rub his hands up and down my body.

I started to push him away and tried to back away but I was pushed against the wall. I was crying and trying to stop his hands.

Brien began to breathe heavy. He climbed on top of me and tried to take off my underwear. I fought him.

"Stop or I will......" I tried to say scream but suddenly Brien started kissing me hard and broke off my sentence.

He had managed to get my underwear off and was trying to open my legs. His body held me down and he never stopped kissing me so I could not scream. I had no choice. I bit his tongue. He yelped and sat up. I took my fist and hit him in his throat. He had blood in his mouth. I screamed as loud as I could. A minute later Krista, Shayla, and Greg ran into the room. Brien jumped off my bed and turned to everyone.

"She invited me and then got mad when I would not agree to be her boyfriend," Brien said to an angry Krista. He sounded kind of funny.

"You whore. Go find your own boyfriend and stop trying to steal mine!" Krista yelled at me as I put my underwear back on.

"I don't want him," I blubbered through my tears.

"Your nothing but a pathetic slut," Krista said as she pushed me hard.

I landed on the floor. I was crying as Krista wrapped her arm around Brien and walked out of my room. Shayla followed close behind them. Greg came close as I stood up and I backed away from him.

"I'm next," Greg whispered.

He leaned close and sniffed me. I just stood there paralyzed in fear. I was raped in this room only weeks ago and the memories flashed in my mind.

"You are going to be so sweet," he said as he roughly rubbed me with his hands before walking swiftly out of Shayla's and then my room.

I was still crying. I was angry. I sat on my bed. I thought about how selfish and cruel Greg and Brien were. They needed to be punished but I was too small to punish them. Brien didn't even flinch when I hit him in the throat. Then I had an idea. I stood up and tiptoed out of the room. I heard noises in Krista's room and Mom's

room. Both doors were shut. I went into the living room. My eyes were adjusted to the light. I saw one of the things I was looking for on a table by the door. I picked up the wallet and opened it. Inside was a driver license with Greg's picture. I took all the money out of the wallet. I took the money and hid it in my room. I then returned and looked for Brien's wallet. I did not find it. I walked to Krista's bedroom door. The noises were still pretty loud. I opened the door a crack and looked inside. The bed was on the opposite wall from the door so they could not see me. Krista was on bottom and Brien was on top of her with his back to me. They were doing it. I went into the room quietly and saw Brien's pants just a few feet from the door. I walked over and grabbed them. I got his wallet. I took the money out and put the wallet back in the pants. I was putting the pants back down when I heard it.

"Samantha, Oh, Yes, SAMANTHA!" Brien exclaimed.

"Fuck, get off of me you bastard," Krista said in surprise as she tried to push Brien off.

I saw Brien slap her hard and then put a pillow on her face. I just stood there shocked as Brien finished. Krista was fighting him but he did not seem to care. He just kept saying my name over and over. Finally he removed the pillow on Krista's face as he seemed to thrust one last time. I quickly left the room and shut the door. I hid the money with the rest. I grabbed my blanket and Hope. I went to the backyard and laid on the back porch under my bedroom windows.

I could not sleep and felt exhausted. I peeked in the window and did not see anyone in my room. I sneaked inside and grabbed the blanket from Shayla's bed and the pillow from my bed. I went back out the backdoor. I walked around the house struggling to carry both covers, a pillow and Hope. I took everything to the front porch. I moved the chairs so I could sit on one and put my feet on the other. I wrapped Hope and I in one of the blankets and sat on the chairs. I put the pillow on the arm of the chair by my head and covered up with Shayla's cover. It was a little warmer and much more

comfortable. I fell asleep thinking I just had to make it through the night. Tomorrow had to be better.

Chapter 35

I was startled awake when I felt someone move the hair that was on my face behind my ear. I sat up quickly. My heart was beating fast as I saw that Brien was crouching beside my makeshift bed. I was terrified. How long had he been watching me? I drew the blankets up to my neck as I looked at him in terror.

"Good morning, princess," Brien said softly.

I looked at the dark sky. The sky was lightening but it was not sunrise yet. Besides it looked cloudy so the sunrise might not be visible. I looked back at Brien suspiciously.

"I think it is time we talk about our relationship," Brien said.

"I don't want a relationship with you," I said trying to sound strong.

"Well, that is not very nice. I can be a really good boyfriend," Brien said as he pulled out the second chair and sat on it right across from me.

I removed my legs from the other chair when he moved the chair. I brought my knees to my chest and sat with the covers wrapped tightly around me. I was pretty sure I was actually tangled in the blankets so I did not try to run. Besides, Brien was too close.

"I don't want a boyfriend," I said.

"Now, that's not very nice," Brien said as he slid a hand into the covers.

Luckily I was wrapped tightly in both blankets so he could not find my actual body. I just cringed away from his touch.

"Please, just leave me alone. Please, Brien, can't we just be friends," I begged him.

"I love you. You are so beautiful that I can't stop myself. Samantha, I can be gentle. You will like it next time. And if you were my

girlfriend, Greg would leave you alone," Brien said softly as he moved closer and stroked my face with his hand.

Brien leaned in for a kiss but I leaned away and buried my face in the cover.

"No, please, just go away," I said, closing my eyes and wishing he would go away when I opened them.

Brien pulled the covers away from my face and grabbed my face in both of his hands. He pulled my face to him and leaned in for a kiss.

"I will bite you," I threatened.

Brien tilted my head and kissed my forehead. He then put his mouth by my ear.

"I will change your mind. One day you will be mine and mine alone," Brien said before kissing my cheek.

He released my face and moved his chair back. He bent down and picked me up blankets and all. He grabbed the pillow with one hand. I tried to push him away. He walked around to the backdoor and went inside. He dropped the pillow on my bed and I worried he would try to hurt me there again. Instead he carried me and my blankets into the living room. I felt Hope still in my blankets and held her close. He grabbed the remote and sat down with me on his lap. He hugged me close no matter how I struggled.

"Relax or I will have sex with you. I am going to show you what a good boyfriend I can be. Relax, I will not hurt you," Brien said.

"I don't believe you," I said stubbornly.

"Listen, if you stay outside you will freeze to death. I just want to warm you up. I will not have sex with you right now. So, stop fighting or you might just make me horny and then I will have to screw you," Brien threatened.

I stopped fighting to get off his lap because I was afraid of what he said. What if I was causing it? Does fighting boys really make them unable to stop themselves? Brien pulled me close to him and turned on the TV. He found some cartoons. The lights were off and the living room was dim. Brien kept trying to straighten the

covers and unwrap them. After a while he uncovered me. He picked me up and moved the blanket out from under me. He then covered us both up with both blankets. He claimed he was cold but I did not trust him. He cradled me in his lap and kept me very close. One of his arms was wrapped around my shoulders. His other hand kept rubbing my legs and belly and chest.

"Please stop, Brien," I whispered as he was rubbing my body.

"I am just trying to warm you up, baby," Brien said softly into my ear. He was breathing a little fast.

"I don't like it, please, Brien, please stop," I begged as I felt him get hard under me.

"Don't worry baby, it is just us," Brien said as he quickly adjusted us until I was laying on the couch and he was on top.

"Brien you promised. Please," I begged as he began to kiss me.

Brien put his hand over my mouth. He leaned down and whispered into my ear.

"Just hold still. I won't hurt you this time. I promise. Just hold very still and I will not hurt you this time," Brien begged.

"Promise?" I asked, realizing I did not have a choice.

"Oh, yes, Samantha, you are incredible, I love you......Oh Samantha.....Samantha...." Brien whispered.

Brien began to rub his wee wee against me. I kept my legs closed as tight as I could. I kept turning my head away from him and tried to look anywhere else but he kept turning my face to look at him. Hope had fallen out of my arms when he moved me. I felt tears run down my face. Brien kept muttering and saying my name. He was breathing hard and kept kissing me. Finally he jumped up and turned away from the couch. White pee shot out of his wee wee. It fell on the carpet. I jumped up from the couch. I grabbed Hope and ran to the bathroom before he could stop me.

I washed my legs where he had rubbed against me. I felt dirty and felt like it was my fault. I should have found a better hiding place to sleep. How did he know I was on the front porch? I felt like it was my fault. I heard a knock at the door.

"Who is it?" I said just loud enough for the person on the other side of the door to hear me.

"I need to clean up," Brien said.

"Step back, I will leave," I said.

I opened the door slowly. Brien was halfway down the hall wearing his pajama bottoms again. I tried to run past him but he picked me up. He carried me into the bathroom. He put me in the bathtub. He closed the shower curtain and I listened as he went potty and washed his hands.

"Please just let me go," I begged when he opened the shower curtain and picked me back up.

"If I let you go you will run outside and freeze. It started snowing outside," Brien said as he carried me to the couch.

He put me on the couch and covered me up. He went to the kitchen and wet a washcloth. He returned and cleaned up his white pee. He then went to the washer off the kitchen and put the washcloth in the washer. He walked back and sat beside me on the couch. He put his arm around me and pulled me close. I pushed away from him but he pulled me even harder against him.

"Stop fighting or I will take it as an invitation to have fun," Brien threatened.

I stopped fighting but as soon as his grip lessened I pulled as far from him as he allowed. I hated that I was not stronger than him. Krista, Shayla and Greg eventually emerged from their rooms. Krista glared at me and did not say anything to me. Shayla smiled when she saw Brien and me. I took the opportunity when everyone got up to run to my room. Shayla followed me with our blankets. We began to make the beds. I put Hope on my pillow at the top of the bed.

"So, is Brien your boyfriend now?" Shayla asked excitedly.

"No, I don't want a boyfriend," I said.

"I think he likes you," Shayla said.

"I don't want him to like me. Isn't he supposed to like Krista?" I said angrily.

"I guess he likes you more. Wait, Greg does not like you, right?"
Shayla said worriedly.

"I hope not," I said shuddering inside.

"I can't believe we both have boyfriends," Shayla giggled as we got dressed for the day.

"I do not have a boyfriend," I said stubbornly.

"You do now," Shayla said as she skipped out of our rooms.

I had just picked out my outfit and looked out the window at the snow falling. I wished Mom would return so Brien and Greg would not try to hurt me. I felt trapped. I looked at the doorway that led to the kitchen and the rest of the house. I wished my room had a door. I turned away from the door and quickly took off my clothes. I put on my dress with tights on underneath. After that I put my shoes on and turned around. Brien was watching me from the doorway. I stepped back. He reached out a hand for me to take. I took a deep breath, I held my head up high and straightened my back. I walked right past him without taking his hand. He chuckled and followed me to the kitchen. I looked in the cabinets but the boys had eaten all the food I bought the previous day and there was nothing to eat. They even finished the peanut butter. I grabbed a soda and sat at the kitchen counter. I did not want to be on the couch.

Brien and Greg left for home about an hour later. Krista watched them go. She was angry because Brien was ignoring her completely. Brien had spent his time sitting by me at the counter in the kitchen while I pointedly ignored him. He had found my attitude cute. He called it foreplay when he joked about it to Greg. I just felt sick. As soon as the boys were out of sight Krista stomped over to me and yanked me off the stool by my hair. I screamed. Krista climbed on top of me and began to choke me. Shayla was trying to pull her off of me. Krista was screaming about me stealing her boyfriend, never letting her be happy, and the fact that Brien had dumped her. I was scratching her but was about to pass out when the front door opened and Benny came in. Benny dropped his bag and ran to me. He pulled Krista off of me right before I was about to pass

out. I saw floating dots. I gasped for breath. I held my throat. After a few minutes Shayla helped me sit up. Krista finally stopped fighting Benny and went to her room. She slammed the door. I was ok. I was dizzy but it was not too bad. Shayla helped me to the couch and brought me my half full soda. It hurt to swallow but the cold beverage also felt good going down. Krista stayed in her room as Shayla, Benny and I watched TV. After a little while I told Shayla where to find the candy and she brought it out to the living room. Shayla and Benny finished the candy bars while I ate two suckers. Then Shayla and Benny finished the suckers. Mom came home with some groceries a few hours later. She also had a pepperoni pizza. Krista came out of her room but did not even look at me. She was back to ignoring me. To her I had stolen her boyfriend. I was her bad guy. I felt sorry but knew she would never listen to my apology. Maybe it was all my fault.

Chapter 36

School started up the next day. The routine that was established before started all over again. We went to school during the day. In the afternoons and evenings I would stay in my room while the bad men visited my sisters. Either Greg or Brien would watch me and make sure the men did not hurt me. That was their job. There was always one or two men who would negotiate to have me. They scared me. Brien would always try to touch me when he thought Mom was not looking. I told him over and over that I did not want a boyfriend but he said it was not my choice but his.

The last few weeks of the semester went by quickly. The kids at school were excited about the holidays. They would talk about all the stuff their family would do. They talked of traditions, presents, and food. My family was different so I just listened a lot. I knew my holiday would not be like theirs. I hated our holidays. I felt safe at

school and wished the break would not happen. No one at school ever tried to hurt me. I was safe at school.

Then it was the break. We had three weeks without school. I remember walking home with my siblings slowly. Every step felt heavy. I got sadder the closer to home we got. I could not decide what was worse, Mom leaving or Mom staying. If she leaves, the boys will come and I might get hurt. If she stays my sisters might have to work and Christmas day will be torture for them. Then I thought about how little food we had and how I was running out of money. I needed more money. I only took money from bad guys. I had a wicked idea to get money. After all, wasn't Mom a bad guy, too?

We got home and Mom sent me to my room like usual. My sisters were sent to their work rooms. Brien showed up a little while later. Soon the men were arriving. I knew I would have to be up really late so I laid down to rest. Brien read me stories until I dozed off. I had all my clothes on and knew Mom would check on me later so I felt safe enough with Brien. He would not try too much with Mom so close. I woke up after dark. The men were still coming and going. Brien was drinking a beer by my door. I sat up and checked myself. None of my clothes appeared to have been taken off. Brien looked over at me and smiled. He flipped on my light. I had to blink a few times for my eyes to adjust.

"Good morning, sleeping beauty," Brien said as he stood up and walked to my bed.

"It is not morning, it is night," I said as I quickly untangled myself and Hope from the blanket before Brien sat down.

"I missed you, that's all," Brien said as he tucked a loose strand of hair behind my ear.

"Are the men going to leave soon?" I asked looking towards the door.

"In a few more hours. Your Mom wants to stay open a few more hours," Brien said without feeling.

"Are my sisters ok?" I said worriedly.

"They're getting used to it," Brien said.

"No one gets used to being hurt. No one likes to be hurt," I said angrily as I crossed my arms across my chest.

"You're wrong. Most people grow to love it. I could show you if you would just let me," Brien said leaning close and putting his hand on my thigh.

"No, thank you," I said leaning away from him.

"Son of a bitch, you just keep teasing me. If you keep teasing me I might just not be able to control myself one day," Brien said as he stood up, finished his beer and stomped out of the room.

I got up and made my bed. I then put my shoes on and then turned out the lights. Brien had not returned yet. I needed to go potty. I sat on my bed and looked at the snow falling outside the window. My room was really cold but not too cold. Finally I could not wait anymore. I got off the bed. I left hope on the bed. I went to the door. Brien was in the living room talking loudly with some of the men. I looked into the kitchen but no one was there. Mom was on the other side of the living room looking at her watch and smoking. I had to go potty. I cut through the kitchen and ran into the hall. I ran to the bathroom and locked the door behind me. I went potty and washed my hands. I was scared to open the door. I shut off the light and looked under the door. I did not see anyone. I stood up and opened the door slowly. I ran to the end of the hall terrified of getting trapped. I was going into the kitchen when I heard Mom call my name.

"Samantha, Samantha, come here," Mom yelled across the room.

I turned and started walking toward Mom. There were three customers and Brien in the living room. All of them turned to stare at me like I was food and they were starving. I felt dirty just walking by them.

"Can I help you, Mommy?" I asked when I reached Mom's smoky table.

"Empty this ashtray and bring me another cup of coffee," Mom said handing me her overflowing ashtray and empty coffee cup.

I took the ashtray and cup into the kitchen. I emptied the ashtray in the trash. I then pulled a chair to the counter with the coffee pot. I climbed on top of the chair so I could reach the coffee pot. I slowly poured the coffee into Mom's coffee cup. Then I got down. I took the ashtray to Mom then went back to the kitchen to slowly carry Mom's hot cup with both hands. I used a washcloth so I would not burn myself on the hot cup.

"I would love a cup of Joe," one of the bad men said.

"Oh, yes," the other bad men piped in.

"$2 a cup," Mom said as she took the cup from me. "Samantha, get each of them some coffee and bring me their money."

I returned to the kitchen. I got down three cups. Then I carefully filled each cup. The coffee pot was empty when I finished. One by one I took the cups to the men. One by one each man would try to touch me or say something suggestive. I felt dirty but did what I was told. When I finished I took the money to Mom.

"That was the last of the coffee," I told Mom.

"Brien, show Samantha how to make some more coffee then take her back to her room. We should be closing in about an hour," Mom then stood up and went to the bedrooms.

While Brien showed me how to make coffee two men left and two of the men in the living room disappeared into the bedrooms. That left only one man in the living room. He stared evilly at me as Brien and I restarted the coffee. Then Brien put the chair away and picked me up and sat me on the counter.

"You have not eaten. Are you hungry?" Brien said.

"I don't want to eat out here," I said, glancing at the man who was staring hungrily at me.

"How about some ice cream? We could eat in your room," Brien said smiling at me.

"Ask Mommy," I said.

I expected Mom to say no but she said yes. Brien made a big bowl of ice cream and grabbed two spoons. It was strawberry and I was excited. Brien gave me the bowl and carried me and the ice

cream to my room. Brien put me on the bed and turned to turn on the light.

"Leave the light off," I said quickly. I wanted to watch the snow.

Brien turned. He sat down right across from me. He put one hand on my leg and took his spoon with the other.

"This is nice," Brien said.

"I like the snow," I said as I pushed his hand off my leg.

I put my pillow on my lap between us. I put the bowl on the pillow. Then I finally took a bite as I looked out the window. I wished Brien was not so close. Brien repositioned himself so I was between both of his legs. He scooted as close as he could. His legs wrapped all the way around me. I just kept my legs criss-crossed and kept the pillow on them. I tried to ignore him.

"You are really beautiful. I want to kiss you," Brien whispered leaning closer.

"No, thank you," I said. "I'm done. You can have the rest." I said as I put the bowl right in front of his face.

He was annoyed and grabbed the bowl. He got off the bed and stomped to the kitchen. I jumped down and grabbed my coat and gloves. I stepped outside just as he returned.

"Where the hell are you going?" He said angrily.

"I am allowed to play in the backyard," I said with as much attitude as I could muster.

"It's snowing," Brien complained.

"So," I said.

"It's dark," he complained.

"So," I replied.

"It's cold," he complained again.

"Snow is supposed to be cold, silly," I said as I giggled and ran out into the magical night.

"Just stay there, I will be right back," Brien said as he disappeared into the house.

I went to the back corner and started making snowballs. Brien emerged from the house with his coat on but he was still

putting on his gloves. He looked around but did not see me. He started looking frantically for me. I let him look for a few minutes while I made a few more snowballs. When he started to yell my name too loudly I threw the first snowball. I was mad at him for trying to hurt me so I pretended I was throwing rocks. I threw until I ran out of snowballs. He knew where I was by then and began to throw snowballs as well. I started throwing snowballs in anger but it was so much fun that I found myself laughing. I totally won that snowball fight no matter what Brien says. Mom found us just as the fight was wrapping up. I threw a snowball at her and she actually joined in the fight. When my mom laughed you could almost forget all the bad things she did. She glowed when she laughed. Soon though Mom made us all go in. I made a few snow angels on my way inside. I loved how the whole time Brien just played and never tried to hurt me.

Brien had told his Mom he was staying at a friend's house so he slept on the couch. Shayla came back to her bed. She was in pain and fell asleep crying. Benny slept with Mom. Krista stayed in her own bed. I was awake. I waited until they were all asleep. I then crept into the living room. I went to Mom's purse where she put all the money. I grabbed as many bills as I could carry. I returned to my room and hid them where I hid the other money. I then went back and did it again. I could not see what bills I was taking so I only took two trips worth of money. I knew Mom would not count the money until tomorrow so this was my only chance. Then I went to bed still wearing all of my clothes. I did not sleep well and woke repeatedly.

Chapter 37

I woke up early to watch the sunrise. The snow had stopped during the night. I got up and put on my coat. I pulled my gloves on and decided to take hope with me. I went out the backdoor and walked around to the front porch. I dusted the snow off a chair and flipped the cushion over before I sat down. I looked out at the

beautiful snow that seemed to coat the entire world with sparkling glitter. The sunrise was perfect. I saw several shades of purple and pink that reflected off the new snow. I was alone and I felt relieved. For a few minutes, at least, I was at peace. Hope thought the sunrise was beautiful and wondered who painted it.

Soon I heard noises in the house. I went around the house and went in the back door. I took off my coat and gloves and made my bed. I put Hope on my pillow. Mom was awake and making coffee. Brien was no longer on the couch.

"Good morning, Mommy," I said as I entered the kitchen.

"Good morning, Sissy. How did you sleep?" Mom said as she bent down to hug me.

"Fine. How did you sleep?" I asked.

"Ok, I just wish the sun wasn't so bright in the mornings," Mom complained as she poured a cup of coffee.

"I'm sorry, Mommy," I apologized.

"Well, I am glad you are up. I have been thinking that now that you are healed we might just begin working you, too. I have been getting a lot of offers from some real nice men who are willing to pay very well just to hang out with you for a little while. I was thinking you could start right after Christmas," Mom said as she sat at the counter and put me on her lap.

"Mommy, I don't want to. It will hurt. Please, Mommy," I begged.

"Well, Sissy, we really need the money. Besides, this would not be like last time. I was mad and may have overreacted. These gentlemen would be really gentle. They will not hurt you," Mom explained.

"Mommy, it will hurt if they put it in my hole. It will. Please, Mommy, can't you find another job. We are too young to work. My other friends don't work," I pleaded.

"You ungrateful, selfish, bitch. Have you been telling all your spoiled friends what goes on here? You will start work the day after Christmas and you better not complain or try to fight or I swear to

God I will kill you! You stupid whore!" Mom said as she pushed me down hard.

Mom took her coffee into the living room. She turned on the TV and sat on the couch. I got up and saw that Brien had been watching from the hallway. I went to my room. I laid down and buried my face in Hopes fur. I began to cry quietly.

I don't know how long I cried. Eventually I heard Shayla start to wake up. I dried my face with my pillowcase. I sat up and greeted her. We talked while she made her bed but I did not tell her what had happened this morning. When she left I grabbed my Barbie dolls and played quietly on my bed. I did not want to be around Mom. I just wished she would go away forever. Maybe I could find a job at the store four blocks away if Mom disappeared forever. I could put food on shelves and sweep. I could carry bags for people and I could take their money and give them change. I imagined how nice it would be without Mom. Brien came in about an hour later. He had to go home and asked what I wanted for Christmas this year. I ignored him. He bent down and kissed my forehead. He whispered he would see me soon. I imagined he would go away too. If he and Greg went away with Mom we could move into Aunt Penny's house and she could make us goulash and apple pie every night. That would be perfect!

Mom worked my sisters that afternoon and evening. However Mom was really angry that neither Brien nor Greg did not show. She stormed around the house until I promised to stay in my room all night. I was afraid to see the men anyway. I wished Christmas would never come. I wondered why they did not come though. Mom paid them well and they always liked coming. Mom always let them drink as much beer as they wanted. Greg usually drank a lot so that by the end of the night he could not walk straight. Mom was mad at them for not working. Still Mom worked my sisters until late. This time when I had to go potty I went outside. It was cold but at least no one stared at me. I waited until all the men were gone to get ready for bed. Mom did bring me a sandwich and a

soda half way through the night. She was nice to me again and even smiled at me. Shayla cried herself to sleep again. I was glad when the day was over. I fell asleep wishing that Mom would disappear forever.

The next morning I awoke before dawn. I crept into the living room and took more money from mom's purse, this time there was just enough light that I only took a handful of twenty dollar bills. After I hid the money, I went to the front porch with Hope to watch the sunrise. This was my time. I felt like I was the only one in the world. Everyone else was asleep in their beds. I wondered what other people were dreaming about. My friends liked to talk about fairies and unicorns and princes in their dreams. I like to dream about peace. Living where bad men did not come to your house. Living in the country with just my sisters and I. That would be perfect. No one to hurt us. We could be free and maybe Krista would forgive me and love me. We could be happy. I thought of this as I watched the sunrise. I did not want to go inside. I stayed outside as the sun rose higher.

I heard Mom wake up. I decided to stay outside longer. I could hear the TV on but still I did not go inside. As long as I stayed outside I could pretend that everything was fine. Then I saw someone coming. Aunt Penny was walking fast towards our house. She looked real mad and was stomping through the snow. I quickly grabbed Hope and got off the porch. I ducked around the side of the house. I thought about running to my room but I was curious. Aunt Penny marched onto our porch and banged repeatedly on our door. I ducked down in the snow and peeked around the corner. Aunt Penny was red in the face and she looked furious. Mom quickly opened the door.

"What the hell is going on?" Mom demanded.

"You bitch! What the hell did you get my boys into?!?" Aunt Penny yelled at Mom.

"What are you talking about?" Mom said quickly.

"I overheard Brien and Greg bragging about it to my son Ramon last night when he came home for the holidays. I confronted them. I will have you know they told me everything. They told me about how you have been using your daughters to run a damn whorehouse. They told me how you have been paying them to work for you. You are a monster!" Aunt Penny angrily yelled.

"What exactly did they tell you?" Mom inquired.

"They confessed everything about what you are doing to your poor daughters. I will have you know I plan on taking them home with me right now and then calling the police so you should just start running, bitch," Aunt Penny said as she tried to push her way around Mom.

"They told you everything, did they? Did they tell you how they have been screwing my girls? Did they tell you how they gang raped my five year old little girl? I am sure the police would love to hear that," Mom threatened as she blocked Aunt Penny's way into the house.

Aunt Penny paused when Mom said that. Aunt Penny just stared at Mom. Mom grinned back at her. I hoped Aunt Penny would call the police and save us. Surely she would save us. She loved me. She said she loved me like a daughter. She would never choose her evil sons over us. Would she?

Mom and Aunt Penny stared at each other for a few minutes. Finally Aunt Penny took a step back and all the anger seemed to leave her.

"I hate you right now. I will never forgive you for what you have done. However, you are right. I love my boys. I am going to send them to live with their father for a while. But.......you have to go. You have to leave. I just can't see this anymore. I can't," Aunt Penny said to Mom.

Aunt Penny turned to leave. Mom watched her walk to the sidewalk. Mom went back inside and closed the door. I went back to my room. Aunt Penny knew and did not care. Aunt Penny just walked away. Aunt Penny said she loved me but she chose the boys

who hurt me so much over me. I was less than them in her eyes. I was nobody. They were bad but better than me. I was no one. I felt betrayed. There was so much sadness enveloping my whole body. I realized in that moment that no one would save any of us. We were lost. We were trapped. We only had each other. We were all alone. We would never be at peace. I laid down. I felt so sad that I felt overwhelmed. My entire hope came crashing down in that moment. I just kept seeing Aunt Penny walking away without even a look back. I will never forget that.

That morning Mom told us all to start packing. She left to find a new place. She did not tell my sisters why we were leaving and I was too hurt to care to tell them. Mom took Benny. She did get us some boxes from the store before she left. Benny and Mom were gone two days. I was so wrapped up in my own head that I barely remember those two days. Krista and Shayla packed up as much as they could from the rest of the house. I packed up mine and Shayla's room. I put two outfits for each of us in our individual backpacks. I felt almost like a zombie. I barely ate. I barely drank. I just felt hopeless and lost. We were all lost.

Chapter 38

Mom returned with a trailer attached to the back of our car. Mom helped us finish packing up the house. I wanted to leave at that point. We loaded up the trailer that night. We spent one last night at the house. The next morning, four days before Christmas, we loaded the last of our stuff and left. I had hidden my money in the bottom of my backpack inside a toy. We drove all day. Mom stopped at a fast food drive through for dinner. Then we drove until dark. Finally we pulled up to a two story house on a very nice street. The house was yellow and had lots of windows. I liked it. We quickly unloaded the car and went inside. We each had our own rooms except Benny who would share a room with Mom. My room was upstairs and faced the

backyard where a big tree was. It was pretty. That night we slept on the floor of our individual rooms.

The next morning we quickly unloaded the rest of the car and the trailer. When the trailer was empty Mom and Benny disconnected it from the car. Then Mom and Benny went to buy furniture while Krista, Shayla and I stayed to unpack what we could. There was no food in the house so Mom promised to bring something home when she returned. Krista was almost nice to me again. Mom was gone most of the day. Men came that afternoon. They said Mom sent them. They carried in a bed and dresser for each room. They also had a table and chairs for the dining room and furniture for the living room. Other men came and set up a brand new washer and dryer. When they left, we were able to finish unpacking as we waited for Mom to return. I liked my new bed. I decided that life would be better here. I spun around my new room and fell face up on my bed with my arms far apart. I felt like a princess.

Mom returned later. She brought groceries and pizza. Krista, Shayla and I were starving. After dinner we all watched a movie on our new TV. Mom was in a good mood. Soon it was time for bed. Mom came up to tuck me in.

"So, do you like your new room?" Mom asked me.

"I love it Mommy. It is so nice here," I said.

"Well, I have some news for you. I chose this place because it is in a nicer neighborhood. I am hoping to attract richer clients. But, it will take some time, Sissy. So it might be a few weeks before we can start working again," Mom said.

"Thank you Mommy," I said as I hugged her.

Maybe she was changing her mind. Maybe she would decide never to sell us again. Maybe she was postponing the work because she finally listened and decided never to hurt us again. Maybe.

"Good night, Sissy. I love you," Mom said as she got up and turned out the light.

"I love you, too, Mommy," I called after her.

Maybe this place will be better. I could be happy with our family if we were never hurt again. Mom was postponing so maybe she would find another job. Maybe. I fell asleep thinking that maybe all the bad stuff was behind us.

The next day dawned bright and early. My new room had a window that faced East so I did not have to go outside to see the sunrise. It was very pretty, even though there was not as much snow here as in our old home. Here they only had an inch or two of snow. The old house had five or six inches of snow. Still the sunrise was full of colors and hope. A new beginning. A new life.

Mom went out the next day and bought a Christmas tree and Christmas decorations. Krista, Shayla and I were really excited. That afternoon Mom left and Krista, Shayla, and I spent the day decorating the house for Christmas and making ornaments for the tree. Benny spent his time exploring the Basement. The previous owner of the house had left boxes and old electronics down there. Benny was so excited. Benny immediately went to work taking apart an old radio. We watched an old Christmas movie before we went to bed that night. Mom was not back before bed. I heard her come home in the middle of the night but luckily she was alone. I locked the door behind her and went back to bed.

The sunrise was obscured by clouds the next morning. However, I was still excited. Christmas was coming. Maybe it would be a good Christmas after all. Mom left that afternoon in a bad mood. She had been upset all morning and yelled at us often. She even slapped Shayla once. We were relieved to see her go. Tomorrow was Christmas Eve. We were excited. We hoped Mom would be in a better mood tomorrow. Mom did not come home that night.

Benny spent Christmas Eve in the basement. Krista, Shayla and I spent most of the day playing outside. We had snowball fights and made snow angels. It was so much fun. When it got dark we went inside. The groceries Mom had bought were already almost gone. We ate dinner in front of the TV. Krista already told me years

ago that there was no Santa Claus. However, when I went to bed I still found myself sending a mental note to Santa that if Mom was in a bad mood he would keep her far away tomorrow. I fell asleep. Early the next day I woke before dawn and took the presents for my sisters out from under my bed. I ran downstairs and put them under the tree. Then I returned to my room and watched the sunrise. I wrapped my best doll for Krista and my best Barbie for Shayla. I hoped they would like them. I could not wait to see them open the presents.

Krista and Shayla were surprised to see the presents under the tree for them. They seemed happy when they saw what was inside the presents. We spent the day playing in the living room and watching Christmas movies on TV. Mom still was not home. We finished the rest of the food. It did not help that Benny ate more than any of us. I knew that I would need to find a store if Mom did not return soon. I just did not know where one was in this new town. I asked Benny where Mom bought the groceries before but he said he did not remember. Mom never returned home that day. It was good because then we were safe but bad since we did not have food for the next day.

I awoke to a loud banging noise. I sat up in a panic. I looked out the window and saw the moon was high and full. The stars reflected on the snow and made everything bright outside. I got out of bed quickly. I crept downstairs toward the noise. The noise was someone knocking on the front door. I walked to the door and looked out a window by the door. Mom was there being half carried by a big man with a potbelly. I opened the door.
"Who are you?" I asked the stranger politely.
"I'm Albert. I am your Mom's new boyfriend," Albert said as he stepped into the house.

I stepped back and looked at this strange new man. He was kind of ugly. He had a wide forehead. He had a potbelly. He was average height and had lost most of his blond hair.
"Which way to your Mom's room, pumpkin?" Albert said.

"Oh, her room is this way," I said showing him the way.

I was relieved when I saw that Benny was not in Mom's room. He must have stayed downstairs last night.

"Are you staying the night?" I asked Albert.

"If you don't mind. It is late," Albert replied, smiling at me.

"Good night," I said and turned to leave.

"Thank you, pumpkin," Albert said as I was walking away.

I went to Krista's and Shayla's rooms one by one and locked my sisters inside their rooms. I then went back downstairs. Mom's door was shut now. I locked the front door before I went down to the basement. It was creepy down there. Benny was sleeping on a blanket on the floor. I covered him up and went back upstairs. I then went to my room. I locked my bedroom door behind me and laid back down. I could not get back to sleep. I kept listening for noises. When the sky started to lighten I watched the sunrise. I went to the bedroom door. I unlocked it. I did not see anyone in the hall. I went to the bathroom. After I finished, I tiptoed downstairs and peeked into Mom's room. Albert and Mom were fast asleep. I went back to my room. I shut the door but did not lock it. I returned to bed and fell asleep in the bright morning light.

Chapter 39

I awoke to the sound of someone opening my door. I sat up in a panic. Shayla was standing there holding a green shirt.

"Does purple pants match green?" Shayla asked.

"Not really. Do you need help?" I asked, jumping off the bed.

"I don't like having my own bedroom. I don't know how to find clothes that match," Shayla said, sounding frustrated.

"Your room is right next to mine. I will always help you. I like having my own room. It makes me feel like a princess in a tower. We can both be princesses," I said as I quickly made my bed.

Shayla and I went to her room. I helped her find some clothes that matched. I then returned to my room and got dressed for the day. I wondered if Mom's friend would still be here. Maybe he would be nicer than Mom's other boyfriends. I went to meet Shayla in the hall and we walked downstairs together. The clock said it was after nine. I did not see Mom or Albert. I went to Mom's bedroom door. I opened it a little and peeked inside. No one was there. I entered the room and checked the bathroom. The bathroom was empty as well. Mom and Albert must have left.

"Did you see Mom leave this morning?" I asked Shayla and Krista when I joined them in the living room.

"Mom left two days ago, remember?" Krista said.

"She came home last night with a man named Albert. I thought they would be here," I said walking towards the door.

"You must have been dreaming. Mom did not come home," Krista said.

"She did come home. She did not have her key so I had to open the door for them," I said.

"Stop lying. If Mom really came home where is she now?" Krista said.

"Fine, don't believe me but I am not lying," I argued as I walked to the door and opened it.

I stepped outside and looked around. I did not see anyone so I went back inside.

"Mom left again. Is there any food?" I asked.

"We finished all the food yesterday," Shayla said.

"We need to try to find a store nearby. Who wants to come with me?" I asked.

"You can't just go to the store. You don't have money," Krista said, rolling her eyes.

"I know how to get stuff from the store. I just don't know where one is. Does anyone want to look with me?" I asked again.

"Forget it, whatever your planning won't work. You are just wasting your time," Krista said, returning her attention to the TV.

"I want to go," Shayla said.

Shayla and I went upstairs. We put on our coats, gloves and backpacks. I made sure to put all the money in the little zipper. Then we headed out. We walked to the sidewalk and turned left. After one block we saw a school. It was a big school and had a big playground. We decided when the weather was warmer we would play there every day. We walked twelve blocks but did not find any stores. We turned around and walked back toward home. When we got back to the house we went inside to warm up.

"Did you find a store?" Krista asked us when we went inside.

"No, not yet. Is Mom back yet?" I replied.

"No, of course not," Krista replied.

Shayla and I got a drink of water and left again. This time we turned right. After ten blocks we saw a gas station. I figured it was better than nothing. We went inside. Shayla wanted a lot of candy. In the end we bought four boxes of cereal, two gallons of milk, some sliced cheese, lunch meat, bread, and four candy bars. We put everything except the milk and bread into our backpacks. On the way home I made Shayla promise not to tell Krista about my money. I explained that it was my emergency money for food. She promised not to tell. I told her to tell Krista that we asked the man for help and he gave us the food. We practiced the lie all the way home so she would remember it.

When we got home Krista and Benny were really happy to see we brought home food. Benny took a cereal box and went back down to the basement. Krista, Shayla, and I ate some cereal in front of the TV. When we were finished I ran upstairs and hid the money in my room. We watched TV and played in the living room most of the day. We had sandwiches for dinner. Mom finally returned right before bedtime with Albert. We all greeted them. Albert was kind but I never really trusted Mom's boyfriends. Stacy always said that Mom only brought home bad guys. I made sure my sister's doors were locked before I went to bed myself.

I awoke several times during the night. However, I never heard anything so I went back to sleep. I woke up before dawn and watched the sunrise. There was something about the peace that comes with the sunrise that always rejuvenates me. I got dressed for the day. Then I unlocked the door and went to the bathroom. After I finished, I went downstairs. The house was quiet and peaceful. I saw that the front door was unlocked and went to investigate. I opened the front door and looked outside. On our front porch sat Albert.

"Good morning, Albert," I said politely.

"Oh, you startled me. Did I wake you up?" Albert said.

"No, I always wake up early," I said, still standing in the doorway.

"Well, come on out and sit with me," Albert said motioning to the other chair.

I went and sat where he indicated. The front porch was really small. I looked out at the street and the house next door. I missed the country. It was peaceful in the country.

"So, why do you wake up early?" Albert said, interrupting my thoughts.

"I like the sunrise," I stated.

"Yes, I like the sunrise as well. So, forgive me, but what was your name again?" Albert said.

"I am Samantha," I said.

He went back to looking off the porch and drinking his coffee. I looked around the neighborhood. Maybe there would be other kids nearby who will be our friends. I liked playing with Lucy and Brian. Maybe I could find friends like them again. I missed them. I got bored so I went inside without talking to Albert again. I went to the kitchen and got a glass of water. I sat at the kitchen table and drank my water. I heard a noise and saw Mom come out of her room. She was wearing jeans and a sweater.

"Good morning, Mommy," I said.

"Good morning, Sissy. Have you seen Albert? He was not in bed when I awoke," Mom said looking around.

"He is on the porch. He made some coffee," I replied.

"Oh, yes. I need some coffee. Thanks," Mom said as she made a beeline for the coffee.

Mom disappeared out the front door. I put my glass in the sink and went upstairs to check on Krista and Shayla. Krista's room was unlocked. I opened it and discovered her still asleep. On the floor near the foot of the bed was a pair of men's underwear. I looked at Krista closely but did not see any bruises. I left her room and went to see Shayla. Shayla was just coming out of her room when I reached her door. We bumped into each other and giggled. After Shayla went to the bathroom, I helped her pick out her clothes for the day. I also helped her clean her room. Shayla liked to hide her messes under her bed. I helped her take her laundry downstairs. Mom and Albert were now in the kitchen. We went by them to the laundry room.

"Why don't we all just go out for breakfast? That way you can do the grocery shopping afterwards," Albert suggested to Mom.

"No, how about we go out to breakfast? The kids can have cereal for breakfast. Then I will go grocery shopping," Mom said to Albert.

"Why can't we all go?" Albert inquired.

"It is too much trouble with all the kids. Some of them aren't even awake and ready," Mom pointed out.

"Well, why don't we take who is awake," Albert insisted.

"Fine, anything you want," Mom replied clearly annoyed, "Samantha, is anyone else awake?"

"Just Shayla and me, Mommy," I answered.

"Ok, go get your coats and meet us on the porch," Mom said.

Shayla and I went quickly to our rooms. When I got my coat and gloves on I went and helped Shayla. Shayla and I went back downstairs and went to the front porch. Mom came out a few seconds later. Albert was behind her. We all got in Mom's car and left. Five minutes later we pulled into a restaurant parking lot. Mom never took us out to eat. We always used drive-ins when we were on the road. I was excited. My first restaurant.

We sat at a table. Mom ordered for Shayla and I. Mom and Albert talked a lot. Albert seemed to really like her. Shayla and I talked quietly amongst ourselves. We looked all around and were fascinated. There was a long counter where people could sit and eat. There were pies and cakes all along the counter. Everything was new. Shayla and I ate scrambled eggs, sausage and fried potatoes. I was good. After breakfast we dropped Albert off at his house. Albert had a job. Then Mom drove us to the grocery store. After shopping, I paid attention to the way Mom took home. Apparently, I needed to go straight five blocks and right four blocks. That is easy. I would remember that for next time. When we got home, Krista was on the porch. She looked mad. We pulled up and she came out to meet us. "Hey, Krista, did you get my note?" Mom greeted Krista.
"Yes, Mommy," Krista replied.
"Help us carry in these groceries," Mom said, opening the trunk.

We all carried in as much as we could. Mom had me stay inside and help her put away the groceries while Krista and Shayla finished bringing in the rest. When everything was put away Mom poured a cup of coffee and went to watch some TV. Shayla, Krista, and I went upstairs. Shayla and I started to tell Krista everything that had transpired that morning. We were so excited. Krista was upset that we did not wake her. She was mad we went without her. Eventually, Krista stormed out and went back to her room. Shayla and I stayed in my room and played house with our dolls.

Chapter 40

Mom had a hard time starting the business. She said that the people in the town were too snobby and that she could not connect with who she needed to connect with. That did not make much sense to me. Albert turned out to be a decent guy. He stayed over many nights. However, I noticed that Krista's room was always unlocked in the mornings when I checked on her. Still, Albert was nice. When two weeks had gone by, Albert helped Mom find a job at the store

near our house. Mom was furious about having to work every day. Whenever Albert was not there Mom would beat us and take her anger out on us. When Albert was around Mom would act sweet and loving towards us. Mom wanted Albert to marry her so he could support us.

Soon, it was time for school to start again. Our new school was only a block away. We discovered that the alley was a short cut. We saw a lot of kids cut through the alley to school. The new school was one level and was long with three different wings. Each classroom opened outside so kids could just go to their classroom door when they arrived. The gym/lunchroom was in the middle. The office was in the first wing. My new classroom was closest to the alley. My new teacher was Mrs. Curtis. She was nice. There were sixteen other kids in my class. I liked school. We got lunch every day in the cafeteria. Everyone was nice.

One of the boys in my class was named C.J.. He lived on the same block as us. There was a small white house behind our house that separated my house from C.J.'s house. There was a creepy old man who lived in the white house. He always was nice to my sisters and me. He would watch us go to and from school. His house was across from the alley. C.J. lived in a two story white house with burgundy shutters. There were four trees in his front yard.

C.J. and I became fast friends. Mom was always at work so C.J. and I would play together after school every day. Our favorite game was sword fighting. We took sticks and used them as swords. We played for hours after school. Being friends with C.J. made me feel free. I could just be a kid. The months went quick. I spent most of my time with C.J.. Shayla and Krista made their own friends. Benny preferred to be by himself.

There was one problem. C.J. did not like the old man in the little white house. His Mom told him the old man was a bad man and to stay away. I thought the old man was nice. He always smiled at my sisters and I. He always had candy for us. He was nice. I should have listened to C.J.. One day I got what my mom and Albert called

a cold sore on my lip. The old man offered me some medicine for my lip when he saw it. He said that the medicine was inside his house if I wanted to come in. I followed him into his house. His house was dark inside with all the blinds closed. It was crammed full of stuff too. I felt claustrophobic. Still I followed him into his very small bedroom where he said the medicine was up on a shelf.

When he got me to his room he sat me on the bed. Instead of getting the medicine he started to take off my dress. I started to fight him but he managed to get my dress around my waist. My chest was exposed. I started to yell and kick him. He pushed me down and put a pillow over my face. I could not breath. I still kicked and fought and screamed. I was losing strength when suddenly the weight lifted on the pillow. I quickly threw the pillow off my face and scrunched into the corner with my knees to my chest. I gasped for air and looked at him. He was sitting by the bed with a sad look on his face. He apologized and let me put my dress on correctly. He offered me the medicine but I told him to stay away from me. I quickly ran out of his house. I saw C.J. as I ran down the old man's porch steps. I did not stop to talk to him. I ran home and to my room. I hid in my closet and hugged Hope close. I stayed in my room all evening. I went to bed that night early. From now on I would stay away from the old man.

The next day went back to the new normal. Mom was getting more and more upset about having a job. She would routinely hit us kids for any perceived slight. I spent more time with C.J.. C.J. asked what happened when I went to the old man's house but I was too ashamed to tell him. A few weeks later I saw the old man talking to Shayla on his porch. When Shayla left I stomped up the porch. I told the bad old man that if I saw him anywhere near my sisters ever again I would tell the world what he tried to do to me. After that he stopped offering us candy. When he saw me coming he just went back into his house.

The school year was almost over. The school was taking a field trip to the botanical gardens. Mom took me to the store and let

me pick out anything I wanted to take for lunch. I picked out all sorts of cupcakes and snack cakes and pies. I even found a teenage mutant ninja turtles snack pie. I also grabbed some chips. The day of the field trip my lunch would not fit into a lunch box so Mom let me take it in a big brown bag. My sisters got only a sandwich, an apple, and a bottle of water. I had a lot of desserts and several different kinds of juice boxes. Krista and Shayla were jealous but I was too excited to really care. The field trip was great. I hung out with C.J. all day. It was the best day ever. We stopped for lunch on a big green hill. I sat next to C.J. on the grass. Before I unpacked my lunch I noticed that there was a boy who did not have lunch and looked sad. I got up and went to him. I sat next to him.

"Where is your lunch?" I asked the boy from another class.

"I don't have one," The boy said looking down at the ground.

"Didn't your Mom pack you lunch?" I asked, confused.

"No," he said as a tear fell from his eye.

"What is your name?" I asked the boy.

"My name is Carl," Carl replied.

"I am Samantha. My mom let me pick my own lunch at the store. I packed a lot of snacks. I can share with you if you like," I told Carl.

"Ok," Carl said smiling at me.

Carl and I shared my lunch. He was nice. I even gave him my Teenage Mutant Ninja Turtles pie that had green slime inside. I had been looking forward to trying it all day but he wanted it and I knew what it felt like to be hungry and not have what you wanted. I enjoyed sharing my lunch with the boy. We played on the hill after lunch. When we got back to school it was time to go home. Mrs. Curtis asked me to stay and help her put the chairs on the desks. When we finished she said she wanted to talk to me. She told me she saw what I did at lunch and she was impressed with what I did. She said she was proud of me. She made me feel like I was a good person.

I still had a lot of leftover snacks in my big lunch bag. I grabbed the bag and headed home feeling happy. All the other kids

were already gone. I headed for the alley. I was only about ten feet into the alley when I saw a shadow and heard footsteps behind me. I turned around expecting to see another kid. However, no one was there. The shadow was gone. I turned back around and started walking again. I once again heard the footsteps. The footsteps were getting closer and I clearly saw the shadow of a person. I was half way through the alley but I was scared. I turned around quickly. I heard a small thump and shuffling as I turned around. Still I did not see anyone in the alley. I stood there looking in the corners where nothing seemed to be moving. I knew someone was there. I knew it. Then I remembered the shadow. I looked down at the ground. At first I did not see anything suspicious. Then I saw a shadow move. The shadow was coming from behind a trash can by a telephone pole. The shadow was clearly a human. The pole was only six feet away from me. I considered looking closer but I was suddenly scared. I turned quickly and ran as fast as I could home. I heard someone running behind me. Luckily I made it out of the alley before I was caught. I ran straight for a group of kids near our house. When I reached them I told them I had snacks leftover and asked if they wanted them. The kids of course said yes. I just wanted people around me. Suddenly I did not want to be alone. I sat on the back porch steps surrounded by the kids. I looked back at the alley. I thought I saw a shadow move but then it was gone. I decided never to go in the alley alone again.

Mom was mad I gave away all the snacks. I got beat really bad that night. However, there was a part of me that was so distracted with what had happened in the alley that I only half felt the beating. A week later, Albert and Mom broke up. It turned out that Mom caught him in bed with Krista. Mom was mad at Krista for seducing him. Mom beat Krista multiple times before I was able to make her stop. As soon as school was over Mom moved us to a new town. Still when I look back at my life, many of my happiest childhood memories were from that place with C.J..

Chapter 41

We moved to a new town. I remember it was several hours away. Our new house was a small three bedroom house. We were on the town limits and the houses were close but not too close. Mom was able to start up the business in just one week. The first week Mom made me serve beverages to the men waiting to see my sisters. I also emptied ashtrays and sold cigarettes. The men would grab my butt as I walked by them. They would whistle and laugh. I thought they were all disgusting. I hated these horrible men. It was summer so Mom would make us work from right after lunch until way past dark. We only got a ten minute break for supper then we went back to work.

The second week Mom told me to stay in her room. She made me wear a white frilly dress. It looked like a little wedding dress. I would have loved the dress if I did not know what it meant. Mom said it was time to start pulling my weight around here. I was angry but knew I could not show Mom. So I turned my anger into annoyance. I told my mom that I would not allow the men to hurt me and that I would fight them off. Mom just laughed and said to try. That night the nightmare began.

I remember my first night of work like a cancer that attacks my soul. I can feel the memories eating me alive. I feel dirty and disgusting just remembering. A child's body was not designed to withstand the abuse I suffered. I was malnourished and small for my age. Every time I was penetrated I felt like I was being ripped apart. Like someone was taking a knife and stabbing me over and over again. I tried to fight them off but it was like a mouse trying to stop a river.

I was sold to four men that night. Mom said I was worth more than my sisters because I was younger. The first man talked to me as he came closer. When I backed into a wall he picked me up and carried me to the bed. He held me down and ???????"slobbered

all over me as he kissed me. I kicked him but he just pushed my legs aside and climbed between them. I tried to scratch his eyes but he just used one hand to hold each of mine. He slowly lowered himself inside me the first time. I screamed as loud as I could but he just kissed me to muffle the scream. Then he covered my mouth with his other hand. He began to thrust so hard that it hurt my stomach and legs. I thought he would break me. I begged for death in my mind. I thought it would never end. Finally he gave a big thrust and then a few small ones. Then he was done and out. I felt broken. He began to kiss me all over my face. He said thank you over and over again between kisses. Then he rose and put his clothes back on. He left with a final thank you.

I could barely move. Everything hurt. I leaned over the bed and threw up as Mom entered the room. She was furious that I threw up on the floor. I was in her bedroom. Mom sent me to her bathroom to clean up. She got mad when she saw how slow I was moving. I went as fast as I could but it hurt so much to move. I threw up one more time in the potty. Mom came in and gave me a sponge bath. I could barely move without hurting so she did it all. She told me to go lay down and rest. I sat on the bed not wanting to lay in the same spot that I was hurt so bad on. Mom finished cleaning up and then left.

I was still sitting there when another man came in a few minutes later. I began to cry and begged him not to hurt me. He laughed and said this was going to be fun. I fought him but I was weak from before. It was not easier the second time. Actually it was worse. He added new bruises and deepened the previous bruises. I did manage to scratch him on the cheek. I felt good that at least I hurt him a little. He did not thank me. He just got dressed and left. I felt like trash, used and discarded.

This time I cleaned myself. As soon as Mom left the room I hid in her closet. I heard the door open and close. I stayed real quiet. I heard the man moving around. Soon he opened the closet door. He saw me hiding in the corner and laughed. I grabbed at the door frame

as he pulled me out of the closet. He just yanked me and laughed. He said it would not hurt. I called him a liar. I kicked his evil penis when he tried to climb on the bed. He got really mad. He hit me so hard I blacked out. I woke up when he thrust inside me. I screamed from the pain. A pain so intense that it blocks out all other pain and thought. I began to fight him off. He leaned down and whispered that I was a sweet little whore. He said he would use me so good that I would always think of him. I was trapped. He had my hands pinned so I spit at him. He laughed and began to thrust harder. I screamed louder and he covered my mouth with his hand and laughed. When he finished he pushed me away like I was garbage. I rolled off the bed and half ran half crawled into the bathroom. I shut the door and wished it had a lock. I cried as I wiped off. I felt sick but only dry heaved in the potty. I hated my life and myself. Why wasn't I stronger?

Mom was mad that I had a fresh bruise on my face. She told me to be nicer to the men. I just ignored her. She was mean. Mom stayed in the room until the next man came in so I would not hide again. The next man came in carrying a book. Mom left and the man approached the bed. He said he just wanted to read me a story. He sat down on the bed and began to read the book. I loved to be read to and found myself moving closer to see the pictures. He had a deep voice. After a few pages I was seated beside him. He read the whole book. Then as he finished he shut the book and set it on the floor. Before I could scoot away he pounced. He used his weight to hold me down as he undressed. He was disturbed that I fought him. He kept telling me to relax. He said if I relaxed it would not hurt. I fought him and even knocked his glasses off twice. He entered me fast and hard. I screamed. He grabbed the sheet off the bed and shoved it into my mouth so hard I began to choke. I tried to take it out but he would not let me. He was done fast though. When he finished he said he would see me in a few days and left. He took his book with him. He said the book was a gift for his niece and he would think of me when he read it to her.

Mom let me take a shower. I felt so dirty. I could not get clean. When I literally could not stand any longer I turned off the shower. Mom changed her sheets and let me sleep there until my sisters were finished. I was so exhausted I fell asleep immediately. Mom woke me up the next day. I was in my own room in my own pajamas. I had fallen asleep in one of Mom's shirts. Mom said it was time for lunch and asked if I wanted anything. I said no and went back to sleep. I was so tired and sore.

I remember being awoken by laughter and noise a few times during the evening. I slept all evening. I woke before dawn the next day. I went outside and watched as the sun rose in the sky. I was crying as it rose. I felt lost and weak. Shayla found me on the back porch when she woke up. She did not say anything. She just sat down beside me and held my hand. I drew comfort from her for a few minutes until I remembered that I was supposed to comfort her not the other way around. I squeezed her hand then stood up. I helped Shayla to her feet and we went inside to get ready for the day. Once we were dressed we went to find breakfast. Mom was on the couch drinking coffee. I went to the cabinet and got the last box of cereal down. Shayla and I ate cereal at the table.

Chapter 42

After breakfast Shayla and I took our Barbie dolls to the front porch to play. I wanted out of the smoke filled house that always smelled like the evil that took place there. Krista joined us later on. Krista told me that it was about time that I had to work too. Krista said that now maybe I would not act all high and mighty all the time. I ignored her as a tear slowly traced a path down my cheek. Krista eventually went back inside.

Shayla and I were playing when a car pulled up to the house. We were about to run to the backyard when we saw that there were three women in the car. We breathed a sigh of relief and sat back

down. The three women got out of their car and smiled as they approached the house.

"Hello," I said as they climbed onto the steps.

"Hello, sweetie, is your Mom home," one of the ladies said as she looked at the front door.

"Mommy is inside. Who are you?" I asked the ladies.

"I am Roxie, this is Sandra, and this is Lucy. What are your names?" Roxie said.

"I am Samantha, and this is Shayla," I answered smiling at these nice ladies.

Mom came out onto the porch shutting the door behind her. She blew her smoke at the ladies. The ladies took a step back from her.

"What do you want?" Mom said rudely.

"Well, I am Roxie and this is..." Roxie began.

"I did not ask what your damn names were. I asked what you want?" Mom interrupted.

"Well, we are here from the Church of Christ in town. We were wondering if you would like to join us this Sunday," Roxie smiled sweetly at Mom undeterred by Moms glare.

I decided I liked Roxie. She was strong.

"We ain't interested," Mom said as she turned to go inside.

"Mommy, can we please go?" I jumped up and ran to Mom pleadingly.

"I am not going to waste my gas taking you to some stupid church," Mom said turning back around to glare at me.

"We have a church van that can pick her up from here if you would like," Sandra piped up.

"Please, Mommy, please. I really want to go," I begged Mom.

"Fine," Mom said as she turned and went into the house.

Mom slammed the door behind her. I turned and smiled at the ladies.

"Can my sisters come too?" I asked the ladies.

"The more the merrier. Are you sure your Mom will let you come?" Lucy responded.

"I think so. Do you pray to God? I had friends who always prayed to a man named God before they ate," I said eager for more information.

"Yes, we pray to God," Roxie chuckled as the other ladies smiled at me.

"The bus will be here to pick you up around nine am on Sunday," Sandra said.

"Ok, we will be ready," I said to the nice ladies.

"Have a wonderful day," Roxie said as the ladies turned to go.

I watched as the ladies got in their car and drove away. They waved as they backed out of the driveway. I felt a surge of hope. The magic house family always prayed to God. Did all prayers go to the same church? George told me once that God could hear and answer prayers? I wondered if I could meet God. Would God help us? I could not wait for Sunday.

That night my siblings and I had to work. I hated it. I fought the men as much as I could but it was to no avail. I had three men from the last time return plus two new men. The more I fought the more excited the men were. I hated all of them. I spat, I kicked, I bit, I scratched, I even head butted a few. Still I could not fight a single one off. Most of them just laughed at my attempts to stop them. I did ask one of them what day it was as he was leaving. He told me it was Friday the 12th of June. When I was finished for the night Mom let me fall asleep on her bed again until all the men were finished with my sisters.

When Mom came in to move me I was still awake. I had been fighting the urge to sleep for hours so I would not forget what I needed to do. Mom sent me to my room. I went in and made sure Shayla was tucked into bed. Then I grabbed a pen and ran into the living room to the calendar on the wall. I stood on a chair. I found the number 12 and put a small smiley face in the lower corner of the square. I then went to bed. I felt hopeful again. There was hope. On

Sunday I would meet God and he would magically help my family. Just like he helped the magic family.

I awoke so sore and stiff that it hurt to move. I still got up and went to the back porch. It was a little cloudy but not too cloudy to see the sunrise. It was beautiful. The sun made the clouds look pink and purple as it rose over the horizon. Once more I found myself wondering who painted the sunrise every morning. To me it seemed like each one was different and unique. I returned to my room. I was excited to see how many days were left until Sunday.

I woke up Shayla and we both got dressed for the day. We had so many bruises that we had to wear pants to hide them. The clothes rubbed against the bruises making them hurt more. We went out for breakfast but there was only one slice of cheese and one piece of bread in the kitchen. Mom and Benny were on the couch eating toast and eggs. They must have been the last eggs. I gave the last of the cheese and bread to Krista and Shayla to share. I approached Mom slowly.

"Mommy, good morning," I said in greeting.

"Good morning, princess," Mom said as she took another bite of food.

"Mommy, we are out of food. When can we go shopping?" I asked.

"God Damn It! Fuck! All you selfish brats want to do is spend money. Money does not grow on trees. You want food then you brats need to earn some more money, damn it," Mom fumed.

"I am sorry, Mommy. I didn't mean to make you mad," I said, backing away from her.

"No, I am sorry. It is ok. You just don't know how hard it is to make money. We don't have enough for food yet but when I go to get the alcohol and my cigarettes for tonight I will pick up a pizza for you kids, if you are good. Then, if you work hard tonight, I will buy some more groceries tomorrow," Mom compromised.

"Ok, Mommy, I love you," I said.

"I love you, too, princess. Now run along and play so Mommy can watch TV in peace," Mom said dismissing me.

Shayla and I took our baby dolls and baby doll clothes to the front porch to play house. Mom left about an hour later. Benny went with her. I jumped up and ran to my room. I grabbed a pen and went to the living room. I marked a little smiley face on the bottom corner of the square. Tomorrow was Sunday. I could not wait. I put my pen away. I went into Krista's room. She was coloring on her bed.

"Hello, Krista," I said as I entered her room.

"Hello, brat," Krista said, not looking up from her coloring book.

"Shayla and I are going to church tomorrow. Do you want to come?" I asked.

Krista sat up on her bed and looked at me.

"What time are you going?" She asked.

"The church bus will be here around nine?" I answered.

"That's too early," Krista said, laying back down and returning to her coloring.

"I can wake you up," I suggested.

"No, I don't want to," Krista said.

"It will be fun," I coaxed.

"I said no, now get out of my room before I make you," Krista yelled.

I left her room and returned to the porch. Shayla was still there playing with the dolls. Mom came home about two hours later. Mom was angry but I did not know why. Mom told us to help her carry everything inside. Shayla and I carried a 24 pack of beer together. It was too heavy for us to lift otherwise. Benny and Mom carried in the rest. I did not see a pizza. We took the beer into the kitchen where Mom was unpacking the alcohol.

"Mommy, where is the pizza," I asked Mom.

"God Damn It to Hell. No, welcome back, no hello, Mom, we missed you, just where is what I want! You ungrateful bitch!" Mom sprang on me.

Mom had knocked me to the floor so I scrunched up into a small ball and covered my face. Mom just kept hitting me. I don't

even know why she was hitting me. Mom hit me hard on the top of my head then stopped.

Chapter 43

The rest of the day seemed to go quickly. We put the alcohol in the refrigerator and cleaned the house while Mom smoked and drank coffee. That evening, Mom sat at the table by the door. The front door was open but the screen door was closed. There were storm clouds outside beyond the door. I had just finished putting up my toys and was returning to the living room.

"Take a shower and clean yourself up. I will put your clothes in the bathroom. Get dressed then come see me," Mom said.

I went into the bathroom and shut the door. I slowly undressed.. The spray of water hurt my bruises as it fell. I winced as I washed myself. I knew I was crying but the shower was a really safe place to cry. When you cried in the shower no one could tell that you had been crying. Finally I was finished.

I stepped out of the shower and began to dry myself with a towel. I looked for my clothes and groaned when I saw them. There on the small counter by the sink was the white dress. I had to work tonight. My stomach and head still hurt and now I would be hurt more. I slowly put on the clothes. I hated my life. No, I hated the work. I had to hold onto my hope. It would be fine. One more day and then I would meet God and he would fix everything. He would give Mommy all the money she needed so she would never get angry again and she would never make us work again.

I walked out of the bathroom and down the hall to find Mom. Mom was standing by her table laughing and giggling with a man. The man was here to see me. I recognized him as the book reader. Mom was touching his arm and talking to him.

"Hello, Mommy," I said to Mom.

"Oh, sugar, come meet Steve. Isn't he cute? Did you know that Steve is the mayor's son. He is an attorney downtown," Mom said as she stood beside Steve holding his hand.

"I met him," I said, taking a step back.

"Well, Steve just asked me out for tomorrow. Isn't he great?" Mom beamed.

"Yes, Mommy," I said as a knot formed in my stomach.

"Well, enough with this. Go in my bedroom and I will send the first client in," Mom said to me.

I slowly walked into her room. I felt sick. I hated my mom for what she did to us. However, she was my mom and I wanted to love her. I needed to love her. I just felt so confused. I immediately hid under the bed when I went into the room. The closet hadn't worked last time. Maybe this time they would not find me.

I saw the door open and close. The man paused after shutting the door. He then went into the bathroom. Then he checked the closet.

"Come out, come out, wherever you are," the man chuckled as he looked for me.

Finally, he looked under the bed and grinned as he pulled me out from under the bed.

"Please don't hurt me. Please," I begged him as he pushed me down onto the bed.

He never answered me. I begged and pleaded. I kicked and screamed. I bit his arm and spat at him. He was undeterred. When he finished he just got up to get dressed.

"Thanks, sweetheart, I will see you next week," He said before he left the room.

I went into the bathroom and cleaned up the best I could. I then went and hid behind Mom's corner dresser. The last guy never looked back here. A few minutes later a new man entered the room. I could not see him from my hiding place but I could hear him cursing and looking around. Then I heard the man leave the room. I heard distant yelling and then Mom entered the room with the man. Mom

began to curse and look around the room. She was getting madder by the minute.

"Samantha, I know you can hear me. Get out here this minute or I swear I will make you regret it," Mom yelled.

I was too scared to move. If I left my hiding spot I would be hurt. If I didn't I would be hurt. I was too terrified to move.

"Fine, you don't care about your own punishment. If you do not get out here immediately I will beat your sister within an inch of her life and then permanently sell her to a biker gang. You will never see Shayla again. Lord knows we would be better off without that beast!" Mom yelled.

"I'm here. Don't hurt Shayla, Mommy. I will be good," I said running out of my hiding place.

Mom stomped over and slapped me hard across the face. She told me if I ever pulled something like this again she would kill Shayla. Then she left cursing as she went. I stood there watching the man come closer. I backed against the wall.

"Are you ok?" the man asked as he knelt in front of me.

"Please don't hurt me," I cried.

The man picked me up and carried me into the bathroom. He got a clean washcloth and ran it under the cold water. He then brought it to my cheek. My mouth was bleeding a little. I was shaking from terror. He cleaned my face. Then he knelt down to kiss my hurt cheek. Then he did not stop kissing me. I pushed him away but my back was against the medicine cabinet above the sink. I was trapped. He spread my legs. His breathing got louder and I tried to fight him. He took both my hands in one of his. He hurt me right there on the sink counter. Then he left like nothing happened. I just felt hurt and angry.

I did not hide from the men the rest of the night. There were two more men. One was one that I recognized from the first night I worked. The last one was Steve. Steve grinned when he came into the room.

"Just call me daddy from now on, sweetheart," Steve joked as he came towards the bed where I was cowered against the headboard.

Steve laughed as I tried to fight him off. He was not so fast tonight. It hurt so much every time he thrust into me. He just kept kissing me. He was holding my hands above my head with one hand and touching me all over with the other. He was holding my hands too tight and it hurt bad. I tried to kick him but it was like a fish trying to stop a wave. Eventually, he was done. He whispered in my ear that he could not wait to do this every night. Then he was gone.

I was done for the night so Mom let me take a shower while she changed the sheets. She was mad that I had gotten blood on them and said she would have to throw them and my dress away. I ignored her and got into the shower. I hurt all over. When Mom finally left her room I got out of the shower. I still felt dirty but the water was too cold to stay in. I shivered as I looked for my clothes. Mom had left me some underwear and a nightgown on her newly made bed. I got dressed and climbed into the bed. I was too tired to care where I slept. I fell asleep immediately.

Mom woke me in the middle of the night and told me to go to my own room. I sleepily went to my bed and climbed under the covers. I fell asleep immediately. My head still hurt.

Dawn woke me up. I saw the light getting brighter in my window and rushed to the back porch to watch it. I had missed half of it but it was still beautiful. It was Sunday. Today I was going to meet God. I rushed back inside to wake Shayla and get ready for church. Shayla and I got dressed for the day in the best dresses we owned. When I went out to the living room Mom was not there. I tiptoed to her door and peeked inside. Benny was asleep in Mom's bed. I heard the shower running and figured Mom was in the shower. I shut her door and checked on Krista. Krista was asleep in her bed. I returned to the living room to Shayla.

"Shayla, go to your room and pick out one baby doll to take with us today," I said.

As soon as Shayla went into her room I ran to Mom's purse. I grabbed her money and took out twelve twenties. That should be enough. I ran to my room and hid the money with the rest of my money stash. Shayla had picked out her favorite baby doll and dressed it in the nicest baby doll dress she owned. I grabbed Hope. Then we went to the porch to wait for the bus. Neither one of us could tell time so we just had to hope we were not too late. While Shayla waited for the bus I went inside to look for food. There was still no food so I returned to the porch to wait for the bus. I was really hungry but tried to ignore my rumbling tummy.

I heard Mom moving around inside the house. Then I saw a nice car park in the driveway. Steve was behind the wheel. Steve winked at me when he saw me sitting there in my best dress. Steve got out of the car and strode to the porch. Mom came outside and they kissed. Then Steve and Mom left. I don't even think Mom saw Shayla and I sitting on the porch. She was so excited for her date with Steve. Mom had been dressed in a very nice dress and heels. I wondered where they were going so early.

Finally, a van pulled into the driveway. I was expecting a big yellow bus so I was a little worried. A man got out and walked toward the porch. I nudged Shayla awake as the man stopped at the bottom of the porch steps.

"Are you the kids waiting for the church bus?" the strange man asked.

"Yes, but that is not a bus," I answered.

"Well, you are right. It is not a bus but we use this van as a church bus," the man laughed.

"Really?" I said.

"Really," the man said.

"How do we know you are not tricking us?" I asked standing up and motioning for Shayla to stand as well. If we needed to run I wanted to be ready.

"Lucy was one of the women who invited you to church, right?" the man asked.

"Yes...." I answered.

"Well, Lucy is my wife and if you look in the windshield right there you will see her talking to a friend in the back seat," the man said pointing.

Sure enough, in the front seat was Lucy. She was half turned facing the back of the van but I still recognized her.

"Ok, I believe you. Let's go Shayla," I said as I walked off the porch.

"My name is Adam, what are your names?" Adam asked as he helped us into the van and buckled us in the first row.

"My name is Samantha. This is Shayla. She is shy," I answered him.

"Well, it is nice to meet you both," the man said as he shut the door.

The church was a big brick and glass building on the main street of the town. There were a lot of cars parked in the parking lot. The bus dropped us off at the main door to the church. Lucy got out of the church bus and walked us inside. There were so many people there. All the people wore really nice clothes and looked so fancy. I looked all around wondering which one was God. Lucy led us down to the basement. The basement had many different classrooms. Lucy introduced us to Becky who asked us some questions about our ages and grades. Becky then led us down a hall. Shayla panicked when Becky said that the third door on the right was my classroom while Shayla's classroom was the last one on the left. I comforted Shayla and assured her it was just like school. Shayla was scared of all the fancy people. Becky and I walked Shayla to her classroom before returning to my own classroom. When we reached the door to my classroom I turned to Becky.

"Where is God?" I asked, eager to meet the man who would answer my prayers.

"God is everywhere, Samantha," Becky said smiling at me.

"Yes, but where? Can you introduce me?" I asked.

"What do you know about God?" Becky asked kneeling down to look me in the eye.

"Well, God is a man who answers peoples prayers. He is going to help my family. But I don't know what he looks like. What does he look like?" I answered her.

"Yes, God does answer prayers but it does not work quite like that. Why does your family need help?" Becky said, really seeming to listen to me.

"Mommy says we need more money. She makes us work. We need money to buy some food. We are out of food again," I explained.

"Oh, sweetie. Is your Mom with you today?" Becky said looking down the hall.

"No, she is on a date with Steve. Steve is a very bad, mean man," I told her.

"Okay. Well, go to your classroom. Your teacher's name is Kelly. Kelly will tell you more about God and help you understand. In the meantime I will see what we can do to help your family. Has your sister or you eaten today?" Becky asked.

"No," I answered.

"When was the last time you ate?" Becky said, looking sad.

"A few days ago. Shayla ate a little yesterday morning though," I answered.

"Okay, Samantha, thank you for talking to me. Is it ok if I hug you?" Becky replied with tears in her eyes.

I nodded yes. Becky scooped me into her arms. Her hug was warm and comforting. I didn't even mind the pain when she squeezed my recent bruises. I felt safe and wished the hug would last forever. I don't know why but I did feel safe here. When she released me she opened the classroom door and introduced me to Kelly. Then Becky and Kelly whispered to each other a few minutes while I sat on the floor with the other kids. My nicest dress looked a little shabby next to some of the girls dresses. Becky left and Kelly began to talk to us about God. I was expecting some magical man who could grant my prayers like a genie grants wishes. I listened raptly as Becky explained about a perfect father who loved us completely and would do anything to protect us. A father who lived

in heaven and who would never hurt us. A father who wanted to protect us. A father who loved me. ME. A father who loved ME. I had never had a father. I listened with a hunger I didn't even know I had. This was better than any genie. I now had a father. God was my father. God would never hurt me like Mom. God would never choke me like Krista. God would protect me as long as I was good. I would be the best girl for God. I was determined.

In what seemed like a very short time, Becky returned with snacks. She had graham crackers with peanut butter and raisins on top. She had fruit in a bowl. She had lots of juice boxes. It looked like a feast. I was so hungry. The kids and I sat around a table as she passed out the food. They prayed over the food and then the other kids and I began to eat. When I was finished with my first graham cracker I raised my hand. Kelly came over and asked me what I needed.

"May I take some food to my sister Shayla?" I asked Kelly.

"We already did. We took them some food before we came here. She is eating right now," Kelly replied.

"May I take the leftovers home then? Krista did not come with us. She is my other sister," I explained.

"I will bag it for you before you leave today," Kelly said, rubbing my back.

Kelly gave me an extra graham cracker before she went to help someone else with their juice box. I was so hungry I ended up eating four graham crackers. I guess I ate too much because I accidently threw up a little on the floor. I was trying to reach the trash can but could not make it. I was afraid they would beat me like Mom would have. Instead they rubbed my back. Then they helped me clean myself up while someone else cleaned up the mess. After I was cleaned up they took me to the kitchen where they had me sip water before giving me a few apple slices to settle my stomach. This time I nibbled the food. I felt better after that. They were so nice to me. It was really nice to have someone take care of me. It made me miss Stacy.

My dress was dirty so they found me a new dress from a pile of clothes that had been donated. The dress was much nicer than the one I had and made me feel like a princess. I thanked them for the beautiful gift. I finally returned to the same classroom. When it was time to go Lucy returned to take us back to the church bus that was not a real bus. When we reached the house I was surprised when Lucy and Adam both got out of the van. Adam opened the back of the van and I saw bags of food and clothes. It was like God really had heard my prayers. Lucy, Shayla, Adam and I carried bags inside. Lucy explained that when I was in church one of the people at church heard about us needing help and had left church immediately and bought us groceries. Mom was still gone so Lucy and Adam put away all the groceries. Then Lucy made us lunch while Adam started to clean the house. After lunch Lucy said she was uncomfortable leaving us alone so together Lucy, Krista, Shayla, Adam and I cleaned the house. We opened the windows to get fresh air inside. When the house was clean and two loads of laundry were washed, dried, and put away, Lucy and Adam took us all out for ice cream except for Benny who was refusing to leave the basement. I wished Lucy and Adam were my parents. They were so nice and considerate. Plus, Adam told the best jokes and never once tried to hurt me or my sisters. Mom was still not back when we got back to the house but Lucy and Adam could not stay any longer. They left us their phone number and told us to lock the doors and call if we needed help.

My sisters and I went back inside. The house smelled so much better now that the windows were open and it was clean. We watched an animated movie on TV while eating dinner. Mom was not back by nightfall so we all went to bed. Unfortunately we did not have locks on our bedroom doors in this house. I hoped we would be safe for the night. I fell asleep watching my bedroom door doorknob terrified it would turn and Steve would enter.

Chapter 44

It was still dark outside my window when I woke up. I sat up in bed and looked around. I was groggy and only half awake. Why was I awake? I pulled back the covers and got out of bed. I walked to the door and listened. Maybe Mom was home. I opened the door and looked out. The hallway had no windows so it was dark. I walked down the hallway and opened Shayla's door. Shayla was asleep. She had kicked the blankets off during the night and I quietly and gently recovered her. I shut her bedroom door behind me. I went to Krista's bedroom door. I opened her door slowly. Steve was holding Krista down and raping her. She was struggling against him but he just kept thrusting into her and panting like a dog. I ran over and jumped on the bed. I grabbed onto his neck from behind and started ripping out his hair.

Steve and I were both screaming. Steve let go of Krista and began trying to get me off of him. He hit me but I would not let go. For one thing, I was afraid to let go because I feared that he would turn on me. For another thing, when he let Krista go he stood up and suddenly I just did not know how to get down. I just kept pulling his hair and trying to choke him. He began to run around the room naked and screaming and cursing. He banged me against the wall several times before I fell off of him. Just then Mom, Benny and Shayla came rushing into the room. Before anyone could react, Steve picked me back up and threw me across the room. I remember flying and then utter blackness. Peaceful slumber. I sunk down into the darkness gladly.

It hurt. I was wandering through the darkness with tall trees everywhere. I was alone but something seemed to be chasing me. I did not see anyone behind me but I knew someone was behind me. I ran faster but the trees were a maze. It was dark among the trees. I looked for the sun or moon but the leaves were too thick. I could not find my way out. Where were the roads or paths? I had to escape. I saw light far up ahead and ran for the salvation. I jumped over a fallen tree. On the other side was a little brown haired puppy. I could

not leave the puppy. I bent down to quickly pick it up so we could run to the light. Suddenly something grabbed me from behind. I woke up screaming in pain and fear.

I quickly stopped screaming and laid back down. My head was pounding. I looked around the room. I was alone. The sun was shining bright through my window. My body hurt everywhere. I had soiled my bed. Slowly the memory of what happened came back to me. I remember the fear and yet the determination to protect Krista. I slowly sat up but the movement made me nauseous. I pulled the blanket off and stood up. I had to check on Krista. I had to. I quickly took the bedclothes off the bed and threw them by the door. I changed into clean clothes for the day and put my soiled pajamas on the pile by the door.

I went to the door and opened it. There was no one in the hall. I went to Shayla's room, it was empty. The house was so quiet. I walked down to Krista's room. The door was open. I stepped into the empty room. I remembered what had happened the night before. I looked around. I walked to the far side of the room. On the wall about four feet from the floor was a big dent in the wall. I slowly raised my hand and touched the dent. I was crying a little and felt the tears run down my cheeks. I turned and walked out of the room. I closed the door behind me. I did not have time to deal with that now. I had to find my sisters. It was my job to take care of them.

I went downstairs. The house was so quiet. I went into the living room but no one was there. I went into the kitchen, it was empty. Where were my sisters? I was thirsty and my head hurt. I got a glass of water. I went to the living room and put the water on the coffee table. I walked to the front door. I opened the door and stepped out on the porch. Mom's car was gone. I looked down the street. I did not see her or my sisters so I went back inside. I was tired. I sat down on the couch and drank some of the water. My stomach hurt but I was too tired. I laid down on the couch. I fell asleep quickly.

I woke up in the dark. I had forgotten to shut and lock the door. I looked out the screen door and saw the dim light of dawn. I got up and walked to the back door. I stepped out on the porch and watched the sun rise. I felt better. I no longer felt nauseous. My head still hurt but not as bad as before. I went back inside. I locked the back door and then went to the front porch. I saw that Mom's car was still gone. I went back inside and locked the door behind me. After going to the restroom, I went into the kitchen. There was some lunch meat so I made myself two sandwiches. I was so hungry. I sat down and ate them quickly. I put my dishes in the sink and checked the house. I even went to the basement. I did not see anyone. I was alone.

Mom did not return for three more days. I spent the time learning to do the laundry and the dishes. Since Lucy and Adam gave us the groceries, I had plenty of food. I actually enjoyed the quiet. I did miss my sisters though. I ran to greet Mom when I finally heard her car pull into the driveway.

"Mommy, Mommy, where were you? I missed you!" I said as I opened the door and ran into her arms.

Mom hugged me for only a second and then she pulled me off of her. I looked up into her eyes. She did not look happy.

"Mommy, I love you," I pleaded.

"I love you, too, Sissy. I just did not know if you would be ok. Is anyone else with you?" Mom said in a funny tone as she looked behind me and then turned to look down the street.

"No one is here. I have not seen anyone since I woke up. Where are my sisters?" I said looking towards Mom's empty car.

"I will tell you everything in a few minutes but first you have to promise me no one is here," Mom said kneeling down and looking me in the eyes.

"I promise, Mommy," I said. I was a little scared. Mom was acting funny and I did not like it.

"I believe you. Let's get inside and I will tell you everything," Mom said as she pushed me inside.

Mom led the way to the living room and told me to sit on the couch. She locked the door and then went room to room checking the house. She eventually came back downstairs and went to the kitchen. She returned with a beer and sat down beside me. I watched her take a big drink.

"What do you remember?" Mom asked me, looking at me seriously.

"I remember Steve hurting Krista and I tried to stop him and he threw me against the wall. I woke up alone, Mommy. Where were you? Where are my sisters? Why did you leave me behind?" I asked as tears slowly slid down my cheeks.

"That is not what happened. I will tell you what really happened but first you have to stop that stupid whining. You know I hate crying. It is fucking annoying," Mom said as she took another drink.

I wiped the tears away with my dress collar. I then looked at Mom and waited patiently.

"Steve did not hurt Krista. Krista seduced him. I punished her good for that. That whore is always trying to seduce my men. She needs to back off or I will kill her one of these days. She is such a whore. I have made her work twice as much since Steve. Maybe I can screw her whorish ways out of her. You walked in on them and Steve just panicked a little. He did not mean to hurt you. Honestly, we thought you were dead. You were so still. We waited a whole day but when you did not wake we thought you were going to die so Steve suggested we leave for a few days to let nature take its course. I felt so bad leaving you like that but what could I do? I put you back in your bed and tucked you in. I have felt so guilty and sad. Steve has been my rock. We figured we would return and deal with the body later. You should see how distraught Steve is over all of this. He has been helping me with the business since we left. He set us up with a place across town and has even brought in more customers. I am glad you are not dead. A few of the customers would love to meet you. I felt so bad. I have been missing you every day. You should not worry Mommy like that," Mom said as she hugged me tight.

I felt so confused. I thought Mom would have known that Steve was the bad guy but she loved him now more than ever.

"Mommy, what day is it?" I said as her words of waiting a whole day before leaving finally clicked. How long did I sleep?

"Today is Saturday, honey," Mom said as she stood up to take her empty can to the trash.

"Are you going to bring my sisters back?" I asked as I followed her.

"I will bring them back tonight after they work. I could use a few days off. I got to tell you, I am exhausted. Running a business as a single woman is hard," Mom said as she returned to the living room and headed for her purse.

"Mommy, are Krista and Shayla ok?" I asked, scared for my sisters. I was here when they needed me to help them.

"Their fine, they are just as spoiled as ever. You should have heard Krista and Shayla crying and complaining because they had to work again. I swear those bitches are so ungrateful," Mom said on her way out the door.

Her words sent a chill down my spine. I was terrified. Mom left quickly. Almost like she was never there. I stared after her car for a long time before I went back inside.

Chapter 45

Mom stayed with Steve for three more months. We commuted to work every other weeknight. We worked every Friday and Saturday, however Mom started to always give us Sundays off. It was a small charity but one I relished. All week long I would countdown to Sunday. My father's day. Mom moved us after she dumped Steve. We moved every 3 to 8 months. Sometimes we would just move to another part of town. Sometimes we moved hours away. Occasionally a man or woman from the government, they always wore business suits or skirt sets, would show up and we would move immediately. Mom said they were family services and wanted to hurt us. We were always moving. I lost Hope when we

moved after Mom dumped Steve. More than once I lost the money I had collected. I was a kid who hid the money in toys. So if I left the toy I lost the money. With all the moving we also lost or left behind a lot of our possessions. We did not have much to begin with so the loss was very noticeable. However, more than once we had to pack up in less than an hour. Things were easy to lose.

Krista became more aggressive as we got older. She repeatedly choked me and often wouldn't stop until I was unconscious. I don't know why she hated me so much. I thought she blamed me for everything that was happening to us, however it was happening to me too. I thought it was Mom's fault. Or maybe Mom was right and it was because we were so poor. Still, I never dreamed of blaming Krista so I did not understand why she would blame me. It made no sense to me. Shayla and I just grew closer together. I took care of her and she grew accustomed to my inability to sleep and would sometimes lay close to me so I could sleep. Sleep grew harder and harder for me. I was so afraid to fall asleep because I did not know who would come into my room next. I had horrible nightmares when I slept. I hated to sleep. I was terrified. My home was not safe. I tried more than once to convince my sisters to run away with me. They always refused. Krista wanted me and Shayla to leave without her. She was convinced that if Shayla and I were not around Mom would treat her better and never make her work again. Shayla decided that Benny was her soul mate and refused to leave him. I could never leave my sisters. I loved them more than I loved myself.

Mom always managed to find a boyfriend in every town we went to. The boyfriends would hurt us girls or ignore us. One of them started to hurt Benny but when Mom found out she attacked the man and the man hurt Mom really bad. Mom recovered and we moved immediately. Benny began to visit Shayla often and Shayla kept saying she was in love. That made me feel really confused. He was our brother. Plus, Benny was always hurting us. He also started creeping around trying to watch us dress. That made me uncomfortable. Benny would also try to rape me. Most of the time I

could get him to leave me alone. However, a few times he succeeded in restraining me and raping me. I did not like him.

So, I am just going to give the highlights of the clients over the next three years. They were always coming. It was like every man on earth had a little evil in them. I could always tell by the way they looked at me which men had given in to their darkest evil. It was the men who looked at me like they were starving and I was a delicious feast. My stomach would churn every time some man looked at me that way. Still, I did not blame the men. The men always told me that they could not control themselves. They said they were unable to endure the temptation. I began to resent my mom though. I still loved her. I needed her. However, if she was not selling us, these men would not be hurting us. She opened the door to these men. She allowed it. She profited from it. She was the cause. I realized that while men are capable of giving in to their evilest desires, it is women who open the door. Women could be more evil than any man. It is women who are capable of creating hell on earth. Women who can be the most untrustworthy. I loved my mother, but I no longer trusted her.

One of the regular clients would call me Mary when he was raping me. I was so busy fighting him that I did not think anything of it until one day when I was playing at the park. I was on the merry go round with a little girl who told me her name was Mary. Suddenly the merry go round stopped spinning and there was the bad man. I was immediately terrified he would grab me and take me away to rape me. Instead, as I sat there in complete terror the girl squealed, "Daddy" he scooped her up and walked away. The girl was just one year younger than me. I sat there staring after them. He took her to a nearby car and she hopped into the back seat. He then turned and smiled back at me. I was supposed to be off work that night. I was getting ready for bed when he showed up at the house that night. He agreed to pay double to have me for half an hour. My mother looked hungrily at the money and took it. He took me into my mom's room and threw me on the bed as I began to cry. I fought him but he just

held me down and yanked my legs apart. He was in a hurry. He was breathing hard and panting like crazy. When he finished he told me how excited he got when he saw me playing with his daughter. He told me the desire was so intense he could barely wait to visit me. He got up and as he walked out of the room he said he hoped to see me at the park again soon. I never visited that park again.

Then there was the guy who tried to get me to call him daddy. When I refused he started hitting me. I still refused to call him daddy. He beat me so bad I was in bed for two weeks. Everywhere was bruised. I could barely move. Mom refused to let him use me again. However, when she threatened to not let him see any of us he showed her a badge. He was a detective or something. He threatened Mom. Mom started letting him see Shayla. Shayla was willing to call him daddy. He only hit her a few times and nowhere near what he did to me. I felt bad for Shayla and a little guilty. Still, I was glad I did not call him daddy. The church had taught me what a heavenly father is and I began to see a daddy as a sacred being. God was my daddy.

The last client I will tell you about is actually one of the worst if you can believe it. Mom usually only sold us for a half hour at a time. However, one day Mom made me pack some of my best clothes for a weekend. She said I was going on a trip. I assumed she was taking me on a special trip for the two of us. Instead, she drove us to a grocery store parking lot. My mom put me in the backseat of a man's big SUV. The man just grinned at me from the front seat. I asked Mom where I was going. She told me that the man was buying me for the whole weekend. She acted like I had won some big prize. She told me I would have lots of fun. The man and Mom talked a few minutes about meeting back in the parking lot in three days. Then the man handed Mom a big envelope. I saw Mom open it and saw it was filled with money. Mom grinned and turned back to our old vehicle. The man started driving. He stopped by a McDonalds after a few hours. He bought me a happy meal. The weird thing was he never talked to me. He just kept grinning at me in the rearview

mirror. I was terrified and did not say anything. I was so scared I could not even eat, even though I had not eaten since the previous day. Finally, the car slowed. We turned into a long driveway. I came over a hill and I saw ten or more cars parked in front of this big house. At first I was filled with hope. With all these cars surely nothing bad can happen to me. There would be too many witnesses. Plus all the cars were really nice and looked new. The house was also really nice. It was one of the biggest and nicest houses I had ever seen. The man parked the car and helped me out of the car. He picked up my suitcase and took my hand. We walked up to the front porch. I was in awe looking at this beautiful house. We went inside. The house looked amazing. There was a large staircase. The man took me down a large hall and opened two large doors on our right. There were about twenty men standing around this bar drinking and laughing. The room got quiet when they saw me. The terror immediately came over me. I was standing in a doorway of a room where all the men were looking at me like they were starving and I was food. It was one of the worst weekends of my life. I remember it all. Sunday didn't even save me that weekend. The men passed me around over and over again. When they were not passing me around they were drinking and smoking big, fat and brown cigarettes. When the man finally said it was time to go I could not even stand. He had to carry me to the vehicle. He had laid down several towels on the backseat and the floor. He said he did not want my blood in his car. I was so sad the tears would not stop. I hurt everywhere. The men had not hit me but they did hurt me. When I finally saw my mom I was actually grateful. Mom only gave me three days off. Most of the time I just spent in bed crying. Shayla would lay beside me and stroke my hair as much as she could. By the fourth day, Mom had lost her patience and informed me I needed to pull my weight in this family. She said I needed to stop pouting. She made me work that night.

Mom was always more abusive if she had to get a job. She only got a job if we moved to a town where she couldn't start her business. She also started getting mad at the government. She said if

the government would butt out of our business then we wouldn't have to move so much. She also warned us repeatedly about the police. She said that if they captured us we would be tortured. One day, I brought home from school a letter letting Mom know that the police would be in school to talk to us the next day. Mom freaked out. She demanded to know everything I knew but I did not know anything. Mom kept me home from school the next day. She said she was saving my life. She said if the police came and took my fingerprints then they would take me away and I would never see her or my sisters again. I grew to be terrified of the police. I did not want them to torture me. I did not want to lose my sisters. My sisters were all I truly had.

Chapter 46

Mom said I was ten when we moved to a small town called LaMonte. We moved to a small trailer park in the middle of town. It was August so school was about to start. Mom was excited to start up her business. I was looking forward to school. They fed you breakfast and lunch at school. Mom would still go days without feeding my sisters and I. Mom and Benny ate several times a day. I was old enough to remember the name of our town and was eager to learn how to read more. I could read a little but we moved so much I could barely read Spot books. In my last school my classmates could read bigger and more colorful books than me. I wanted to read better this year.

We had the weirdest trailer we had ever lived in. It had four rooms. There was even an upstairs. The living room was at the front of the trailer. The living room door was the only door in or out of the trailer. Off the living room on one side was the master bedroom on the other side was the kitchen that opened up to the living room. The bathroom was beside the kitchen through a sliding door that looked like the paneling throughout the trailer so that when the door was

shut it was hidden. Past the kitchen was a very small hallway that ended in a very small bedroom. This bedroom had two sets of built in bunk beds on each side. There was only about three feet of space between the beds. There was also a built in Armoire with two drawers and a cabinet to hang our clothes. This was Shayla's and mine room. Beside the door to the room was a small stairway. This stairway led to the upstairs. When you went upstairs there was a small room on the right with a built in bed and a built in dresser. This was Krista's room. To the left of the stairs was a space that looked like a large shelf. This area was meant to be for storage but Mom put a mattress up there for a bed. This would be Benny's room whenever he did not sleep with Mom. Mom had Benny just keep his clothes in boxes beside his mattress.

I liked the new house. I hoped it would be too small for Mom to start up her business. That made me feel safe. School was starting soon and Mom said we were close enough to walk. She drove us to school on the first day so that we would know the way. I had worn some of my best clothes for the first day of school. The last place we lived we had to leave in a hurry and I had lost most of my clothes and all my toys but one. Still, I tried to wear my best. It was an old and worn plaid dress. I also had a bow in my hair. I had dressed Shayla in her favorite shorts and t-shirt. Krista wore a jean skirt and a tight top. I was so hopeful to start school. We arrived early so we could eat breakfast. I sat with Shayla but Krista went to sit with a bunch of girls across the room. I looked around at the other kids. There were only about fifty kids in the large room. They all wore nicer clothes than me. I hoped they would like me. I felt nervous. After breakfast a teacher took Shayla and I to our separate classroom.

My teacher was named Mrs. Wilcox. She looked nice and smiled at me sweetly. She introduced me to the class. Two girls in the second row whispered to each other and giggled. They were looking at me. I felt self-conscious and blushed. Mrs. Wilcox showed me to my seat. I sat down and watched as the teacher got me

a workbook and supplies to put in my desk. I had nothing. Mom never bought us school supplies. She always said she never had the money but she always had money for cigarettes and alcohol. The teacher asked me if I had a backpack. I told her no. She gave me an extra one that she had. She put it on a hook in the back of the room. Then the teacher began class. No one talked to me. I felt shy. At recess, we all went outside. Unfortunately, Shayla's class had a different recess time. Whenever I asked if I could play with someone they would run away or say no. I felt sad so I went over to a corner of the playground. I sat on the grass and began making dolls out of the grass and flowers.

"What are you making?" a girl with sandy brown hair was standing just a few feet away.

I hadn't even heard her approach. I was a little startled but she was smiling at me.

"Their dolls. The grass dolls are boys and the girls are flowers," I answer smiling back at this kind girl.

She sat down across from me and picked up one of the girls and one of the boys.

"These are cool. Can I play with you?" The girl asked.

"Yes, that would be fun," I answered, blinking back tears.

"Your name is Samantha, right?" She asked.

"Yes, what is your name?" I asked, eager to make her my friend.

"My name is Missy. Do you want to play princess and prince with your dolls?" Missy asked.

"Sure," I said smiling.

We played together until the end of recess. None of the other kids bothered us. I made one friend. We went back to class. The rest of the day we stayed in the classroom. Missy sat across the room but she would occasionally look at me and smile. None of the other kids were nice to me. Most of them ignored me. At the end of the day, I met Shayla at the front of the school. Shayla had had a bad day. The other kids had made fun of her all day and called her a retard. I tried to comfort her as we waited for Krista. Eventually Krista came out to

meet us. She was smiling. We began to walk home and Krista told us all about her day. She talked nonstop. She said all the girls were snobby but one. She had a new friend named Becky. Becky was cool because she had a hamster for a pet. Then she told us that she met a boy at lunch. He said he wanted to be her secret boyfriend.

"What's a secret boyfriend?" I asked, confused.

"A secret boyfriend is a boyfriend you don't tell anyone about. He is a senior and does not date eighth graders. He also has another girlfriend. But he says I am so beautiful and he loves me. He says it was love at first sight," Krista explained.

"Why doesn't he break up with the other girlfriend if he loves you?" I asked, even more confused.

"He will, he just is going to wait for the right time. He does not want to hurt her. Oh, did I mention he has a truck. He can drive," She squealed with excitement.

After that we listened as Krista told us how they had snuck away and made out. I felt suspicious about the guy but was afraid to voice my doubts. Krista was so excited. When we got home Mom and Benny were not there so we let ourselves in. Krista went to watch TV. Shayla and I went to our room. I showed Shayla my new book bag and told her about all the supplies my teacher gave me. I also told her about my new friend Missy. Shayla then told me about the mean boys who had picked on her at recess. She told me that the girls in her class had made fun of her and pulled her hair. We sat on my bed as I hugged her while she just cried. She asked me what retard meant and I told her I didn't know. I guess Krista had been listening because suddenly she appeared in the doorway.

"A retard is a stupid moron," Krista said matter-of-factly, "It means that you are broken and can never be smart."

Shayla began to cry harder. Krista just turned and walked away. I heard her in the kitchen looking for food. Shayla and I stayed in our room. Shayla cried until she finally dozed off on my lap. I slowly moved out from under her and went to the living room.

Chapter 47

"Is Mom home yet?" I asked Krista who was watching TV in the living room.

"Does it look like she is home?" Krista replied sarcastically.

"Did you find any food?" I asked.

"No," Krista said looking at me finally.

"Is there a phone book?" I asked.

"Yes, it is in the drawer in the kitchen," Krista said.

"Do they deliver pizza here?" I asked.

"Why? We don't have any money," Krista said.

"I have a little," I said.

"Give it to me," Krista demanded standing up.

"No," I said trying to stand taller.

I knew if I gave Krista the money she would take it for herself. I wanted to make sure Shayla got food too.

"GIVE IT TO ME OR I WILL KILL YOU," Krista screamed.

"No," I whimpered terrified, taking a small step backward.

I didn't even see her fist until it struck me. I fell backward and Krista jumped on me and began to choke me. Then suddenly Krista flew off of me. Shayla must have heard Krista yell at me because Shayla had tackled Krista. Shayla hit Krista. I ran to my room and grabbed my new backpack and threw the stuffed animal with the money hidden in its underwear into the bag. I ran back to the living room. I grabbed Shayla's hand and we ran out of the house. We ran to the end of the trailer park and then paused to look behind us. Krista was not following. I remembered that there was a gas station a few blocks away. We began to walk that way.

"Thank you for saving me," I said, still holding Shayla's hand.

"Why did she hurt you?" Shayla asked.

"I told her about the money and she wanted it. I told her no because I knew she would not share the food if she took it." I answered.

"Are we going to get food? I am hungry," Shayla said.

"Yes," I answered.

We walked the rest of the way in silence. We got to the gas station just a few minutes later. It was a Casey's. According to the sign they had pizza. We went inside and ordered a large pepperoni pizza. As we waited for the pizza we walked around the store. We finally bought the pizza and also some donuts. Then we walked home. I held the pizza while Shayla held the donuts. She ate one as we walked. When we got home I saw Mom's car in the driveway and knew we would be safe from Krista. However, I should have known not to underestimate Krista.

We entered the trailer. Krista and Benny were watching TV in the living room. Krista looked up and grinned at me evilly. I quickly put the pizza on the counter and took off my backpack. "Shayla, go to our room and shut the door. Hide!" I whispered to Shayla as I gave her my backpack.

I watched Shayla run to our room just as Mom stepped out of her room with a shredded belt and an angry expression on her face. I felt terrified.

"Hey, Mommy, your home. I missed you," I said as sweetly as possible while I put a fake smile on my face. I could hear my voice tremble.

"DON'T TRY TO ACT ALL INNOCENT! TELL ME THE TRUTH YOU LYING, STEALING WHORE! DID YOU STEAL MONEY FROM ME!" Mom yelled as she rushed over and grabbed my hair.

I saw Krista smiling at me from the couch.

"No, Mommy, I swear. I would never steal from you. I promise," I begged.

Mom slammed my head onto the counter right next to the pizza box. I felt the impact through my whole body. My entire head felt pummeled.

"THEN WHERE THE HELL DID YOU GET THIS FUCKING PIZZA BITCH. PIZZA DOESN'T JUST FALL OUT OF THE FUCKING SKY!" Mom yelled bringing my face right in front of hers.

"I stole it. At the store. The pizza was sitting on the counter with a ticket that said it was paid for and that it belonged to the Bakers. I told the clerk that I was Samantha Baker. She gave me the pizza and the donuts and said they had been paid for already. We grabbed it and ran. I swear, Mommy. I would not steal from you. I love you," I whimpered.

Baker was the last name of a girl in my class. I prayed that Mom would buy the story.

"KRISTA, GET YOUR ASS OVER HERE NOW. ONE OF YOU BITCHES IS LYING AND I WILL HAVE A GOD DAMNED ANSWER!" Mom said as she threw me to the floor and turned to look at Krista.

Krista was no longer smiling. Instead she was glaring at me as she rushed over to Mom.

"Yes, Mommy," Krista said quickly.

"YOU TOLD ME THAT SHE HAD MONEY! YOU FUCKING BITCH HAD BETTER NOT BEEN LYING TO ME!" Mom yelled at her.

I stood up quickly. I knew Mom was angry. I looked quickly down the hall. Our bedroom door was shut so I knew that Shayla was safe at least. Now that I was not in Mom's clutches I took a moment to take in everything. Mom smelled funny again so I knew she had been drinking. That must have been where she had been. This was not good. Mom was always worse when she had been drinking. I did not know how to calm Mom down. Why had Krista told her? Krista must have known what would happen.

"I wasn't lying, Mommy. She told me she had money," Krista said.

"DO YOU HAVE MY MONEY?" Mom yelled at me.

"No, Mommy, honest," I whimpered terrified of the way Mom was looking at me.

"BENNY, GET YOUR ASS OVER HER AND SEARCH THIS WHORING BITCH!" Mom yelled.

Benny ran over and started rubbing his hands all over me. He was grinning as he did it. He ran his hands up my dress and felt up my privates. I pushed away. Finally he stood up.

"No money," He told Mom.

The slap came out of nowhere. Mom hit Krista so hard that she flew backwards. She fell on the ground and before she could recover Mom began swinging the shredded belt. Krista rolled over into a ball.

"I WILL TEACH YOU TO LIE TO ME. I SHOULD HAVE KNOWN YOU WERE MAKING UP STORIES. MY ANGEL WOULD NEVER STEAL FROM ME. YOU ARE A WORTHLESS FUCKING WHORE. I NEVER SHOULD HAVE HAD YOU. YOU DO NOTHING BUT CAUSE ME SHIT!" Mom yelled as she swung.

"Please, Mom, that's enough. Remember school," I said as I jumped forward and grabbed Mom's other hand.

It was the only thing I could think to say. It must have worked though because she stopped swinging the belt and went into her room. She slammed the door behind her and left Benny, Krista and I alone. I half expected her to return and beat me too. Instead I heard the TV in her room turn on. I went to Krista and knelt beside her.

"Are you ok?" I asked as I put a hand on her shoulder.

Krista looked up at me with pure hate. She shoved me away and stomped off to the bathroom. She had blood on the side of her mouth. I went to our room and got Shayla out of the Armoire where she sat trembling. She actually yelped when I opened the door to the Armoire. We returned to the living room. I got down two plates. Benny was on the couch watching TV with four pieces of pizza on a plate on his lap. I got Shayla two pieces and a donut. Then I got two pieces and a donut on the second plate. I sat Shayla in the living room to eat and then took the second plate with me. I went to Mom's door. I needed to calm her down somehow. I knocked softly on the door.

"WHAT THE FUCK DO YOU FUCKS WANT?" Mom yelled through the door.

I opened the door.

"I just wanted to bring you some food. I am sorry you are mad, Mommy," I said softly.

"Oh, baby, you are sweet. Come in and sit with your Mommy," Mom said as she patted the bed beside her.

Mom had a bottle of alcohol in her lap. Half of the bottle was empty. I stepped inside and shut the door behind me. I walked to the bed and handed Mom the plate before I climbed up to sit beside her. "I never should have believed that bitch of a sister of yours. You would never have stolen from me," Mom said as she began to eat.

Mom watched TV as she ate. I was starving but I knew better to leave without being dismissed. I just waited patiently. Mom was watching some western on TV. When Mom finished eating she gave me her empty plate and thanked me for being such a good angel. She told me to go so I quickly left the room. Krista was on the couch eating pizza and donuts. Benny was sitting on the floor with Shayla. They were all watching TV. I took Mom's plate to the sink. I got down a plate for me and went to get some pizza. I opened the box and discovered it was empty. I opened the donut box but that was empty as well. I put my plate in the cabinet. I then went back to my room. I laid down on the bed. I hugged my last toy, my stuffed animal, tightly to my chest and cried.

Chapter 48

The next day I woke up early. I went outside and watched the sunrise.

"Daddy, please help me," I prayed quietly.

I hoped that one day God would bless my mother with all the money she needed so she would stop hurting us. I wanted God to also bring us an Earthly father who would never hurt us and would always protect us. Still, I liked having God as my father. That made

me a princess. I sometimes dreamed that God would ride down from heaven on a winged horse and carry me and my sisters to his castle in the clouds where we would see Stacy again. Stacy would apologize for leaving us and we would all live together in peace forever. I sighed just thinking about it. I turned and went back inside to wake up Shayla.

Shayla and I were putting our shoes on when Krista came downstairs. I grabbed my backpack and the three of us went outside. Krista walked too fast. Shayla and I rushed to keep up with her. When we were close to school Shayla and I slowed down to catch our breath. Krista didn't even slow down as she crossed the street and rushed inside. Shayla and I crossed the street together and walked to the cafeteria by ourselves. I was starving. We got breakfast and sat down. I immediately put the apple and the juice in my backpack. I wanted to save them for later just in case Mom still didn't buy groceries. There was not a grocery store in this town so it wasn't like I could just buy food myself. We finished our breakfast. When we finished, Shayla asked if she could go to my class with me but the teachers said she couldn't. Shayla looked so sad when she walked to her class. I went to my class alone.

School was actually worse. The other kids picked on me. One girl who was very popular was named Tina. She had brown hair like me and had an older sister in the sixth grade. Tina actually put gum in my hair when the teacher was not looking. The teacher had to cut it out. When I told the teacher who did it, Tina denied doing it. The teacher said I should not make up stories about others and told me that for lying I would not be allowed to go out for recess. Tina and the other girls just snickered and laughed. Missy sat with me at lunch. She saw me put my fruit cup in my pocket and offered me hers as well. Missy was nice to me. That afternoon we got to go to P.E.. There was this black haired boy with goggle-like glasses who was in our class. His name was Matthew but he went by Matt. He was so cute and really good at basketball. I told Missy in the locker room that I thought he was cute and liked him. The other girls overheard and began to tease me. I felt embarrassed.

Finally, school ended. I was so happy to get to leave but was sad that I wouldn't get to see Missy until the next day. I met Shayla at the front of the school. She had had a worse day than I did. As we waited for Krista, Shayla told me that some of the boys in her class

had cornered her at recess. They had groped her and called her retard. They pushed her in the mud and one of the boys had spit on her. At lunch they knocked her lunch tray out of her hands and she had to stay to clean up the mess.

"Didn't you tell the teacher what the boys had done?" I asked her.

"I was too scared to tell. The boys said they would punch me if I did. Samantha, I am scared," Shayla whimpered.

I hugged her as she began to cry. We walked across the street to wait for Krista as Shayla continued to cry silently beside me. The buses left before Krista finally came out of the building. She saw us and ran to our sides.

"You guys are going to go home without me today. Lucas is going to drop off his girlfriend and then come pick me up. He is going to take me to his house. We are going to watch a movie," Krista said excitedly.

"Mom, won't like it if she finds out," I said worried.

"Tell Mom I am studying with a friend. If you don't I will make your pain far worse than any pain Mom will give me," Krista threatened.

Krista ran back into the school after the threat. Shayla and I just turned around and walked back home slowly. When we got home Mom's car was in the driveway. Shayla and I walked up the steps and onto the small porch. The door was unlocked. I had forgotten to get the key from Krista. I was glad Mom was home. I went inside. Mom was in the kitchen unloading some groceries. I was glad that we would have food in the house again. Yet this also worried me a little. When we moved to a new place Mom would wait to buy groceries until she either had a job or had found a way to restart her business. I hoped it was because she had a job.

"Hi, Mommy, do you need some help?" I asked with a fake smile on my face.

"Sure, Sissy, you can take the groceries out of the bag. Hey, where is that slut Krista? Didn't she walk you home?" Mom said.

I turned to give Shayla my backpack to take to our room and looked at her seriously for a minute. I turned and walked over to the stools to climb up so I could help Mom. Shayla rushed to our room so that she could hide.

"Krista had to work on a school project with Becky," I lied as I took the food out of the bags.

"So, how was school today, baby?" Mom asked.

"It was ok. How was your day?" I asked hoping she had found a job.

"I found a job. It is temporary. It is in a factory in the next town. I am still hoping to start up the business but we need the money until I can," Mom answered as she threw the bags in the garbage.

"Mommy, do you have to start the business up again?" I asked, looking down at the counter.

I always asked Mom but it never stopped her in the end. Yet, everywhere we went I asked hoping to persuade her not to sell us again.

"Oh, princess, you know I don't have a choice. We need the money and I can't support us on my own. Maybe if I found a man to marry who could support us all then I wouldn't have to work all the time. However, with your slut of a sister seducing every man I find that may never happen. Anyway, I am going to go watch some TV," Mom said as she walked out of the kitchen.

I got down off the stool and went to my room. Shayla was not there. My backpack was on my bed. I took the food out of it that I had saved from school. I put the food in the bottom of our Armoire. I then put my backpack on the top bunk for tomorrow. I went upstairs to find Shayla. She was in Benny's room. Benny and Shayla were kissing.

"Mom is downstairs. You should not do that when she is home," I cautioned Shayla.

"What did you tell Mom about Krista?" Shayla asked as she sat up and wiped her mouth off.

"I told her that Krista went to Becky's to study. Come on, Mom is watching TV. We should go watch TV with her," I said pulling on Shayla's hand.

Shayla gave Benny one more kiss before allowing me to pull her downstairs. I still did not like the relationship between Benny and Shayla. It just felt wrong and gross to me. Anyway, I hoped that if Mom saw Shayla in the living room she would feed Shayla some food at dinner. Lately, half the time Mom cooked dinner she only made enough for herself, Benny and I. A fourth of the time she would feed Krista, herself, Benny and me. It was mean the way that she would exclude Shayla as if she did not belong to the family. I just would hide as much of my food as I could to feed Shayla later. Shayla and I went into the living room and watched TV with Mom.

Shayla sat on the floor while I sat beside Mom on the couch. Mom was smoking one cigarette after another as she watched a western on TV. When the movie ended Mom got up and began to make some spaghetti for dinner. Krista showed up just as Mom put the dinner on the table.

"Did you eat at your friends house?" Mom asked her in greeting.

"I told her you went to study at Becky's," I whispered to Krista quickly as Mom looked down to fill the plates.

"Oh, uh, no. We did not eat," Krista answered Mom quickly.

"Well, you and Shayla can eat at the counter. I don't want to have to look at you while I eat," Mom said harshly.

Shayla and Krista took their plates and went to sit at the counter. Mom sat so she could see the TV in the living room. I sat on her right while Benny sat on her left. Mom smoked and watched TV as we all ate. My back was to my sisters but at least they were allowed to eat dinner tonight. Mom did not like us to talk, so we all ate in silence. After dinner Mom made Krista and Shayla clean the kitchen. I asked if I could help but Mom said I was too young and not allowed. I sat on the couch beside Mom as she watched more TV. When the kitchen was clean Shayla, Krista, and I all went up to Krista's room. Krista was so excited to tell us all about her after school date. We stayed in her room while she talked about them making out on the couch while they watched a movie.

That night I laid in bed waiting for sleep to come. Shayla was snoring as she slept. Mom and Benny had retired to Mom's room. The house was quiet. I thought about the differences between my sisters and me. Shayla liked to have sex with Benny. She said it felt good. Krista was willing to have sex with lots of people. I was ten and thought all sex was painful and gross. Was something wrong with me? Or was something wrong with them? I could not imagine sex feeling good. To me, it always felt like someone was stabbing me. It felt like someone was trying to rip me apart. I shuddered just remembering it. Maybe I was broken. Mom said it was normal for parents to sell their children. When she couldn't start a business somewhere she always said it was because there was too much competition in the area. I did not want to believe Mom but I also had no proof she was lying. Was every family like ours?

Chapter 49

School continued as before. The other students were cruel so I tried to avoid them as much as possible. Missy was my only friend. We began to hang out sometimes after school. Mom was gone most afternoons and evenings. She had the second shift at the factory. Shayla eventually made a few friends but still the other kids called her moron and retard every day. Krista began to make us leave early for school. She would walk with us to her boyfriend's house. She would make us wait outside while she had sex with him inside before school. For the next three months things were kind of nice. Because of her schedule, we rarely saw Mom. She came home long after bedtime and we left before she woke up. Mom was meaner than usual on the weekends when she was home though so Shayla and I tried to stay out of the house as much as possible. Mom was tired of working. She couldn't start up the business so she had to work. Krista spent as much time as she could with her secret boyfriend. The rest of the time she spent with Becky.

In mid November a new student moved to town. She was in my class. Her name was Sarah. Sarah was mean and snobby to everyone. She said that her father owned Mighty Melt in Sedalia and that made her better than most of us. However, the other kids treated her just as badly as they treated me. Missy said we needed to be nice to her. She said that it was mean to leave her without a friend even if she was mean. So, we befriended her. She was mean to me but she liked Missy. So the three of us became friends.

At the end of November Mom brought home a new boyfriend. He was going to be living with us from now on. His name was Travis Cooper. He had moved here from Michigan and he worked with Mom at the factory. When he met me he immediately gave me the hungry look so I was immediately scared of him. Luckily he worked the same shift as Mom at the factory. Mom was always home when he was there. However, on the weekends he would always try to get me to sit on his lap or take a nap with him. I started to avoid the house at all costs when he was home. Thankfully, Missy liked for me to hang out at her house and she did not mind if I brought Shayla.

Our house settled into a precarious peace. Mom was trying to convince Travis that they should get married. Mom was being extra nice to us kids so that Travis would think she was a good Mom.

Travis was getting frustrated that I was avoiding him. He began to fight with Mom. Two weeks after Christmas everything exploded. I was at the dining table with Shayla coloring in a coloring book. Mom and Travis were fighting in the doorway to Mom's room.

"It is a fucking nap," Travis finally yelled.

"We both know it is not just a fucking NAP! You don't get shit for nothing!" Mom yelled back.

"You shut the fuck up. How the Hell are You Going to Stop me!" Travis yelled.

"If you think I am just going to stand back and allow it you are fucking crazy!" Mom screamed in his face.

"I will move out and you can kiss my fucking money goodbye," Travis yelled.

"Then take Shayla. She is worthless anyway!" Mom said a little quieter.

"I don't want the retard. I want Samantha," He was still yelling.

Shayla and I just watched in horror.

"No," Mom yelled at him.

Suddenly he slapped her. I wondered how long he had been hitting her. She just grabbed her cheek. I did not want him to hurt my mom. My mom was not a good mom but she was still my mom. I jumped up and ran over to them.

"Mommy," I said hugging her.

Mom sobbed as she held me. Travis grinned at me.

"Come Samantha," He demanded as he pulled on my arm.

"Mommy?" I asked in a whimper.

"Just a nap?" She asked Travis.

"That's what I fucking said," Travis snarled at Mom.

Travis pulled me to Mom's bed. I watched Mom pull a chair into the bedroom doorway to watch. Travis laid down on the bed and pulled me against him. He held me too tight. Mom watched me with tears in her eyes. I felt Travis's wee wee get hard against my bottom. I struggled out of his grip and scooted to the other end of the bed. Travis was pretending to be asleep so he couldn't hold me too tight. However, he rolled over and scooted against me again. He began to rub me through my clothes. I struggled out of his grip and went back to the other side of the bed. I knew there was only so much he could do if Mom was watching and he was pretending to sleep. He rolled over and scooted against me again. His wee wee poked at my

bottom. I was grateful that I was wearing jeans. I struggled out of his grip and ran to Mom.

"I am not tired, Mommy," I said loudly.

Travis stayed in bed and gave Mom and me the evil eye. Mom shut the door and carried me to the couch. We sat down and watched TV. I feared that next time Travis would win. I tried not to think about it. The next day Travis was gone. Mom said he went back to Michigan to live with his Mom. Mom was sad but I was glad.

In January Mom moved us to a house on the other side of town. The house was a three bedroom. Mom put a bed on the glassed in porch for Benny's room. Shayla and I got the room next to Moms. Krista got a bedroom upstairs in the attic bedroom. Krista's room was huge but a little creepy. Mom also bought me a few new toys. I loved our big white house. It was a corner lot with a big backyard. It was farther from Missy's house but Mom gave each of us a bike so we could go around town.

Because of our new house we had to ride the bus to school. I always sat next to Shayla on the bus. The other kids would shout insults at Shayla and occasionally throw things at her. They called her retard and an idiot. They also called her white trash. Shayla would get so mad she would sit sideways in the seat by the window and yell back at them. I felt so small and helpless. I begged Shayla to just ignore them. Her behavior just made everything worse. I began to wish I could disappear. School was hard for me. The other kids were mean. The teacher discovered that I could barely read and began to keep me in at recess to work on my reading. The teacher said I needed to read at home as well but we did not have books at home. Missy and I were inseparable. Sarah was jealous of Missy and my friendship and began to try to get us to fight. Sarah stole one of Missy's favorite dolls and tried to blame it on me. Thankfully Missy believed me when I said I didn't take it. Sarah refused to return the doll until Missy's Mom called Sarah's Mom. Sarah refused to talk to us for a week. I was happy but Missy felt guilty.

Krista's boyfriend promised to take her to prom but then broke up with her two weeks before. Krista was heartbroken. She was also mad. The day it happened she came home and stepped on one of my toys. She got so mad she broke five of my Barbie dolls and threw them at me.

A week before school ended for the year Mom came home with party invitations. She told me I would have my first birthday party. I asked her when my birthday was. She told me it was June 13th. I immediately decided that the number 13 was my favorite number because that was the date of my birthday. I was so excited. I had never had a birthday party. Krista was furious. She asked Mom when her birthday was and Mom told her it was in September and that Shayla's was in October. Krista was enraged. Krista stormed out of the house and took off on her bike. Mom just ignored her.

Together Mom and I filled out the invitations. On each invitation Mom wrote on the back that I wanted money for a large present that I wanted to get myself. Mom had me take the invitations to school the next day. Everyone got an invitation including the kids in Shayla's class. The next Sunday Mom had me take more invitations to church. I was excited. Mom said she had ordered a cake and that there would be ice cream. I was going to have my first birthday party. Shayla and I were practically bouncing with excitement. Krista was furious and jealous. Every time Mom was not home she would hit me and hurt me. I began to avoid her at all costs. School ended and Shayla and I spent as much time as possible with Missy. Sarah would pick on Shayla whenever she thought no one was looking. I decided that Sarah was just an ugly person.

The day of my party, the sunrise was perfect. There were only a few clouds in the sky. We set up tables in the backyard. Mom had gotten princess table cloths for all the tables. My cake was a princess cake that had Belle, Cinderella, and Aurora on it. It was big and pink with blue writing. I loved it. The party began at 2. Missy, Sarah, and Becky came. Occasionally a car would pull up and Mom would go over to take a card from the occupants of the car. Mom had bought me a new Barbie doll as a present. Missy gave me a makeup set for a present. Sarah gave me a card with a $5 bill inside. Mom had brought out a boom box so there was music blaring. Missy and Sarah opened the makeup set against Mom's wishes. Missy and Sarah did my makeup. They put on bright blue eye shadow, bright red blush, and bright orange lipstick. They said I looked great. I thought I looked like a clown but kept that opinion to myself so I would not hurt their feelings.

When they finished they began to work on Shayla. I took my new Barbie doll into the house. I sat on my bed and began to play

with her. Mom eventually came in to tell me my friends were leaving and it was time to say goodbye. I went out and hugged Missy. I waved goodbye to Sarah. Mom took the leftover cake and ice cream inside. I stayed outside to watch my sisters and brother clean up the party. Mom said I could not help. I felt so happy. My first birthday party. Wow.

The rest of the summer went by quickly. I spent most of my time with Missy and Sarah. Shayla stayed with me whenever Mom was home but if Mom was not home she spent her time with Benny. Krista ignored me most of the time. She told me she hated me and she wished I would die. Mom was gone most of the time. She worked at the factory in the afternoons and evenings and then she went out whenever she didn't go to work. Mom took all my money from the birthday party and never gave it back. She also stopped buying groceries. When she did bring home groceries it was only for her and only enough for a day. She only fed us twice a week. Finally, at the beginning of August Mom stopped coming home. It was not unusual for her to be gone a week or so, so we didn't think anything of it. However, our neighbors noticed. One day they asked me when I was playing in the yard where my mom's car had been lately. I said I don't know. Shayla was with me and without thinking about it Shayla told them that Mom hadn't been home in days.

The next afternoon, some friends of my mom came by to pick us up. They were in a hurry. They dropped Krista and I off at their house and went to pack our stuff from the house. They said we would be staying with them for a few weeks. When we went inside, Krista was furious. She said she had planned to steal some stuff from them but now I had ruined her plans. She slapped me and knocked me down. She said she was going to kill me. She began to choke me. Just before I blacked out there was a frantic knock at the door. Krista cursed and rushed to the door. It was Mom's friends. They said that the police were at the house and they thought they had followed them back. They told us three girls to hide. Benny was too old so he didn't need to hide.

Shayla hid under a cot in the living room. I hid around the corner. Krista was around the other corner. The police knocked on the door and began to argue with Mom's friends. Shayla began to cry out because her hair was trapped in the springs of the cot. I rushed over and detangled her hair. We hugged each other close and

watched the argument. Suddenly, Krista ran out of the house and around the corner. Two officers followed her. Only two officers were arguing in the doorway now.

"Shayla, we have to run. Meet back at the house. Go the opposite way I go," I said to Shayla quickly.

Shayla nodded quickly and I took off. I ran as fast as I could down the street. I passed the old trailer park we used to live in. A police man was about one block back running to try to catch me. I knew if I could make it to Missy's house I could borrow her bike and outrun the cop. I looked behind me. The cop was across the street still a block away. I quickly crossed the street at an angle. The cop grabbed me just as my feet touched the sidewalk on the opposite side of the street. I was wearing a dress and he held me where everyone could see my underwear. I kicked at him and tried to hit him. I yelled that my underwear was showing. He told me to stop fighting and he would let me cover up. I stopped fighting. I was captured. I would be tortured and killed. He refused to put me down. He carried me right to the patrol car and put me in the backseat. I tried to open the door but it would not open. Soon my sisters were in the backseat beside me. The officers got in the car. We drove slowly away. I stared at the small crowd of people watching me be driven away to my death. I turned and gripped Shayla's hand tightly as I stared straight ahead and tried not to think about the pain I knew was about to happen.

Dear Reader,

I want you to know that I changed every name in this book from the original name. The purpose of this book is not to punish anyone. I wrote this story about the real life story of Samantha, not her real name, because she asked me to. The story is as close to reality as possible. She wants her story told. Most importantly she wants to raise awareness of a horrible problem living in America. Many people have the erroneous opinion that sex trafficking only happens in the big cities or abroad. Samantha never lived in big cities. She lived in small town America, in the heartland, in the bible belt. This problem is closer than many people think. This should never happen. Please stand with her and me and find a way to stop this from happening.

Since Samantha is still young, many of the people who hurt her may see themselves in this book. Samantha wants you to know she forgives you. She hopes you never hurt another child again and that you will make your peace with God. Samantha forgives you for all your evil and prays for your soul.

Printed in Great Britain
by Amazon

40118619R00139